Horsehide, Pigskin, Oval
Tracks and Apple Pie

Horsehide, Pigskin, Oval Tracks and Apple Pie

Essays on Sports and American Culture

edited by James A. Vlasich

McFarland & Company, Inc., Publishers

Jefferson, North Carolina, and London

Library of Congress Cataloguing-in-Publication Data

Horsehide, pigskin, oval tracks and apple pie : essays on sports
and American culture / edited by James A. Vlasich.
    p.   cm.
    Includes bibliographical references and index.

    ISBN 0-7864-2397-8 (softcover : 50# alkaline paper)

    1. Sports—United States—Sociological aspects.   I. Vlasich,
James A.
GV706.5.H666   2006
306.4'83—dc22   2005031112

British Library cataloguing data are available

On the cover: apple pie ©2005 Clipart.com; football and
baseball ©2005 PhotoSpin

Manufactured in the United States of America

McFarland & Company, Inc., Publishers
  Box 611, Jefferson, North Carolina 28640
    www.mcfarlandpub.com

For my daughters,
Brooke Thieu and Ming Lyn,
who have learned to indulge their father
in his love for the National Pastime

Acknowledgments

I did not start out to be a sports historian, but it seems a rather natural consequence given my love for the games— especially baseball. I grew up in southern Illinois, and, though never a fan of the Cardinals, I spent many evenings listening to Harry Caray broadcast their yearly struggles in the 1950s. Of course, I tried my hand at playing, but I was limited to Little League and a Midwestern favorite known as corkball. There were other attempts at football and basketball, but they proved equally daunting for one of such meager talents. Still, I followed the exploits of the University of Illinois, Gillespie High School, various NFL teams and my favorite: the Brooklyn Dodgers. This last bond was so strong I named my daughters after them.

It wasn't until after I received my Ph.D. that I began to contemplate an academic investigation of sports. I was fortunate to come into contact with Donald Cleland of Las Vegas, Nevada, and I owe him a great deal of thanks for starting me in the sports direction. His grandfather, Alexander Cleland, originated the Baseball Hall of Fame. Using his papers, I wrote my first book on the origin of the organization. That experience led to a keynote speech at the first Cooperstown Symposium on Baseball and American Culture in 1989 and an article published from that experience. I also gave a paper on the subject that same year at the Popular Culture Association Conference in St. Louis. Thus began my association with the organization and its Sports Area chair, Douglas Noverr from Michigan State University. In 1997 he became president of the organization, and I took over his position. A major thanks goes to Doug for his support and friendship over the years. He also helped with the preface of this book.

Others contributed to the finishing touches of this publication. My wife, Grace Hong Vlasich, used her computer expertise to make my communication with authors more feasible. Larry Gerlach, sports historian and great friend (in spite of his Yankee rooting), critiqued my introduction. I should also like to express my gratitude for the work of our department secretary, Kaylene Irwin, and her student assistants Jamie Orton, Kristina Oliverson, Melinda McGuire, and Heather Plumb. They made sure that the typing chores and computer manipulations were done efficiently and correctly.

Finally, I would like to express my special appreciation for all of the authors who made this volume possible. Their impeccable research and entertaining writing styles are all the more appreciated because they were working in a vacuum. None of them was aware of the works included in this volume or the approach that others were taking. The result is surprisingly uniform and coherent. They were also extremely patient with an editor who was a bit overwhelmed coordinating the efforts of 18 different authors.

Contents

IV. FOOTBALL

V. CAR RACING

VI. SPORTS NOT FOR MEN ONLY

Preface

At the 1985 Popular Culture Association and American Culture Association National Conference in Louisville, Kentucky, professors Douglas A. Noverr and Lawrence E. Ziewacz became the co–Sports Area chairs at the invitation and support of Ray B. Browne, the secretary-treasurer of the organizations. From two sessions at that conference, they quickly expanded to nine for the 1987 Montreal conference, and between 1987 and the 1996 conference in Las Vegas, they scheduled an average of 10 sessions annually, with the high points being 12 sessions at two different conferences. Each year's conference involved 30 to 35 participants in the Sports Area.

As sports became an established area for research and publication and as courses developed in the field, participation increased. The guidelines to proposers of presentations were simple: Make them lively and interesting, engage the audience, and ground the work in solid research. The Sports Area participants developed a steady core of "regulars" complemented by newcomers. As a result of regular contacts at the conferences, a network of connections developed from friendships and new acquaintances, with research expertise and knowledge readily exchanged. Most important, a friendly and supportive atmosphere encouraged further work and future participation. The conferences also afforded opportunities for the group to tour baseball parks, local sports venues such as Churchill Downs and the Louisiana Superdome, and even the offices of *The Sporting News*.

Professors Noverr and Ziewacz also became co-editors of a Sports and Culture book series for the Bowling Green State University Popular Press, and a number of the books in that series were written by Sports Area participants. Numerous other books and articles came from presentations made at the conferences. In 1997, after 13 consecutive years of serving as co-chairs for the Sports Area, Noverr and Ziewacz passed the chairmanship to professor Jim Vlasich, who has continued the work with the same atmosphere of scholarship, fun, and supportive collegiality.

Most of the papers in this book came from the 2003 conference in New Orleans and the 2004 conference in San Antonio. It is the editor's hope that future conferences will provide interesting stories that will excite the sports audience while enticing new scholars into the area. With good fortune, this activity will expand the horizons of the sporting public and allow it to view the nation's history through the perspective of the games people play.

Introduction

Thirty-seven Popular Culture Association presenters submitted their papers for consideration in this volume, which made the choices difficult. The 16 articles included in this book span a wide variety of topics and sports from academic contributors throughout the country. They look at sports past and present, traditional and modern, and aspects historic and innovative. All of them reflect the explosion of sports-history courses that have spread throughout college campuses around the nation. What was once deemed unimportant or frivolous by traditional academicians has become a new area of study that students find exciting and relevant as sports becomes an ever more important segment of American life. These papers give new meaning to sports in our culture and demonstrate why these activities reflect the fabric of American society with all of its heroes and flaws.

It is no surprise that baseball receives significant coverage in this book. Over the years no area has received as much attention at the conference. A sport so rich in tradition and records that it was once labeled the national pastime, it was bound to attract the attention of more erudite academicians who attached themselves to a thinking fan's game. It isn't surprising then, that the first sports doctoral dissertation focused on baseball and that it has become an academic staple. Our contributors give us a look at the climactic contest that ends a season and a unique view of one of the game's greatest stars.

No one does a better job in bringing us contemporary accounts of past World Series than Bruce A. Rubenstein. He has provided numerous appraisals of long-ago championships as seen through the eyes of the writers who witnessed them. Rather than quoting less talented sportswriters from the past half century, Rubenstein looks at the earlier period when some of the best writing was done by authors who, for a period of their careers, focused on the games people play. The result, evidenced by his rendition of the famous 1941 Series, is fascinating, humorous, and highly readable. Reading Rubenstein, even young sports fans can experience the frustration of the Boys from Brooklyn who felt the first of many stings from the Yankee juggernaut.

Joseph Stanton is both art historian and poet. As such, he offers unique insight into his favorite baseball hero, Stan Musial. The author understands that such talented athletes simply elude definition, which is the key to their success. Thus Stanton chooses poetry as the way to view both the statistical facts and the mysteries of the "perfect knight" with the ultimate goal of revealing the core of one of the game's purest players. The result is both enlightening and spiritual and perhaps the most intriguing way of understanding someone who towers above others in the pursuit of athletic perfection. Stanton offers eight poems that explore "Stan the Man" at different times in his career and demonstrates the factual and emotional sides of the Cardinal great.

The subject of ethnicity has become a major area of academic study, and, once again, baseball serves as the background for how this emphasis applies to sports. Actually, this is no new concept for fans of boxing who have observed pugilism's stepladder serving Irish immigrants in their struggle for equality in the late 19th century. There are two papers dealing with diverse ethnic groups crossing oceans on opposite sides of the continent during the early and late parts of the 20th century to participate in America's pastime. Both the Italians and the Japanese faced doubters of their ability, but the former came with no expertise and the latter with questions concerning quality. While both performed at high levels, the Italians changed perceptions in America while their Asian counterparts had an even greater impact back home.

Joseph Dorinson shares a love for Italian culture and is well versed on the plight of Italian immigrants who washed up on America's shores almost a century ago. As a nationally recognized expert and sponsor of a conference on the 50th anniversary of Jackie Robinson's breaking of baseball's color barrier, he demonstrates his versatility with prose whose roots stretch back to the boot of Europe. Citing the early discrimination during an era of xenophobia, Dorinson demonstrates how the sons of Italian immigrants, with no real baseball tradition, came to master the nuances of the game while adjusting to the vicissitudes of life in another cultural milieu. As the author points out, the challenge was complicated by the rise of Mussolini and the associated fear of spreading fascism. It is little wonder that Joe DiMaggio lifted Italian Americans and gave new hope for those who followed him to the big leagues. Dorinson's work also expands from players to umpires, managers, and even the commissioner of the game.

While the early Italian players struggled to prove themselves to a critical American audience, those from Japan faced additional opposition from fans at home. As Yasue Kuwahara points out, Japanese baseball players were bucking cultural traditions by exercising their talents across the Pacific. Post-war Japan, much like the United States, emphasized conformity. In both countries, however, affluence led to changing values among the young. Whereas their fathers clung to the same company with excessive devotion, the Japanese version of Generation-X questioned traditional values and placed a much greater emphasis on pleasure and self. The traditions of hard work and perseverance persist, but now the rewards are sought in an American game that is more aggressive, power-oriented and focused on the individual. All of this required a major shift from Japanese traditions and, surprisingly, the islands' fans are adapting similar attitudes. Unlike people from Italy, who lacked an appreciation for baseball, those from Japan are following the lead of their favorite players by demanding that the local game end its stodgy style of play and adopt the American way. Oddly, what started out as a game emulating a foreign national pastime has become a means of shifting Japan's national values.

For decades golf was seen by many as a rich white male's sport. Even the apparent breakthrough by Babe Didrickson more than a half century ago and Lee Elder about a generation later did little to end discrimination against women and minorities. While both groups made slight advances, they remained shortchanged and virtually nonexistent on the more exclusive courses. As America began to change with the Civil Rights movement of the 1960s, gradualism reluctantly gave way to inclusion, albeit not without some stiff resistance. With the movement toward recognizing the country's diversification in the 1990s, golf reluctantly began to open the closed doors of the sport's past. Perhaps the most elitist of sports, golf's purists put up a fight against a talent that could no longer be denied.

The athlete who most personified the recent trend and became golf's poster boy for diversity was, of course, Tiger Woods. In her review of this phenomenally successful master of the links, Donna J. Barbie traces the reasons for his astronomical rise to the top of the game, which has catapulted Woods past Jack Nicklaus and Arnold Palmer in the hierarchy of the sport. Ironically, the very ethnic background that denied previous minorities in the sport has played in Woods's favor. Ethnic groups and champions of the underdogs who previously saw no one to rally around flocked to the greens and television sets to follow their new hero. Given the revenues that followed this support, the media began to court the rising star. Barbie adds a personal touch to her article by describing the audience around her during a Woods round and how the aura of his persona attracted such a wide following. Finally, she points out that his athletic ability was not just a natural consequence but rather a byproduct of a strenuous workout routine. Thanks to Woods, a sport once thought to be the home of out-of-shape duffers is now embracing the physical conditioning of contact sports.

Lagging behind the racial breakthrough by Tiger Woods was a case of gender discrimination in the new millennium. Tom Cook, a women's golf coach, traces the events surrounding the controversy initiated by Dr. Martha Burk of the National Council of Women's Organizations in 2002 when she complained that the Augusta National Golf Club had ignored women in the Masters since it was founded 70 years prior. What started out as a minor protest exploded into a major battle when the tournament's chairman took a rigid and confrontational stand against inclusion of the opposite sex. In a game of one-upsmanship, the two sides exchanged barbs and threats that attracted nationwide media attention and left the situation still unresolved. Ironically, Woods found himself in the middle of the contest and had reasons to support both sides until he gradually moved toward backing women's rights. In addition to his excellent, detailed coverage, Cook also cites philosopher John Rawls, who laid out his principles of justice and how to remove injustice. He then applies them to this issue in an attempt to resolve the problem. The result might leave some women's-rights supporters unsatisfied but might also help to solve the issue when it raises its ugly head in the future.

In many ways football lagged behind baseball in terms of popularity until the explosion of televised contests in the 1960s. Still, similar problems plagued both sports. The question of integration was, surprisingly, brought to the nation's attention in football's college game a decade before Jackie Robinson broke the racial barrier in the national pastime. However, the number of African American players remained small until the Civil Rights Movement. Once again reflecting social trends in America, political correctness of the 1990s questioned heretofore acceptable mascots and nicknames. Some schools acquiesced to the rising tide of complaints while others held on to campus traditions — much to the chagrin of opposition leaders. In professional football, the question of geographic expansion threatened owners much the same way it did in baseball. While the latter was able to hold off the formation of competitive leagues, the former used expansion and absorption as a means of regulating the industry.

College football had undergone integration in the late 19th century, but the number of nonwhite players was small, and there was seldom more than one on a team. With the advent of the 1939 UCLA Bruins, all of that changed in a rather dramatic fashion. As Lane Demas points out, there was no single Jackie Robinson type in this process, but rather a collective movement that paralleled the broader Civil Rights movement of the post–World War II era. Ironically, though, Robinson also played a significant role at the college level eight years before he broke baseball's color line. The other major players at UCLA, Kenneth Washington and Woody Strode, helped to integrate the professional game, and Strode later became a well-known Hollywood actor. Thus the story of the Bruin 11 served as a stepping stone for three men who went on to establish themselves in other professional arenas. This drama was played out against a stubborn Jim Crow that continued to deny black players their opportunity in the Deep South. The reader is left wondering if the powerful Tennessee squad would have faced UCLA had it qualified for the Rose Bowl or whether it would have simply ignored an integrated team.

While the question of racial inclusion came to the fore in the early days of college football, the race issue had still not faded away more than half a century later. This time the exclusion factor involved the use of mascots that were deemed politically insensitive to a particular minority that was on the outside looking in. Arthur J. Remillard investigates the controversy that engulfed Florida State University in recent years and demonstrates the religious fever that gripped both sides. To the university's supporters, the figure of Osceola mounted on a horse with spear in hand represented the symbol of strength in battle. Detractors found it demeaning, historically inaccurate, and racially insensitive. To many people, the real issue is political correctness and whether it expresses the whining of the left or the heavy-handedness of the right. Remillard emphasizes the religious bases of both sides in the hopes of coming to an amicable resolution.

Before adding new teams, baseball extended its base by moving the Dodgers and Giants to the West Coast. The National Football League, on the other hand, was forced to expand due to competition from the rival American Football League. The question was which city would be announced as the new hub of NFL activity. In his article on New Orleans's quest to become a "big league" city, Michael S. Martin demonstrates that its success in this venture resulted from political maneuvering both at the local and national levels. Modern-day sports fans might be taken aback at how the Superdome was approved by Crescent City voters with relative ease in the 1960s. The excitement of attracting a major league team back then would receive strong opposition by today's tax critics, as fans noticed with the recent relocation of the Montreal Expos to the nation's capital.

Auto racing has excited fans at the local level since the invention first hit the American scene, and it remains a fascination on small tracks around the nation. Many of the dirt tracks used in the early stages of racing were built on old horse racing tracks, and they remained unpaved for hard-core enthusiasts. Those who remain loyal to dirt over asphalt see their sport from a purist point of view and disdain the trendy NASCAR explosion on national television. Dirt-track racing peaked in the immediate post–World War II era and stirred great interest in small communities through the 1950s. However, local owners struggled against the rising tied of entertainment alternatives, especially television. Some people integral to the sport on the national level still find an attachment to the world of dirt-track racing. Its grass-roots appeal continues to draw interest from those who will always feel the attraction of car racing at its basic level. Still, one cannot ignore the explosion of NASCAR on the American sports scene and the evolution of the sport as it tries to accommodate the fans who cheer their favorites to a national championship.

The meaning that dirt-track racing has to hard-core fans is vividly described by Daniel Simone and Kendra Myers. They emphasize how the traditional form of racing became part of each community's fabric and an institution to those who support it at the local level. The authors show the roots of dirt-track racing, the importance of the kind of dirt that cars race on, the disdain for asphalt tracks and the pressure to compete with the enormous growth of NASCAR. The sport faces additional challenges from environmental groups and expanding suburban communities who complain of dust and noise. Still, the link that enthusiastic fans have for local-level racing is forged through longtime traditions that fulfill the need of those seeking the intimate thrill of car racing. Their satisfaction goes beyond the excitement of the race and relies more on the passion that has developed from a community bonding.

After the Second World War, stock car racing grew tremendously as Americans sought to entertain themselves after almost two decades of war and economic deprivation. Racetracks sprang up in rural areas throughout the South, and Brian Katen traces these developments in the state of Virginia. He is particularly concerned with the impact of these speedways on the state's landscape and how some of them remain a symbol of its racing heritage. Originating in numerous fairgrounds, they spread out to embrace convenient topographical features that allowed for banked turns and crowd protection. Lacking trained designers, they simply fit the contours of a site chosen for its adaptability to the sport. There was also a sense of mystery and anticipation in the location as fans would typically drive through areas that hid the tracks until the last moment. Here families and friends experienced social gatherings that forged community bonds, which created the foundation for NASCAR dads of today.

Keith Simmons represents the transition between dirt-track racing and NASCAR. While he has been very successful as a major engine builder on the circuit, his heart is still in local-level racing. No one could capture this better than David "Turbo" Thompson, who has researched the subject of racing for years and even participates in events. It took Thompson three interview attempts to capture the rather reclusive Simmons, but the results provide a blueprint for those who would take on the challenging task of running a dirt-track raceway. Simmons notes the hardships of turning a profit amidst the competition from alternative events in the battle for the entertainment dollar. Even more problematic is the weather; every track owner is just one storm from washing out a race that might have been months in the planning. Economic concerns aside, a racing enthusiast can't put his work first without his family and other relationships suffering. In spite of those shortcomings, the reader will be drawn into Simmons's passion for the track, which goes far beyond the sport and compels his devotion for something he loves.

In spite of the purists' love for the dirt tracks, NASCAR's popularity has gone off the charts. No sport has grown so dramatically in recent decades, and there is not a ceiling in sight. Or is there? Barbara S. Hugenberg and Lawrence W. Hugenberg express their concern for the sweeping changes that have altered the traditional base of the sport and led the organization to ignore its long-standing fan base for a new one. In this transition, gone are the "redneck" roots and in their place a more high-tech future. Yuppies in the far West and the Northeast have displaced the Southern families. Electric rock replaced country. The roots of the sport have given way to new locations with higher populations, and a change in determining the point system for champion awards has elevated late-season success over the struggle of the long haul. The reason for those alterations is, of course, television (read: money); corporate interests have replaced the traditional base. Other sports have gone through similar changes. Indeed, the wild-card winner in baseball (set up to expand playoffs and profit) has become the favorite to win the World Series. Rewarding the winner over the long season has given way to the team that paces itself for the last leg of the journey. The Hugenbergs have struck a chord that has reverberated throughout the world of sports, and there appears to be no end in sight.

In the final section of the book, we look at sports that have traditionally been confined to the male bastion — hockey, fishing and boxing. It is, however, a whole new world, and all three articles look at these sports from a fresh angle. In the realm of ice hockey, expansion followed the examples of other sports, but it required a unique experiment in advertising in order to sell the sport to an expanding audience unfamiliar with it. While most of us think of fishermen as anyone with a rod in hand and bait on the hook, they come in different classes. Finally, the boxing world has a unique brand of heroes whose courage leaves an imprint on followers of the ring, and even in the twilight of their careers, those heroes summon an inner resolve that still resonates years later.

Marketing in the modern age of sport has become so sophisticated that promoters from the early days simply pale in comparison to those presently hawking their product. Hockey especially faced a tough challenge because it was always considered a Canadian or regional American sport. Expansion meant that it was now moving into areas of the country that were totally unfamiliar with the game and its players. Hockey promoters could no longer appeal to just a knowledgeable audience; they had to focus on groups never thought of before. As a theater professor intimate with the nuances of reaching an audience, Kimberly Tony Korol deconstructs recent local and national hockey commercials to show how they are designed to reach unique segments of the audience with a special focus on women. The results are both eye-opening and humorous. The reader is left with the strong desire to view the commercials and perhaps even become a hockey fan in the process. The recent shutdown of the game might destroy much of these promotional advances and create yet a new challenge for marketing experts.

While advertisements for fishing tend to focus on a male audience, there is a certain class distinction for both genders that embraces method. It's no secret that fly fishermen see themselves apart from and above those who use live bait or cast a plug. Once again, the reader will observe the struggle between the purist and the pragmatist that creates controversy in other sports. For John F. Bratzel, the position of those who deal in fly fishing is simply elitist. Their claims of being more natural are disputed by the author, who denies any spiritual quality for those using a fly rod over a casting one. Bass fishing might seem too common for the fly crowd, but Bratzel feels that their sense of superiority is simply unwarranted. His refreshing look at a sport that has become a major hobby for many Americans might open further academic investigation of a leisure-time activity most have heretofore ignored.

Finally, Pete Williams reminds us why Muhammad Ali rose to icon status. He had not one defining moment, but many — so many, in fact, that he left his fans believing that his self-proclaimed title of "the Greatest" was no exaggeration. In his inimitable fashion, Williams describes the former champion's fight against Leon Spinks through the phrases of the two greatest wordsmiths of the era — Jim Murray and the champ himself. This is no unusual feat, for the author is unmatched in his stylistic accounts of the former heavyweight icon. The reader will be left wanting more, and rightfully so. Our final article, then, demands a sequel, and as sports becomes even more engrained in our society, the reader will look forward to equally investigative examinations of the contests that attract our attention and stir our competitive spirits.

All of these articles demonstrate that a new area of research has opened up to scholars around the nation over the past two decades. The authors' research has delved into the sports that Americans love but many felt were too frivolous for academic study. This collection of their works provides slices of the sporting experience and thus points the way to future research. They give sports a new meaning in our culture and have expanded the interests and curiosity of everyone who reads this book. Students have found a new way to look at American history, and the general reader will be entertained by their efforts.

I. BASEBALL

1

The Fireman and the Mitt: The 1941 New York Yankees– Brooklyn Dodgers World Series

Bruce A. Rubenstein

As the dark clouds of war over Europe drifted toward the United States in 1941, baseball brought forth a ray of sunshine for the American people. Joe DiMaggio's 56 game hitting streak, Ted Williams's successful quest to bat over .400, and the return of the New York Yankees to the championship of the American League offered hope that, at least on the diamonds of the national pastime, all was normal.

Manager Joe McCarthy's Bronx Bombers avenged their third-place finish the previous year by amassing a 101–53 record to finish 17 games ahead of the second-place Boston Red Sox and 26 games above the defending league champion Detroit Tigers.

The Yankees' opponents were the Brooklyn Dodgers of manager Leo "The Lip" Durocher, the brash, dapper 35-year-old clotheshorse who formerly played shortstop for the Yankees, Cincinnati Reds, and St. Louis Cardinals. Under Durocher's driving influence, the "Bums" won their first league title in 21 years with a 100–54 record, nosing out the Cardinals by 2½ games.

On the eve of the Series, odds-makers, despite overwhelming fan support to the contrary, established the Yankees as 12-to-5 favorites in the upcoming struggle that John Kieran of the *New York Times* characterized as "…the common people against the aristocrats; the unwashed against the precious; the revolt of the masses against the luxurious overlords of established authority."[1] The ever-erudite Kieran added, "This Series shapes up like one of those old-fashioned 'town and gown' fights in some university town. The rough and ready ragamuffins against the college dandies in their academic costumes. The butcher boys against the bespectacled students. It's the crowd from the wrong side of the railroad tracks invading the restricted residential area bent on mischief."[2] As for the baseball fans' expectations, he concluded, "The Yankees are water coming out of the water tap. Good water. Pure, high-grade water — but just what was expected. The Dodgers, winning after all these years — are sparkling wine 'with beaded bubbles winking at the brim,' coming out of an old water tap from which not even very good water ran for years. Practically submerged in the general countrywide wave of enthusiasm over the Dodgers, the Yankees are paying something in the nature of a luxury tax. They are the rich boys, the aristocrats, the chaps brought up to dine off silver service. They have a baseball family tree of magnificent tradition. Their ancestors were 'kings — the powerful of the earth — the wise, the good.' They are paying for all that now. They are neglected — or placidly accepted — while the Dodgers ride high as the 'peepul's choice' — the team of kaleidoscopic color. The Dodgers of destiny. It may irk the Yankees to the extent that they will go looking for revenge on the flanneled causes of this revolt of the masses."[3]

In a less intellectual and poetic, but equally symbolic, fashion, the *New York Times* put the value of the Series in another perspective by editorializing: "The poor wretch who prides himself on being realistic says that two gangs of mercenaries will meet this afternoon at the Yankee Stadium. What, he will inquire, glancing bitterly at the passing throngs, is Manhattan or Brooklyn to them? Aren't they bought and sold like horses? Isn't it a business? Will anything be proved by the victory of either team? We say let those who despise the passions of a people keep to their ivory towers. We pause in the midst of the world's alarms. Did someone inquire as to the future of the human race? We'll take up that question next week."[4]

Early morning saw dark, threatening skies over the stadium, but by game time the clouds had parted and a bright sun warmed the record crowd of 68,540, a majority of whom were invading Dodger rooters who eagerly awaited Commissioner Kenesaw Mountain Landis to toss the ceremonial first pitch to Bill Dickey to signify the beginning of the contest.[5] As the managers met with the umpires to discuss the ground rules, Durocher, to the delight of the spectators, playfully leaned over and planted a kiss on McCarthy's cheek.[6] That gesture symbolically demonstrated what the Yankees already knew — the Dodgers were not intimidated by their foe. Lefty Gomez, in his ghost-written column, had warned that this Dodger team was not the typical October Senior Circuit sacrificial lamb, saying, "I've noticed that in some previous years the National Leaguers seemed to be afraid of the Yanks even before the Series started, but not this Brooklyn bunch. They act as if they were playing the [last-place] Phillies."[7]

To the delight of the Yankee partisans, the home team, behind the 37-year-old Red Ruffing's six-hit pitching, defeated Curt Davis and the Dodgers 3–2, despite having DiMaggio, Charlie Keller, and Tommy Henrich going hitless. This was, according to *Detroit News* columnist Bob Murphy, the equivalent of "passing a bill in Congress without FDR's Democrats having a vote."[8] However, as Grantland Rice sagely observed, "That's the way the Yankees have been for years. You can stop some of them all of the time, but you won't stop all of them any of the time, even with the use of tanks and machine guns."[9]

New York took a 1–0 lead in the second when Joe Gordon lined a home run into the lower left-field stands. Just as the ball landed, someone close to the spot fired three blank shots from a cartridge pistol, which led a Yankee fan from the Bronx to pronounce gravely: "T'ree Dodger fans has just blew their brains out."[10] The Bombers added solo runs in the fourth and sixth frames to more than offset the single tally the Dodgers made in fifth; however, the turning point of the came in the seventh when the Dodgers reverted to the daffy base-running tactics that had long been a hallmark of the Flatbush franchise. Cookie Lavagetto began the inning by reaching first on a bad throw by Phil Rizzuto and was singled to second by Pee Wee Reese. Pinch-hitter Lew Riggs singled to drive Lavagetto across and move Reese to third. Jimmy Wasdell, another pinch-hitter, was sent to the plate, with Durocher telling him, "Jim, Ruffing is trying to steam that first pitch past us, so take a cut at it. If you miss the first one, get the sign on what to do."[11] Wasdell swung and missed at the initial offering and, on the next pitch, swung again and lofted a foul fly behind third. Red Rolfe caught the ball, whirled, and threw to Dickey at home in time to tag out Reese, who foolishly tried to score after the catch. The rally was ended, and with it all the Dodgers' hopes for a triumph.

After the game, which marked the tenth straight Series victory for the Bronx Bombers, most scribes and baseball men ignored how close the Dodgers had come to victory, choosing instead to marvel at the men in pinstripes. Author and playwright Irvin Cobb gushed that the Yankees reminded him of the bourbon from his native state of Kentucky — "smooth but potent."[12] Humorist Arthur "Bugs" Baer said, "The Yanks took 'em as neat as a nurse's cap.[13] Billy Herman, who had faced the Bombers in two previous Series, moaned, "Those Yanks have more power than the Luftwaffe."[14] It was venerable Connie Mack, the 78-year-old manager of the Philadelphia Athletics, who verbalized best the thoughts of most observers when he said softly to reporters, "It was a nice Series, wasn't it?"[15]

The losers' clubhouse was a swirl of controversy and finger pointing, mostly aimed at Durocher. Baer spoke for most writers when he questioned Durocher's choice to start the 37-year-old journeyman Curt Davis, instead of either of his 22-game winners, Kirby Higbe or Whitlow Wyatt, saying, "It seems that if you put your best foot forward you won't get your corns stepped on."[16] Reese admitted that he tagged up and ran on his own and he sat with head bowed, telling reporters, "I thought I could make it. I was wrong that's all. It's all my fault."[17] Wasdell, who had been verbally assailed by his manager for missing the sign to lay down a sacrifice bunt after his first swing, was a mixture of tears and fury: "They [Durocher and third-base coach Charlie Dressen] say I missed a bunt signal, but I say I never saw any such signal! But there must have been one because Durocher bawled the hell out of me in the dugout. So it must have been my fault."[18]

After a shower and some introspection, Durocher told reporters regarding Wasdell's at-bat, "We blew our chance that inning. That's when we should have come through, but we didn't. What the hell! It's just one of those things. It's baseball. Sure it was a tough time to miss a sign like that, but it's not his fault. I'll take the responsibility. Don't blame Wasdell."[19]

Hearing his manager's "damning with faint praise" comment, Wasdell grew even more unhappy as it seemed Durocher was placing the loss squarely on him.[20] Coming to Wasdell's defense was his former manager with the Washington Senators, Bucky Harris, who told reporters, "I managed Wasdell for three years. Jimmy wasn't a smart ballplayer, but he never missed a signal. I doubt if Durocher gave him one."[21]

These internal Dodger recriminations led Lefty Gomez, the Yankee ace whose sore arm was preventing him from pitching, but not from wisecracking, in the Series, to assure reporters, "Nobody will ever steal the Dodgers' signals. They can't get them themselves."[22]

Durocher selected Wyatt to face Spud Chandler in the second game, and the long, lean Georgian, whose mediocre previous hurling for Detroit, Chicago, and Cleveland had led Grantland Rice to dub him "a stray vagabond, a wandering minstrel around the American League," responded by holding the Yankees to nine hits in a 3–2 Dodger triumph.[23] For the first four frames, Chandler had the Dodgers, who had been portrayed as "fire-eaters and smoke-belchers," appear as "quiet, respectable, and decent as nine gas meter readers" as he cruised along with a 2–0 lead.[24] However, "Durocher's Dandies" came to life and scored two runs in the fifth to tie the score and won the game with a run in the sixth.

The crowd of 66,248 sat in disbelief as the Yankees lost a Series game for the first time in so long that, as Henry McLemore of the United Press wrote, "The only men who remember it are so ancient that they are also able to give a firsthand account of the battle between the *Monitor* and the

Merrimac and F.D.R.'s first inauguration."[25] McLemore added cynically, "Not since the midget jumped into J. P. Morgan's lap and asked for the time of day have power, wealth, and dignity been so affronted as they were today when the Brooklyn Bums from the other side of the river licked the New York Yankees. It was like watching the scrubwoman shove Mrs. Astor out of her box at the Diamond Horseshoe at the opera or a swayback mule catch Whirlaway at the stretch and beat him at the wire."[26]

The Dodger clubhouse was exuberant after the victory. Club president and general manager Larry MacPhail, garbed in his familiar sunglasses and racetrack coat, boomed, "Those Yankees haven't a chance! We can beat that ball club easily. They had the breaks, but we won the game."[27] Equally arrogant, Durocher boasted, "This Series ought to be in the bag for us right now. We should have a 2–0 lead in games instead of being here with everything square if we hadn't blown that game yesterday! But we'll win, so why bother with it?"[28] Pug-nosed Kirby Higbe derisively sneered, "Those Yanks are just another ball club, and I'd just as soon pitch against them as the Phillies. Where'd they get all that stuff about Yankee invincibility anyway?"[29]

Brooklyn's gleeful predictions, based on a single victory, seemed premature to Yankee skipper Joe McCarthy, who greeted reporters in his clubhouse office with a sardonic, "You fellows haven't come in here on a loser in a long time, have you?"[30] "Marse Joe," looking pale and fidgeting with his hair as he sat in his arm chair, forced a weak smile as he explained his team's loss, saying gruffly, "They got all the breaks and we didn't. Yesterday was the other way around. They're happy, and we're not so happy. Guess you can't win 'em all."[31] Arthur "Bugs" Baer, noting that Wyatt issued five walks as well as surrendering nine hits, wrote, "All afternoon Wyatt was in more hot water than a washerwoman's thumb" and "had to bear down like the old lady who tried to put the pig in a market bag."[32] Baer said the only reason the Dodger ace survived was because his defense gave him "more support than a five-legged table" and "fielded like a farmer with two pitchforks."[33]

Ebbets Field, filled nearly to overflowing with 33,100 hatless, coatless, and shirtless Dodger faithful, was described by a stunned Meyer Berger of the stodgy *New York Times* as "a psychiatrist's nightmare."[34] Berger related, "If you turned your back on the diamond and looked into the heaving surf of parboiled faces, bare and sweating torsos, frantically glaring eyeballs, and watched the restless and violent gestures of the astonishing amount of alcoholics roaming through the stands, the effect was startling."[35] The scene was such that even a longtime ballpark usher admitted, "They look like someone left the cages open in the county asylum."[36]

Durocher's selection of the venerable 5'11", 185-pound, 40-year-old Fred Fitzsimmons to go against the Yanks' Marius Russo seemed to be vindicated, for he was, in the words of Baer, "going like syrup and waffles in the South on a frosty morning."[37] Henry McLemore noted that Fitzsimmons was working with only his heart, "because outside of his tricky knuckle-ball, his stuff went out with Hoover."[38] In the seventh inning, however, the aged hurler fell prey to his enthusiasm for the game. Russo laced a low line drive back up the middle of the diamond. Fitzsimmons should have stepped aside and let the second baseman field the ball, but the old warhorse instinctively tried to stop the ball himself. Unfortunately, before he could get his glove down, the ball struck his left kneecap with a sickening thud and bounded 70 feet into the air, which allowed shortstop Pee Wee Reese time to race in and make the inning-ending catch.[39]

Fitzsimmons's injury was more painful than serious—a bad bruise barely above the kneecap—but it was the beginning of the end for the Dodgers.[40] Hugh Casey, the Brooklyn relief ace who had pitched two-thirds of an inning of hitless ball in the first game, was called on to take the hill in the eighth. Casey, who had tossed only a few warm-ups in the bullpen, retired Johnny Sturm on a soft fly to center to start the frame, but then Red Rolfe drilled a single to right. Tommy Henrich beat out an infield roller between first and second when Casey failed to cover first base, which led Sid Feder of the Associated Press to belittle the pitcher: "Hugh must have been reaching for a fresh chaw and forgot."[41] This mental lapse was compounded when, pitching from the stretch to the next batter, Joe DiMaggio, Casey could have picked off Rolfe at second but chose instead to concentrate on retiring DiMaggio. This proved to be flawed thinking when "Joltin' Joe" lived up to Baer's prediction DiMaggio would end his hitless Series by "busting out like the fat boy's pantywaist" and laced a single to center, giving the Bombers the lead.[42] Charlie "King Kong" Keller, whose bat was jokingly said by admirers to be "so big that squirrels often mistook it for a tree and stored nuts in it," lumbered to the plate and bashed a single through the box, driving in a second Yankee run and sending Casey, who a reporter said "had a glazed look in his eyes that you see in Joe Louis' victims," to the showers.[43] The Dodgers countered with one run in their half of the eighth but were retired in order in the ninth, making the Yanks a 2–1 victor.

The fourth battle was waged on another sweltering, sunny day before 33,813 fans, many of whom were still shell-shocked by the events of the previous afternoon. However, even more amazing events awaited the unwitting Flatbush faithful. Entering the bottom of the fourth inning, the Yankees had amassed a 3–0 lead off Kirby Higbe. In the home half of the fourth, however, pinch-hitter Jimmy Wasdell atoned for his purported sin in the first game by doubling home two runs off Yankee starter Atley Donald and cutting the Bomber lead to a single tally. In the fifth, Dixie Walker doubled, and league batting champion Pete Reiser smashed a towering home run over the scoreboard to give the Dodgers a 4–3 lead.

Durocher then offered Casey an opportunity to redeem himself, and the big Georgian rose to the occasion masterfully. Entering the game in the fifth inning with two outs and the bases loaded, he doused the Yankee threat by inducing Joe Gordon to pop a soft fly to left. Casey deftly protected the slender margin through the eighth, but then Lady Luck once again turned her back on him and his teammates. Casey started the ninth by inducing Johnny Sturm to tap harmlessly to second, and Red Rolfe hit weakly back to Casey for the second out. "Old Reliable" Tommy Henrich strode to the plate. Casey glowered at the batter as he fired two fastballs past him for called strikes. As the third pitch neared the plate, Henrich let loose with a mighty swing and missed. However, the ball eluded catcher Mickey Owen's mitt, and Henrich beat Owen's tardy throw to first in an attempt to complete what should have been an inning-ending strikeout. His head now bowed in disbelief, the shaken Casey then surrendered a single to DiMaggio and a long double off the left-field wall by Keller, which drove in both runners and gave the Yanks the lead. Now both shell-shocked and heartbroken, Casey walked Bill Dickey. Gordon followed with a double over Wasdell's head in left, which drove in the final two runs of the frame. The crowd sat in stunned silence, not totally comprehending what their eyes had seen, for, as Meyer Berger noted in his parody poem, "... there is no joy in Flatbush. Fate had knocked their Casey out.⁴⁴

The drama surrounding Casey's pitch and Owen's muff overshadowed the fact that when they occurred Henrich represented nothing more than the potential tying run and perhaps merely was forestalling the inevitable Dodger triumph. No Yankee viewed it as a prelude to certain victory.

Durocher manfully shouldered the blame for the disastrous events— at least from a Dodger perspective — that followed. "I pulled a rock. I should have called time and gone to the mound to remind him [Casey] that he still needed only one out to end the game," an uncharacteristically humble Durocher confessed. "To slow him down, in other words, until I was absolutely sure that he was in full control of himself. He pitched to DiMaggio almost as soon as he had the ball in his hand, and Joe hit a bullet into left. The next batter was Charlie Keller, a left-handed hitter. Given everything that had been happening, the situation screamed for me to replace Casey with Larry French, a veteran left-handed pitcher. I did nothing. I froze. For the first time in my life, I was shell-shocked. Casey got two quick strikes on Keller and again we were only one strike away from winning. I should have gotten off the bench and gone out to the mound to talk to my pitcher. In a spot like that, especially after what happened, I've got to go out there and talk to the pitcher, slow him down. I've got to say to him,

'Look, you got him where you want him. Take your time. Waste a couple of pitches; maybe he'll go after a bad one.' Instead, I just sat on my ass and didn't do anything. I let Casey come right back with the pitch that Keller hit for the game winning double. I asked myself what could be gained by going out and getting everyone jumpy? I was guilty of defensive, timid thinking. It will kill you every time."[45]

Durocher exacerbated the situation by not yanking the embattled Casey even after Dickey walked and Gordon doubled across the Yankees' final two scores in a 7–4 triumph that put them within one game of enabling McCarthy to pass Connie Mack's record of managing five world championship teams. "Bugs" Baer sympathetically summarized Casey's plight, observing, "He blew higher than an alto clarinet, but I don't blame the poor old mugg. He's a country doctor who is only called when someone's in trouble. When the country doctor is in trouble there isn't any one he can call."[46]

Baseball scribes sat at their typewriters eagerly pounding out words to express their astonishment over how the Yankees scored four runs after three were out. Baer said, "It's the most amazing end to a baseball game I ever saw, and I've been around ever since there have been taxes. Nobody goes back farther than that."[47] Glib Henry McLemore, who confessed that only once a year did he "not try to be cute, funny, or a good man with a phrase," mused, "From now on don't let anyone tell you that water doesn't run uphill or that fish do not make fine mountain climbers or that blood is not easily extracted from turnips. After that victory of the Yankees nothing is impossible. If someone came up and told me that Hitler had been awarded the Nobel Peace Prize and that Sally Rand had just been elected national president of the Girl Scouts it wouldn't surprise me one bit."[48] A non-bylined scribe for the wire services proclaimed, "It was as though the condemned man jumped out of the chair and electrocuted the warden."[49] John Kieran was, for once, virtually speechless: "Baffling! Bewildering! But truly Brooklyn baseball of the old whirling dervish tradition."[50] Staid John Drebinger concurred with his more colorful *New York Times* colleague, saying, "It couldn't, perhaps, have happened anywhere else on earth, but it did happen yesterday in Brooklyn."[51] Red Smith echoed, "It could only happen in Brooklyn. Nowhere else in this broad, untidy universe, not in Bedlam nor in Babel nor in the remotest psychopathic ward nor the sleaziest padded cell could The Thing be. Only in the ancestral home of the Dodgers could a man win a World Series game by striking out."[52]

The losers' clubhouse was a mixture of sadness, disbelief, and anger. Durocher absolved his battery from all blame, criticizing instead police who charged onto the field for crowd control the moment umpire Larry Goetz called the third strike on Henrich. "Why, one stupid sergeant was standing on home plate," Durocher fumed. "Owen never could have thrown

Henrich out through all those cops."[53] Still stunned by the rapid turn of events that gave him the unenviable record of being the first pitcher ever to lose World Series games on consecutive days, Casey said merely, "I figured I'd throw Henrich a curve and put everything I had on the pitch. I bore down especially hard. The ball really had a great break on it."[54] Owen, a brilliant defensive backstop who had gone almost a year without being charged with an error, sat on the trainer's table sobbing. "It wasn't a good ball to hit," he explained. "It was a low inside curve that I should have had. It wasn't a spitter. It was a great breaking curve that I should have had, but I guess the ball hit the side of my mitt. It got away from me, and by the time I got hold of it near the corner of our dugout, I couldn't have thrown anybody out at first. It was an error. I don't mind being the goat. I'm just sorry I cost the other guys money."[55]

Publicly, most Dodger players blamed bad luck for the defeat. Dixie Walker said disgustedly, "I tell you those fellows have got all of the luck on their side. I never saw a team get so many breaks as they have."[56] Jimmy Wasdell sneered, "There are angels flying around those Yankees, I tell ya."[57]

Away from newspapermen, however, some players were less charitable toward their battery duo. Pee Wee Reese confided that the errant pitch was because "Mr. Casey might have given Henrich the wet slider. Casey could throw a spitball and get it over at any time. We had that game in our pocket, and I'm out there thinking, 'It sure looks like we're gonna get our ass beat now.' And we sure did."[58] Billy Herman never wavered in his blame of Owen, saying the backstop "might have 'nonchalanted' the ball, putting his glove out for it instead of shifting his whole body to make the catch. Owen had a habit of doing that."[59] Herman's assessment was seconded by minor league manager Billy Meyer of Kansas City, who felt that Owen tried to catch Casey's throw "with his knees together rather than with a shift of his body."[60]

Amid the moans and whispers came the most fitting epitaph for the day. John A. Heydler, longtime president of the Senior Circuit, asked reporters plaintively, "Must these things always happen to the National League?"[61]

As was to be expected, the visitors' clubhouse rang with cries of jubilation. Coach Art Fletcher set the tone, loudly urging reporters, "Go get a story from Owen. He's always giving out stories to papers. He's got a pip tonight."[62] Henrich laughed and yelled, "I bet Owen feels like a nickel's worth of dog meat."[63] Joe Gordon shouted, "The game is never over till the last man's out, eh?"[64] Even the usually quiet DiMaggio piped in: "Well, they say everything happens in Brooklyn. They'll never recover from this one."[65] Reflecting on how Owen had tried to spike Rizzuto earlier in the Series, DiMaggio spoke for his teammates by adding somberly, "As long as there has to be a goat, I'm glad it's Owen. We're not a bit sorry for him."[66] Lefty Gomez wisecracked, "It was just the way we planned it. We've been working on that play for some months on the quiet, but we didn't have it perfected until today."[67] To a man, no one in the room that late afternoon would have challenged "Bugs" Baer's proclamation that now "the World Series is a strawberry on the Yankees' shortcake."[68]

The Dodgers were a thoroughly demoralized squad the next day when they faced Ernie Bonham before 34,072 Ebbets Field partisans who acted as though they were attending a funeral. As Billy Herman later admitted, "We were licked before we went out on the field. We couldn't have beaten a girls' team."[69] The wake like atmosphere was broken briefly when Owen came to the plate in the bottom of the second and received a 30-second standing ovation from the forgiving fans.[70] However, by then the Yankees had a 2–0 lead, and were on their way to a 3–1 victory and their fifth world championship in six years.

The only excitement on the field came when Whit Wyatt, who once boasted, "If DiMaggio was playing in the National League, he'd have to swing while he's flat on his ass," deliberately threw high and inside to the Yankee outfielder in each of his first two at-bats, once knocking him down with two consecutive pitches. After the second close shave, DiMaggio shouted, "What the hell are you trying to do? " Wyatt responded, "Joe, if you try to dig in against me again, you'll be in a squat position the rest of your life."[71] Whether intimidated or not by Wyatt, whom he referred to in later years as the "meanest guy I ever saw in my life," DiMaggio fanned his first two times at bat, the only time he had struck out twice in a game all season.[72] With one out in the fifth inning, Henrich drove a long home run over the right field wall. Furious, Wyatt, urged on by teammates shouting, "Stick it in his ear, Whit!" sought revenge against the next batter, who happened to be DiMaggio, knocking him down once again before the Yankee Clipper lofted a fly to center.[73] As he loped past Wyatt on his way back to the Yankee bench, the usually mild-mannered slugger jibed, "The Series is over, boy, so take it easy." Wyatt replied, "If you can't take it, you Dago son of a bitch, why the hell don't you get out of the game."[74] DiMaggio shouted back, "Okay, we've whipped your team, so I might as well whip you," and started toward Wyatt.[75] Owen charged out from behind the plate to intercept DiMaggio and both dugouts emptied, but the umpires converged on the potential combatants before any blows were struck.[76] This incident, according to Bill Boni of the Associated Press, "made DiMaggio as popular with the crowd as the girl with the picture hat who sits in front of you at the movies."[77]

In the Dodger dressing quarters, the players' analysis was that they had been victims of fate rather than their own poor play. Dixie Walker, who hit only .222 in the Series, moaned, "I've played for and against the Yankees, and they're the luckiest club that ever stepped onto a ball field. It doesn't seem right that one club should get all the luck."[78] Dolph Camilli, who had led the National League in homers and runs batted in during the regular season but batted a miniscule .167 with six strikeouts in the Series, said, "If we'd gotten just half the breaks, not all of them, the Series right now should be no worse than three games to two in our favor."[79]

Club management was more gracious, and honest, than the players. Chief scout Ted McGrew lauded the Yankees, saying, "They played five games without making a mistake."[80] Durocher said only, "I think my boys played some good baseball, but they beat us. We just simply didn't have quite enough. But we gave them one helluva fight, didn't we?"[81] Then, wearing only his underwear, Durocher rushed through a private door to the visitors' clubhouse to congratulate McCarthy.[82] Even owner Larry MacPhail was uncommonly temperate, telling reporters, "They beat us because they were a better team."[83] Asked about Durocher's fate, MacPhail said of the man he had oft threatened to fire during the season, "He will be second-guessed, but he has managed for me in this World Series, and he'll manage for me in next season's 154 games, too."[84]

The Dodgers' president took the defeat very hard, however. His drinking increased and his mental stability grew more uncertain, and in September 1942, MacPhail resigned his post before he was to be removed and entered the United States Army as a lieutenant colonel. Ironically, MacPhail returned to baseball in 1945 as co-owner of the Yankees and guided them to more post season championships over his former team. Equally ironic was the tragic fate of hard-drinking, melancholy Hugh Casey, who ended his career in 1949 as a Yankee, and two years later used the hunting rifle his appreciative Brooklyn teammates once had presented him to commit suicide.[85]

The Yankee clubhouse was joyous mayhem. James P. Dawson of the *New York Times* described the scene: "It looked like a free-for-all fight. Punches were flying, bodies were swaying, trunks were being banged around, benches were pushed out of place, towels were thrown through the air, and the noise was terrific."[86] Amid champagne, beer, and cigars, coach Art Fletcher stood upon a trunk, screaming, "We moidered duh Bums! We moidered duh Bums!"[87] Fletcher then led the traditional Yankee victory theme "East Side, West Side," and followed that with a rousing, off-key rendition of "Roll Out the Barrel."[88] Only DiMaggio remained aloof, sitting on his stool, smoking, and watching the revelry with a wan smile.[89] McCarthy, sitting on a trunk in front of his locker, told reporters, "I'm glad it's over, and I'm glad we won. I never go into any Series that I didn't expect to win four straight — nuts to those fifth and sixth games."[90]

Among sportswriters the general feeling was that the best team won and for some that the Series victory had elevated the Yankees of 1941 to the plateau of greatness. Cy Peterman of the *Philadelphia Inquirer* gushed, "The Yankees are the greatest ball club of modern times."[91] Bill Dooley of the *Philadelphia Record* was only slightly more restrained, writing, "Probably there have been better ball clubs than this Yankee one, but this edition will do."[92] Shirley Povich of the *Washington Post* claimed that they were no longer suffering the post–Ruthian hangover of being viewed simply as winning through sheer power, noting, "The Yankees buttress their power with slick fielding, smart base running, and the fire of National League clubs."[93]

However, many scribes agreed with the whining Dodgers that the new champions were simply lucky. Havey J. Boyle of the *Pittsburgh Post-Gazette* said, "The Yankees are a good club, but something this side of an immortal galaxy."[94] Frank Lewis of the *Cleveland Press* concurred, writing, "The Yanks are not a great ball club. Luck was running with them, as luck invariably runs with the Yanks. The Dodgers might have won the Series in four straight had the breaks gone their way."[95] Herbert Simons of the *Chicago Daily Times* acknowledged the Dodgers' bad fortunes as well: "Sure the Yankees got the breaks this time. As weird an assortment of ill-luck dogged the Dodgers as had hounded any World Series team."[96]

Such assertions raised the ire of McCarthy and Yankee president Edward Barrow. The usually placid McCarthy griped to veteran New York writer Dan Daniel, "I believe that for aftermath bologna the 1941 Series set an all-time record. You would think we had no pitching and no hitting, and that the Brooklyn club handed us everything on a platter. The dope shows that we had: 1) the better run making team; 2) the stronger hitting team; 3) the stronger fielding team; 4) the better pitching; 5) the better poise and confidence; and 6) the old Yankee style. But some of the reviewers of the Series say our title was tainted. I wonder if they know the definition of the word 'tainted'? They say we were lucky. Some of the writers accuse Mickey Owen as if the poor fellow was Judas Iscariot, Jesse James, and Benedict Arnold all rolled up into one. The fact is what got away from Owen was a wild pitch. Henrich should have walked on it, but he swung. By being fooled badly on a sharp breaking curve that was too low to catch, Henrich turned Owen into the goat. Owen put Henrich on first base, not the scoring dish. That failure to get the third strike meant putting the tying run three bases away from home. The Dodgers did not lose the fourth game. We won it. DiMaggio singled. Keller doubled. Dickey walked. Gordon doubled. It was a rally. But our title is tainted! Was there ever such drivel written by competent men who ought to know better?"[97]

Barrow seconded his manager, defiantly telling the editor of *The Sporting News*, J. G. Taylor Spink, "What is luck in baseball? Any club which wins is lucky. Luck, my eye! Why not give credit to the Yankees for taking advantage of the breaks? Why not recognize the fact that the third strike that got away from Owen was a wild pitch? Why not admit that the ball which struck Fitzsimmons would have gone out to center for two bases with a run in? Luck, my eye! This 1941 team of ours is greater than anybody has given them credit for being. It's a winning organization — balanced on the field, balanced in the clubhouse, balanced at home, and managed by a remarkable leader."[98]

Perhaps "Bugs" Baer explained the outcome best, saying, "The Dodgers learned you can't win a war with no triggers on your muskets, but the Yankees won mostly because they have a Sunday punch for every day in the week."[99] However, Associated Press writer Bill Boni put the Series, and American innocence, into perspective, writing two months to the day before the attack on Pearl Harbor, "OK, boys, put the war news back on page one. The real battle is over."[100]

Notes

1. John Kieran, "Sports of the *Times,*" *New York Times,* October 1, 1941.
2. *Ibid.*
3. *Ibid.*
4. Editorial, *New York Times,* October 1, 1941.
5. John Drebinger, "Yanks Down Dodgers 3–2 in Opener," *New York Times,* October 2, 1941; Gene Schoor, *The History of the World Series* (New York: William Morrow and Co., 1990), 183.
6. John Kieran, "Sports of the *Times,*" *New York Times,* October 2, 1941.
7. Lefty Gomez, "Dodgers Unafraid of Us," *Detroit Times,* October 2, 1941.
8. Bob Murphy, "Bob Tales," *Detroit Times,* October 2, 1941.
9. Grantland Rice, "Old Red Ruffing a Winner Again," *Detroit Free Press,* October 2, 1941.
10. Meyer Berger, "25,000 at Gates Early in Morning," *New York Times,* October 2, 1941.
11. "Ah, Yes! It's a Dodger Play," *Detroit Free Press,* October 2, 1941.
12. Pat Robinson, "Wasdell Burned," *Detroit Times,* October 2, 1941.
13. Arthur Baer, "Blames Durocher," *Detroit Times,* October 2, 1941.
14. Robinson, "Wasdell Burned," *Detroit Times,* October 2, 1941.
15. *Ibid.*
16. Baer, "Blames Durocher," *Detroit Times,* October 2, 1941.
17. Leo Macdonnell, "Reese Takes Rap for Boner Play," *Detroit Times,* October 2, 1941; "Gossip of the First Game," *The Sporting News,* October 9, 1941.
18. Pat Robinson, "Reese Admits Fault," *Detroit Times,* October 2, 1941; Roscoe McGowen, "Brooklyn Squad Angered by Loss," *New York Times,* October 2, 1941; Gerald Eskenazi, *The Lip* (New York: William Morrow and Company, 1993), 134.
19. McGowen, "Brooklyn Squad Angered by Loss," *New York Times,* October 2, 1941; Eskenazi, *The Lip,* 135.
20. McGowen, "Brooklyn Squad Angered by Loss, *New York Times,* October 2, 1941.
21. Eskenazi, *The Lip,* p. 135: Robert Creamer, *Baseball in '41* (New York: Viking, 1991), 296.
22. J. G. T. Spink. "Looping the Loops," *The Sporting News,* October 9, 1941.
23. Grantland Rice, "A Smart Attack and Wyatt Cash In," *Detroit Free Press,* October 3, 1941.
24. John Kieran, "Sports of the *Times,*" *New York Times,* October 3, 1941.
25. Henry McLemore, "Dignity Dealt Blow by Dodgers," *Detroit Free Press,* October 3, 1941.
26. *Ibid.*
27. John Henry, "Dodgers to a Man Figure Series in Bag," *Detroit Free Press,* October 3, 1941.
28. *Ibid.*
29. *Ibid.*

30. James P. Dawson, "McCarthy Points to Day's Breaks," *New York Times*, October 3, 1941.

31. *Ibid*; Leo Macdonnell, "Rain Halts Yank, Dodger Third Game," *Detroit Times*, October 3, 1941; "McCarthy Ain't Feeling Right," *Detroit Free Press*, October 3, 1941.

32. Arthur Baer, "Wyatt Got More Support Than a Five-Legged Table," *Detroit Times*, October 3, 1941.

33. *Ibid.*

34. Meyer Berger, "Brooklyn Frenzy Hits a New High," *New York Times*, October 5, 1941.

35. *Ibid.*

36. *Ibid.*

37. Arthur Baer, "Series Tighter Than a Dude's Collar," *Detroit Times*, October 5, 1941.

38. Henry McLemore, "Fat Freddie Fitzsimmons Betrayed by a Heart That Was Two Sizes Too Full of Courage," *Detroit Free Press*, October 5, 1941.

39. *Ibid.*

40. Creamer, *Baseball in '41*, 303.

41. Sid Feder, "Even Yankee Fans Sorry to See Fitz Knocked Out, *Flint Journal*, October 5, 1941.

42. Baer, "Wyatt Got More Support Than a Five-Legged Table," *Detroit Times*, October 3, 1941.

43. McLemore, "Fat Freddie Fitzsimmons Betrayed by a Heart That Was Too Full of Courage," *Detroit Free Press*, October 5, 1941; Eskenazi, *The Lip*, p. 136; Creamer, *Baseball in '41*, 306.

44. Meyer Berger, "Casey in the Box — 1941," *New York Times*, October 6, 1941.

45. Durocher, *Nice Guys Finish Last*, 130; Creamer, *Baseball in '41*, 311; Eskenazi, *The Lip*, 139.

46. Arthur Baer, "Dodgers Torpedoed in Home Waters," *Detroit Times*, October 6, 1941.

47. *Ibid.*

48. Henry McLemore, "Casey's Defeat After He Had Won Proves There Is Nothing Impossible Anymore," *Detroit Free Press*, October 6, 1941; Henry McLemore, "Gordon Is Difference Between Yanks and Dodgers," *Detroit Free Press*, October 7, 1941.

49. Curt Smith, *Voices of the Game* (South Bend: Diamond Communications, 1987), 51.

50. John Kieran, "Sports of the *Times*," *New York Times*, October 6, 1941.

51. John Drebinger, "Yanks Win in Ninth," *New York Times*, October 6, 1941.

52. Red Smith, *Red Smith on Baseball* (Chicago: Ivan R. Dee, 2000), 3.

53. "Gossip of the Fourth Game," *The Sporting News*, October 9, 1941; Roscoe McGowen, "Owen Shoulders Entire Blame for Blunder," *New York Times*, October 6, 1941; Dom DiMaggio, *Real Grass, Real Heroes* (New York: Zebra Books, 1990), 220.

54. McGowen, "Owen Shoulders Entire Blame for Blunder," *New York Times*, October 6, 1941.

55. *Ibid*; "'I Should Have Had It,'" Sobs Owen," *Flint Journal*, October 6, 1941; Creamer, *Baseball in '41*, 312.

56. McGowen, "Owen Shoulders Entire Blame for Blunder," *New York Times*, October 6, 1941.

57. *Ibid.*

58. Eskenazi, *The Lip*, 140; Golenbock, *Bums*, 74.

59. Donald Honig, *Baseball When the Grass Was Real* (Lincoln: University of Nebraska Press, 1975), 152

60. J. G. T. Spink, "Looping the Loops, *The Sporting News*, October 9, 1941.

61. Frederick G. Lieb, *The Story of the World Series* (New York: G.P. Putnam's Sons, 1965), 278.

62. James P. Dawson, "Facetious Pair Perfected Play," *New York Times*, October 6, 1941; Harold Parrott, "There'll Be Changes Made, But Not for Durocher," *The Sporting News*, October 9, 1941.

63. Mario Amoruso, *Gil Hodges: The Quiet Man* (Middlebury: Paul S. Eriksson, 1991), 35.

64. Dawson, "Facetious Pair Perfected Play," *New York Times*, October 6, 1941.

65. *Ibid*; Eskenazi, *The Lip*, 140.

66. Creamer, *Baseball in '41*, 312.

67. Dawson, "Facetious Pair Perfected Play, *New York Times*, October 6, 1941; "Gossip of the Fifth Game," *The Sporting News*, October 9, 1941.

68. Baer, "Dodgers Torpedoed in Home Waters," *Detroit Times*, October 6, 1941.

69. Honig, *Baseball When the Grass Was Real*, 152.

70. Eskenazi, *The Lip*, 141.

71. Creamer, *Baseball in '41*, 313; Honig, *Baseball When the Grass Was Real*, 306–307.

72. Honig, *Baseball When the Grass Was Real*, 306; Eskenazi, *The Lip*, 141.

73. Tom Meany, "The Yankee Clipper," *Sport Magazine* (August 1959), 75.

74. Dom DiMaggio, *Real Grass, Real Heroes*, 214–215; Roscoe McGowen, "Bombers Lauded by Dodger Scout," *New York Times*, October 7, 1941; Michael Seidel, *The Streak* (New York: Penguin Books, 1988), 213; McLemore, "Gordon is Difference Between Yanks and Dodgers," *Detroit Free*

Press, October 7, 1941; Frank Graham, *The Brooklyn Dodgers* (Carbondale: Southern Illinois University Press, 2002, reprint of 1945 edition published by G.P. Putnam's Sons.), 213.

75. McLemore, "Gordon Is Difference Between Yanks and Dodgers," *Detroit Free Press*, October 7, 1941.

76. *Ibid*; John Kieran, "Sports of the *Times*," *New York Times*, October 7, 1941; Creamer, *Baseball in '41*, 313.

77. Bill Boni, "Present Yankees Different from Others," *Flint Journal*, October 7, 1941.

78. "Gossip of the Fifth Game," *The Sporting News*, October 9, 1941.

79. McGowen, "Bombers Lauded by Dodger Scout," *New York Times*, October 7, 1941.

80. *Ibid.*

81. *Ibid*; "Gossip of the Fifth Game," *The Sporting News*, October 9, 1941.

82. Parrott, "There'll be Changes, But Not for Durocher," *The Sporting News*, October 9, 1941.

83. Gayle Talbot, "Luckless Dodgers Admit They Were Beaten by a Better Team," *Flint Journal*, October 7, 1941.

84. Parrott, "There'll Be Changes, But Not for Durocher," *The Sporting News*, October 9, 1941.

85. Golenbock, *Bums*, 62.

86. James P. Dawson, "Jubilant Yanks Pound Each Other," *New York Times*, October 7, 1941.

87. Eskenazi, *The Lip*, 141.

88. Dawson, "Jubilant Yanks Pound Each Other," *New York Times*, October 7, 1941.

89. Richard Ben Cramer, *Joe DiMaggio* (New York: Simon & Schuster, 2000), 89.

90. Charles Dunkley, "Usually Staid Yankees Let Their Hair Down," *Detroit Free Press*, October 7, 1941.

91. "Experts Perform an Autopsy," *The Sporting News*, October 16, 1941.

92. *Ibid.*

93. *Ibid.*

94. *Ibid.*

95. *Ibid.*

96. *Ibid.*

97. Dan Daniel, "Giants Asking for Trade Offer," *The Sporting News*, October 16, 1941.

98. J. G. T. Spink, "Looping the Loops," *The Sporting News*, October 16, 1941.

99. Arthur Baer, "Bonham of Bonham and Bailey," *Detroit Times*, October 7, 1941.

100. Boni, "Present Yanks Different from Others," *Flint Journal*, October 7, 1941

2

Eight Ways of Looking at a Musial

Joseph Stanton

This inquiry addresses a question that has no definitive answer. Great athletes, like great works of art, are ultimately indefinable. That is, in fact, what makes them great. An athlete that is solvable, that is easily comprehended and resolved is without difficulty for his or her opponents and is therefore easily defeated. My examination of a number of poems looking at one of the best hitters ever to play the game, Stan "The Man" Musial, is meant to explore the possibility that poetry might have its uses in addressing the mystery of the great athlete. These Musial poems are taken from my book, *Cardinal Points: Poems on St. Louis Cardinals Baseball.*[1]

Among the tributes issued when Stan Musial retired was Ford Frick's: "Here stands baseball's perfect warrior. Here stands baseball's perfect knight."[2] Frick's allusion to Wordsworth's poem "The Happy Warrior"[3] to underscore his esteem for a much-idealized athlete is indicative of the role poetry can play as we endeavor to capture what we think and feel about great athletes.

The title of my essay, "Eight Ways of Looking at a Musial," echoes, of course, the title of Wallace Stevens' classic poem "Thirteen Ways of Looking at a Blackbird."[4] It is useful to consider Warren Goldstein's declaration in his essay "Inside Baseball" that baseball narratives can be boiled down to two basic varieties: Sometimes they are "linear, chronological narrative[s] that [deal] mainly with the material stuff of the game," and other times they are "cyclical, generational [narratives] organized around the emotional response to baseball." In other words when we write about baseball, we tend to choose between the dryly factual and the mythically celebratory. Even

28

though he is a historian and a prose writer, Goldstein goes on to say that the form of writing in which the contrary tendencies toward fact on the one hand and legend on the other are best reconciled is in poetry: Goldstein argues that "the narratives with the subtlest and strongest grasp of baseball's simultaneous thing-ness and mystery, fact and emotion, lie in poetry."[5]

In my examples you will see that I ask my poems to address both of the polarities defined by Goldstein. I expect them to move up and down the spectrum between external facts and the interior truths. Some of my poems endeavor to characterize the legendary mystery of Musial; others are content to refer to it without trying to consider its nuances. I make no special claim for my poems. They do not come close to exhausting the many ways that poetry might consider great players, but the diversity of this batch of poems is illustrative, I think, of a range of possibilities.

"Stan 'The Man' Musial," the first baseball poem I wrote back in 1980, attempts to catch the essence of the legendary hitter by attending to the facts of his play, the fascination he held for his fans, and the effect his performance had on pitchers who needed to try to get him out. Using references to the oracles of Apollo and the riddle of the sphinx, I present Musial as inscrutable, unsolvable, seemingly undefeatable. This theme is picked up in several of my other Musial pieces, but here it is presented most centrally. This poem, in which the Musial legend predominates, was my first attempt to capture the essence of Musial. I strove to achieve an essential Musial without reducing the potency of his legend.

STAN "THE MAN" MUSIAL

He made it look easy
so we tried twisting
our little-leagued bodies

into the incipient
violence of his pose,
a spring pulled tight,

crouching deep in the box.
But we could not invoke
the swift accurate stroke

that sent the balls
where they needed to go.
All pitchers feared him,

this gentle, soft-spoken,
line-drive-making machine
who shaped himself

into a question

they could not resolve
no matter how sharp their answers.

There was no hurled prayer
this smiling, chewing oracle
could not fend off.[6]

In "The Space-Time Continuum and the Slow Eye of Stan 'The Man,'"
I take the legendary prowess of Musial for granted, and the focus is on the
marvelousness of great hitting, of which Musial's is just one example. This
poem addresses a particular legend concerning the nature of such great hitting skill — namely the idea that the most successful hitters are able to see
the ball more completely than other hitters by means of their knack for
somehow slowing down the approaching ball in the mind's eye. This poem
attempts to do justice to both the fact of great skill and the transcendent
nature of its performance. Musial inhabits my words here as a supreme
instance, but the poem is concerned with all the great hitters who might,
perhaps, possess the gift of the "slow eye."

THE SPACE-TIME CONTINUUM AND THE
SLOW EYE OF STAN "THE MAN"

"Well, you wait for a strike. Then you knock the shit out of it."
— Stan Musial's advice to Curt Flood on hitting

The greatest of hitters, legend has it,
have learned the trick of the slow eye:
a magic that contrives to see in slowed

emotion every turn and twist of hurled
white sphere that rotates its seams
in heightened view for those who've found the way

to note the ball's in-flight curve or swerve
or straight and narrowed path, heart-to-heart,
so that the bat can be administered

precisely dead-on through the line of fire,
for the sake of the sweetest intersection
that sends the pill back the other way,

remaking its career, and the pitcher's, too.
It's as if history were rewriting itself
on the way to the plate; as if the ball

destined for a soft home, a shelter,
a tender pocket of comfort and desire,
were snatched of a sudden by death's

harvesting swing, which must be seen though,
in this case at least, as just another life
arising in what some eyes have come to know.[7]

In a few of my baseball poems I endeavor to capture some distinctive remarks by players, shaping and arranging the lines to accentuate the key point made in the famous statement. These could be characterized as "found poems." In the case of "Preacher Roe on How to Get Musial Out," I am treating Musial's inscrutability entirely from the point of view of a famous pitcher. In Preacher Roe's little joke it is assumed that there is no conventional way that even the most excellent pitching might defeat this remarkable hitter; thus the trick of walking him and then attempting to pick him off first provides the means to sidestep the problem of his insolvability at the plate by transforming him into a baserunner. An interesting minor point to this joke is that it implies that Musial, though a fast runner in his youth, is not regarded as godlike on the basepaths. One would not, of course, have made such a remark about certain other superstars— Lou Brock, for instance. Rowe's joke proposes that Musial's legendary status resides in his amazing hitting, with the tangential implication that Musial might be a normal human being in other facets of his game.

PREACHER ROE ON HOW TO GET MUSIAL OUT

> I throw
> four wide ones,
> and then
> I try to pick him off first.[8]

The legend of the kindly baseball star patiently signing autographs for large groups of excited children is a cliché that is not routinely true. In practice few players have the patience to stand around signing endlessly on a regular basis, and one can understand why. It is a wearying activity and has nothing to do with winning ballgames and advancing one's career. John Falter's much-reproduced *Saturday Evening Post* cover captures the fact that Musial was one of the few veterans who would do this sort of thing. Thus, while Falter's picture represents the mythic relationship between a baseball star and his young fans, Falter also happens to be giving a fairly truthful presentation of Musial's heroic patience. My prose poem "John Falter's *Saturday Evening Post* Cover (May 1, 1954), Showing Stan Musial Signing Autographs for Kids" is a small memoir that endeavors to recall what I personally know about this aspect of Musial. I make no attempt to rhetorically enhance my recollection to render it poetical. My exercise here is kept quite prosaically factual to testify to the plain truth of this little bit of legendary lore. Part of what was going on, of course, was that Musial was participating in the creation of his own legend. He understood that he was doing a wonderful thing and also realized that he was earning admiration for doing it. But the speaker in my poem, who is primarily a recollected younger version of me, sees no selfish motive on Musial's part. I present my speaker unambiguously as a devotee of the legend of Saint Stan.

John Falter's *Saturday Evening Post* Cover (May 1, 1954), Showing Stan Musial Signing Autographs for Kids

One of those kids might have been me. At any home
game we could count on him. If we waited beneath the
ramp where the players had to pass, autographs would come
to some of us for as long as the guys were willing to
stop and sign. Almost always it was Musial and the
rookies who lingered longest. The rookies loved to be
asked, though we seldom really knew who they were. Often
we were still not sure after long scrutiny of their
hurried scrawls. Their names were sometimes not even
listed in the infrequently updated rosters we had in
hand. Sometimes they were long gone back to one of the
Bush Leagues by the next week.

But Musial was something else. Even his signature
was classic and classy with those big rounded loops that
lent drama to his calligraphic swings of the pen.
Looking back, his patience defies belief, his kindly
leanings to the clamorous beseechings from which most of
the other stars quickly fled. Game after game that was
the way it was on the ramp: the Man and the Kids. It
seems too Norman Rockwell to be true, but it was.

And down through the years my collection of Musial
signatures grew, even after he retired. It seemed every
year or two we ran into him somewhere — at the shopping
mall where my mother worked, at a Hawks game, in Forest
Park, at every sort of St. Louis place. When he saw you
recognized him, he flashed that wide friendly smile, and,
if you asked, he would sign almost anything. Most of
mine were on things like soiled scorecards, popcorn
megaphones, napkins, paper bags. I never seemed to have
a decent piece of paper when we ran into him.

All those kindly signings are gone now, perhaps lost
in a flooded basement or the sale of my parents' house.
I'm not sure where they went or when or why, but I can
never forget Stan the Man's lightning smile, a signifying
gesture that said he never took himself too seriously but
understood why we kids would never stop pursuing him.[9]

Images of star players can come to be religious icons of fandom. Many
of the most revered baseball images have been photographs, but memorial
statues and plaques have long served in various stadiums and regional halls
of fame as important monuments, which are often genuinely cherished by
the community of fandom. My "Stan the Statue" is somewhat eccentric in

its treatment of a memorial statue and its subject. My poem rudely declares this huge, gawky tribute to Musial an artistic failure and yet finds it a fitting tribute, nonetheless. I argue that the very fact of the statue's failure as a work of art paradoxically makes it successful as a memorialization of the essential feature of the Musial legend. The Man's inscrutability becomes, in my poem, the point the statue's failure underscores: This awkward, earnest sculpture cannot do justice to Musial's peculiar stance, just as two decades of pitchers could not solve the question posed by that stance and by the hitting potency that was coiled within it. Thus the statue's failure is an appropriate tribute to Musial's grand unsolvability.

S<small>TAN THE</small> S<small>TATUE</small>: O<small>N THE</small> M<small>ONUMENT AT THE</small> S<small>TADIUM</small>

> It looks nothing like him
> and makes nothing of its
> artistic license beyond
> a lurid failure
> to resemble.
>
> We want to say The Man
> deserves better than this.
> But maybe the tribute
> fits the subject
> in an odd sort of way.
>
> The sculptor could no more
> figure out The Man than
> could two decades of pitchers.
>
> The inscrutably perfect,
> impossible stance
> blasts, once again,
> a screaming line drive.
>
> No manner of Art
> can breeze one past him.[10]

　　"Harry Caray's Voice" is a tribute to the long time, once-upon-a-time "Voice of the Cardinals," who subsequently became the voice of the Cubs. Musial is referred to only in passing—as the maker of timely line drives. This comment takes for granted Musial's prowess as a line-drive-making machine, an important aspect of what a voice of the Redbirds would have to take note of again and again. The legend implicit here is the consistent nature of Musial's relentless hitting, even in most of his later seasons. The focus in this poem stays on Caray and his voice, and the tribute to Musial is implicit and secondary, but Musial's greatness is firmly asserted in the form it presented itself in the late years of his career. The poem is set around 1962 or 1963, an era in which one might expect the power to come from

Ken Boyer or Bill White, but even in his concluding years, Musial was still expected, this poem implies, to continue hitting an amazing quantity of timely hits.

HARRY CARAY'S VOICE

His voice rising garish, garrulous
above our barbecue pits was summer.
His deep voice high pitched
to a blue-sky falsetto
when the game was on the line.

Those excited moments stick
to the mind beyond memory of what
happened and why it mattered,
if it did. The excitement
was a game unto itself.

Hearing his voice on my way
to somebody's backyard
or while rounding
some corner on my bike —
I could not know whether

Boyer had slammed a homer,
Musial had laced a timely
line drive, Gibson had drilled
a hole in McCarver's glove
for a third strike on Clemente,

Banks, or Matthews. It was not
the hearing that was so wonderful,
but the overhearing. That voice —
its rise and fall, the chatty
silliness of its commentary,

the outrageous confidence
of its insane predictions
(that so strangely often came true) —
that outrageous, unlovely voice
so wonderful to overhear

from a distance while rounding
a corner on a bike — that voice
meant summer was still out there
like a big, slow Curt Simmons curve
that might never stop floating.[11]

In "Dreaming with the Great Rookie, Albert Pujols," Musial is again mentioned as a side note for the sake of talking about someone else. Musial is treated as a vocabulary item. One of the things Musial means in the history of baseball has to do with the phenomenon of his extraordinary success when brought up to the major leagues for the first time. In order to indicate the the the sensational nature of Pujols's rookie performance, my poem suggests it is comparable to Musial's great showing in the closing days of the 1941 season.

DREAMING WITH THE GREAT ROOKIE, ALBERT PUJOLS

As the summer of 2001 draws to a close,
Albert Pujols seems manna from heaven.
A fearless, extraordinary young man —
equally at home in infield and outfield
who hits for power and for average —
he's a kid that doesn't act his age.
As they said about Musial his first year,
"How can anybody be this good?"
Dreaming grandeur for a just-begun career
can be a risky game, but it is what
we should do, what we need to do.
As with the butterfly and Chuang Tzu,
what might turn out to be true is real, too.[12]

"Musial, Mize, and DiMaggio in Moiliili" concerns the feelings of fans who live far from the cities where their teams play but can sometimes make connections with their team or its stars in such regional activities as minor league games and barnstorming exhibitions. For instance, on the island of Oahu, we can take note of the remarkable fact that many big-league players played here on armed forces teams during World War II. Although the Navy did not keep Musial in Hawai'i very long, my poem catches a retrospective glimpse of him as a participant in the games in Honolulu Stadium, a no-longer-existing structure not far from the university where I work. That stadium, which was still in use when I first came to Hawai'i, has now been replaced by an open space known as Stadium Park. Although Joe DiMaggio is the central figure in my poem, Musial's presence is crucial for me. My awareness of his brief 1940s sojourn on Oahu connects the life of my current place to the world of Musial and his legendary achievements. Of course, Musial's inscrutability remains fully operative here. Although I know he was here, not much information has ever been available about exactly what he did here. If I had known more about Musial's Navy baseball doings on Oahu, I would probably have made him the star of this poem instead of giving the spotlight to Joltin' Joe. Musial's Hawaii time is a blank space in all the biographies, a situation that could lead me to write yet another Musial poem.

MUSIAL, MIZE, AND DIMAGGIO IN MOILIILI

During World II
major league stars

battled in the Pacific theatre
of Honolulu Stadium
for inter-service bragging rights—
the Army may have had Joltin' Joe,
but the Navy had his brother Dom
and guys like Stan The Man
and the Big Cat, Johnny Mize.

Even the little town
where I live now
was, in those days,
a major league metropolis—
the redoubtable Aiea Hilltoppers
sported pro stars.

It's hard to hold in mind,
but good to know, that —
were I seated in my Honda Accord,
parked in a certain spot
on Isenberg Street

on a certain day in June of 1944 —
a prodigious homerun
by the great Joe DiMaggio
would have blasted through my window.[13]

As I continue to speculate about the mysteries of Stan "The Man" Musial, it seems quite possible that I might eventually arrive at 13 ways of looking at a Musial, and perhaps even more beyond that. A book-length collection of Musial pieces could be my next step. My Musial poems attempt to capture Stan "The Man" in the life of my mind; they are perfomances of his place in my thoughts and feelings. A baseball poem can be a unique opportunity to report on the facts of a baseball occurrence while also endeavoring to do justice to the legendary dimensions of the event. Poetry's unembarrassed receptivity to the mythos of the moment gives it a certain advantage over more prosaic treatments.

Notes

1. Joseph Stanton, *Cardinal Points: Poems on St. Louis Cardinals Baseball* (Jefferson, NC: McFarland, 2002)

2. Ford Frick. Quoted in Bob Broeg and Jerry Vickery, *The St. Louis Cardinals Encyclopedia* (Chicago: Contemporary Publishing Group, 1998): 258. This quotation, in slightly altered form, has become familiar to St. Louis fans in an inscription on the statue of Musial that is commented on in one of the poems included in this article. See note 10 below.

3. William Wordsworth, "The Happy Warrior," *One Hundred and One Famous Poems*, edited by Roy Cook (Chicago: Reilly & Lee, 1958): 27–29.

4. Wallace Stevens, "Thirteen Ways of Looking at a Blackbird," *The Emperor of Ice Cream and Other Poems* (Mineola, NY: Dover, 1999): 20–22.

5. Warren Goldstein, "Inside Baseball," *The Gettysburg Review* 5.3 (1992): 411.

6. Stanton, 33.

7. Stanton, 35.

8. Stanton, 34.

9. Stanton, 40.

10. Stanton, 41. The 10-foot bronze statue on a 10-foot base on prominent display outside Busch Stadium was the work of Carl Christian Mose, a Danish artist who also sculpted a statue of General John J. Pershing for the Missouri State Capitol in Jefferson City. For an account of the controversy surrounding the statue, see James Giglio, *Musial: From Stash to Stan the Man* (Columbia, MO: University of Missouri Press, 2001): 280–82.

11. Stanton, 45.

12. Stanton, 98.

13. Stanton, 30.

II. Baseball and Ethnicity

3

"Poosh 'Em Up, Tony!" — Italian Americans and Baseball

Joseph Dorinson

While baseball has served as the nation's pastime since the mid–19th-century, it has also offered opportunities for minorities to advance in American society. For African Americans, the game, albeit subject to "Jim Crow" apartheid, provided avenues of social mobility to be sure; but the national pastime also promoted self-esteem at a critical juncture in American history for an oppressed minority — Italian Americans.

Before Joe DiMaggio, things were dramatically different. To appreciate this drastic transformation, one is compelled to examine the historical context of the Italian American experience.[1] From 1850 to about 1880, 80,000 immigrants came from northern Italy. Fairly prosperous, highly skilled, and lighter skinned (and thus more acceptable to many Americans) than their southern counterparts, the *contadini*, they came in pursuit of *la dolce vita*, i.e., a living wage, less warfare, and a brighter future for their children. Prior to 1880, Italian immigrants posed no threat to WASP hegemony. They were relatively small in number. Census data from 1850 identified only 3,645 residents as Italian-born, primarily situated in New Orleans and San Francisco.[2] Later, they gravitated to Boston, New York, Philadelphia and westward ho to Chicago and on to the California vineyards. The cult of Columbus, quite prevalent in early–19th-century America, endeared the newcomers to those born on "native grounds." American *cognoscenti* (intellectuals) gloried in the Italian Renaissance as the hallmark of modernity and western values.[3] To Europeans of literary sensibility, Italy represented a respite from the harsh realities of industrialization and the cruel constraints of Max Weber's Protestant Ethic.

Then something — economic disaster — happened. Citrus crops in Florida and California eclipsed Italian orange and lemon exports. Disaster also visited the Italian wine industry between 1870 and 1900. France, a less than friendly neighbor to Italy, boosted tariffs, and phylloxera, a virulent plant disease, decimated the vineyards. This tragic turn of events coupled with a cholera epidemic, volcanic eruptions, earthquakes, and a massive flood in 1908 propelled a vast exodus out of Italy.[4] Nearly 4.5 million immigrants, now primarily southern Italians, streamed into the United States.

The large-scale immigration from southern and eastern Europe fanned the flames of xenophobia. Far from gay, the 1890s witnessed an upsurge in anti–Semitism, anti–Catholicism, and phobic racism. Spurred by class conflict, labor unrest, crippling depression, and the "New Imperialism" at the turn of the century, Americans vented against newcomers, particularly the Italians. Referred to as "black dagoes," "wops," and worse, Italians endured negative stereotypes. They were labeled — indeed libeled — James S. Olson documented in a perceptive study, as "ignorant, inferior, and superstitious; lacking ambition and social taste."[5] Crime aroused fears and provoked equation with the advent of the so-called Black Hand or Mafia. Notwithstanding sociologist Daniel Bell's insightful observation that crime is "an American way of life" and "a queer ladder" for success, ethnic crime continues to carry Italian baggage.[6]

The alleged national conspiracy to control crime served as a convenient cover to step up violent acts against Italian immigrants starting in the 1870s. Olson catalogues the murder of four Italian "scabs" (strikebreakers) by union-affiliated miners in Pennsylvania, the 1886 lynching of an Italian in Vicksburg, Mississippi, the roundup of 325 Italian suspects for an 1888 murder of a fellow immigrant in Buffalo, and the worst-case scenario in New Orleans, where 11 Italians were lynched after a trial by jury in 1891.[7] Eight years later, the "dear hearts and gentle people" of Tallulah, Louisiana, murdered five Italian storekeepers for paying black workers the same wages as their white counterparts. Moreover, "lynch law" continued to victimize Italian Americans in West Virginia (1891 and 1906); Altoona, Pennsylvania (1894); Tampa, Florida (1910); and Johnson City, Illinois (1915).

The high (or low point depending on one's vantage) point of anti–Italian hysteria surfaced in the so-called Roaring Twenties, allegedly another decade of bliss, with the Sacco-Vanzetti case. Arrested, tried, and convicted for a murder/robbery on April 15, 1920, the two Italian anarchists, Niccolo Sacco, a shoemaker, and Bartolomeo Vanzetti, a fishmonger, languished in limbo on death row for seven years. Despite evident improprieties in the investigation and pleas for mercy by many dignitaries, including the Pope, the two immigrants were electrocuted on August 22, 1927.[8] Their judicial murder prompted novelist John Dos Passos, speaking for a legion of disillusioned Americans, to write, " ... all right ... you will kill the brave men our friends tonight ... all right, we are two nations."[9]

To overcome the patent prejudice visited on their ethnicity, young Italians pursued alternative avenues toward Americanization. Sports, for example, served as a passport to social acceptance. Ironically, historians, until the 1970s, paid little or no attention to the role of sports in our culture. And the interaction between Italians and baseball has been almost totally neglected. Author Carmelo Bazzano questioned this cavalier disregard of five million people. He noted the linkage of English immigrants with love and knowledge of various games, the Germans' fondess for gymnastics, the Irish penchant for boxing, Scotch-Irish preference for track and field, and the Scandinavians' inclination toward snow sports. But where are the Italians, Bazzano asks rhetorically. The third-largest immigrant group in America carved out a niche that blended cultural identity and mainstream America. Sports would serve as a socializing agent and a source for validation of self-esteem.

In Italy, the more affluent northerners had sufficient leisure to lavish on games. The great poet Dante noted foot races in Verona. Indeed, a sport culture flowered during the Renaissance. There were schools for fencing, mass games on holy days and boxing matches that were banned by the Duke of Urbino as a threat to the social order. Sports federations sprang up in the 19th century: one for gymnastics in 1869 followed by swimming in 1892, weightlifting and wrestling in 1902, fencing in 1909, and boxing in 1919.[10]

This spurt in sports activity, primarily in the north, coincided with mass migration from the south as four million-plus Italians left between 1899 and 1924. Most of these newcomers— approximately 80 percent — remained along the East Coast in New York City, Philadelphia, and Boston. Because of grinding poverty and massive oppression, southern Italians put a premium on work, not play, in order to survive. In addition to the already mentioned crop failures, the *contadini* (peasants) were plagued by uncaring absentee landlords, prolonged poverty, pest proliferation, and governmental malfeasance. Southerners brought bocce (lawn bowling) to America as their principal recreational outlet along with wrestling and cards. Gradually, however, immigrants and their children, often heavily concentrated, with 200,000 squeezed into less than one square Manhattan mile, took to bicycling in 1900. *Unione Sportiva Italiana*, which met at 254 West 54th Street, attracted 250 members with 80 outstanding cyclists.[11]

Sports took off in the second generation during the Progressive Era,

1900–1917. According to historian Camillo Cienferra, the progressive reformers viewed sports as a vital agency, along with the then-popular concept of "muscular Christianity," to accelerate the race toward Americanization. Translated, meant team play, assigned roles, self-sacrifice for the collective good, and a healthy body fused with a healthy mind. Suddenly, the American-born Italians experienced conflict with their European-born fathers, who viewed sports as secondary to work and who distrusted anyone outside the family. "Get a job and contribute!" they insisted. *Questo gioco e la rovina della famiglia.* (This play is the ruination of the family.)[12] Before his sons reaped financial rewards from their play, Giuseppe DiMaggio, patriarch of the clan, once bellowed, "Baseball, what is that? A bum's game! Whoever makes a living at baseball. All it does is wear out shoes."[13]

Schools provided a counter-message. Recreation ruled the roost in settlement houses as well as in the Public School Athletic League. There, Italian children were exposed to baseball, basketball, cross-country, swimming, tennis, lacrosse and even rifle shooting. Above all, baseball, the national pastime, beckoned. As early as 1909, an Italian team won the state championship of Vermont. From Barre, Vermont, to Tontitown, Arkansas, from San Francisco, California, to New York, New York (Greenwich Village to be precise), Italians played baseball. The West Coast became a hotbed of Italian baseball.[14]

In their excellent study, sociology professors Richard Renoff and Joseph A. Varacalli identify the Italian American pioneers in baseball. They cite Vincent "Sandy" Nava, who played for Providence in the National League and Baltimore in the American Association from 1882 to 1886, as the first. They also claim that Joe Tinker, of the Cubs famous double play combination, was Italian American.[15] Ed Abbaticchio, the player who is mentioned most often as the first Italian, hailed from the middle class. His father, a successful entrepreneur, wanted Ed to enter business after college. He preferred baseball, joining the Philadelphia Phillies in 1897. After a five-year stint in the minors, Abbaticchio returned to the National League's Boston team, the Braves, as a shortstop/second baseman in 1903. He retired in 1905 but came back in 1907 to play alongside the immortal Honus Wagner and form a dynamic keystone combination in Pittsburgh. That year, he earned $1,000 more than Wagner, a four-time NL batting champ. He left baseball in 1910 to resume a career in hotel management.[16]

Contrary to some pundits' predictions and others' fears, Italians gradually moved into Major League Baseball before the 1930s. Born in 1888, Francesco Pezzolo, a name he anglicized to Ping Bodie (the first name derived from the sound of his bat minus cork or pine tar as he belted line drives), followed Abbaticchio into the majors. His family had migrated to San Francisco in 1877. Playing for the local Seals team in 1910, he hit 30 home runs. In 1911 he moved up to the Chicago White Sox, where he hit .289 with 97 RBIs. Improving to .291 in 1912, Bodie slipped to .265 and .229 in the following two years. Traded to the Philadelphia Athletics, he regained his batting eye. In 148 games, he hit .295 with 7 home runs and 74 RBIs. Sent to the Yankees in 1918, Bodie finished his major league career in New York. His best year was 1920, when he hit .295 in 129 games. Although only 5'8" tall, Bodie's squat 195-pound frame packed considerable power and included a strong throwing arm. Considered the most colorful character on the Yankees until Babe Ruth hit town, Bodie actually roomed with Ruth or, as Bodie put it more accurately, with his suitcase. Italian fans probably crafted Ruth's nickname, the Bambino, Italian for child or babe.[17] Italian players such as Abbaticchio and Bodie had their names abbreviated or changed to accommodate mainstream America's prejudice and sportswriters' inability to spell long surnames with an abundance of vowels.

Rinaldo Angelo Paolinelli did not change his name, technically. He merely shortened it to Babe Pinelli. Pinelli, like Bodie, hailed from San Francisco. Following a solid career in the Pacific Coast League, he became the second of 17 Italians to make the majors from the Bay area between 1911 and 1950. Pinelli moved up to Cincinnati in 1921 and replaced the popular German American Heinie Groh at the "hot corner." A fine fielder and solid batsman, Pinelli hit .276 over eight years, with an impressive .306 average and 23 stolen bases in 1924, his best year. After his playing days ended in 1932, he turned to umpiring. In 1935, he became the first Italian American umpire in the majors. He encountered many ethnic slurs, some from no less a figure than Babe Ruth. Despite his short stature—5'9" and 165 pounds—he stood tall and worked steadily in 3,400 games over 22 years. Pinelli went out in a blaze of shared glory with Don Larsen and fellow *paisan* Lawrence Peter "Yogi" Berra. Behind the plate on October 9, 1956, Pinelli called a high third strike on pinch hitter Dale Mitchell to climax Larsen's perfect game, the only no-hitter in World Series history. Lawrence Baldassaro, a noted expert on Italian Americans in baseball, cogently argues that by exemplifying authority "with dignity and skill, [Pinelli] gained respect and conveyed a positive image of his ethnic group to everyone involved with big league baseball."[18]

While Sacco and Vanzetti sat in federal prison waiting for the end, the first Italian American star entered center stage, as it were, at Yankee Stadium in 1926. Born in San Francisco in 1903, Anthony Lazzeri left school at age 15 to gain employment as a boilermaker. This work beefed up his biceps, which generated enormous power from a 5'11", 160-pound frame. Lazzeri hit 60 home runs and knocked in 222 runs for Salt Lake City in the Pacific Coast League. That amazing record over 197 games earned him a promotion to the Yankees. As a rookie, he hit 18 home runs with 114 RBIs.

Italian fans flocked to the Bronx to cheer for their hero with cries of, "Poosh 'em up, Tony!" He did not disappoint, hitting at a .292 clip during a stellar 14-year career. At second base, he anchored arguably baseball's greatest team: the New York Yankees, vintage 1927. Stigmatized by a famous strikeout, after nearly hitting a home run, in the 1926 world classic, Lazzeri proved a vital spark to a club dominated by two German American stars, Ruth and Gehrig. Among his many accomplishments were two grand slams in a single game with 11 RBIs in 1936. In the 1932 World Series against the Cubs in Chicago, he hit two home runs as he led the Yanks to a four-game sweep. Lazzeri combined speed with power, excellent defense with potent offense. In his final year in the majors, he played for two local teams in the National League: the Dodgers and the Giants. Lazzeri had an outstanding career despite the scourge of epilepsy, which probably led to his premature death at age 42 in 1946.[19]

During his tenure with the Yankees, Lazzeri set the pattern for other Italian players to put on pinstripes. That point was driven home on February 13, 2002, when the *New York Times* published an obituary of Frank Crosetti. Born in San Francisco in 1910, "the Crow" — his Yankee moniker — joined the Bronx Bombers in 1932, one of many Italian Americans who hailed from the Bay Area and made it to the bigs. He played shortstop as a regular from 1932 to 1940 and as a reserve after Phil Rizzuto replaced him in 1941. In fact, he helped Rizzuto take over, a rarity among players in any era, let alone the grim years of Depression and war. Retiring in 1948, he became a coach, a career that lasted another 20 years. Thus, he participated in 23 World Series and collected 17 winner's shares totaling $142, 989.30.[20]

In Italy, Crosetti's ancestral home, athletics was deemed a waste of time. Hunting in the old country was an aristocratic preserve. But here in America, youngsters such as Crosetti gravitated toward sports because it offered inexpensive entertainment, a channel for adolescent energy, and a ladder for social mobility, argue Italian coauthors Jerre Mangione and Ben Morreale. [21]

From the early 1900s, ethnic diversity received more than lip service. Baseball's chief organ, *The Sporting News*, frequently harped on this theme, which it equated with democracy, author G. Edward White observes.[22] Indeed, longtime sportswriter Frederick G. Lieb, of German American extraction, presumably argued that "next to the little red school house, there has been no greater agency in bringing our races together than our national game, baseball ... our real melting pot."[23] Italians as well as Jews received the most attention. Editors did not seem to mind that authors continually misspelled ethnic names; thus Lazzeri became La Zerre or Lizzeria. As Ku Klux Klan activity mounted including the revelation in 1923 that pitcher Robert Hasty was a man with a hood, *The Sporting News* sang the praises of polyglot players and extolled the merit system. "It matters not what branch of mankind the player sprang from, with the fan, if he can deliver the goods.[24] In the 1930s, as the number of Italian players increased, *The Sporting News* warned the Irish players, half facetiously, that their jobs were insecure. In a more serious vein, noted baseball historian Charles C. Alexander points out that the Italians, waiting in the wings, were vying for "racial superiority."[25] Articles invariably mentioned the ballplayer's ethnic origins and linked them with certain stereotypic traits. Oscar Melillo, for example, became "the small Italian." By contrast, Ernie Lombardi was "the big Italian." Ernie Orsatti emerged as "the colorful wop."[26]

Although almost all of the early Italian American major leaguers hailed from the Bay Area, San Francisco did not have a monopoly on Italian talent. St. Louis also produced outstanding players. In Gary Mormino's study of the "Dago Hill" area, we learn that after World War I, Italians came from Lombardy and Sicily in search of employment in St. Louis brickyards. With an assist from "bootlegging" during Prohibition, Italian families earned enough money to buy homes and build a new church. The Roman Catholic Church played a pivotal role in promoting sports. Father Kaceno, a third-generation Bohemian priest with a conveniently Italianate name, shepherded youngsters into sports, especially baseball.[27] From the Hill came Ernie Orsatti, Joe Garagiola, and Yogi Berra.

Fifteen Italian American players appeared on major league rosters in 1934. The best of this bunch included the Giants' Gus Mancuso, Cubs' Dolph Camilli, Cardianals' Ernie Orsatti, Dodgers' Tony Cuccinello, Reds' Ernie Lombardi, Yankees' Tony Lazzeri and Frank Crosetti and the Browns' Oscar Melillo. Of these illuminaries, two were catchers, ten infielders, and two outfielders.[28] Only 2 percent of that year's major league rosters, Italian Americans represented 8 percent by 1941.[29] In the intervening years, a dramatic change occurred in public perceptions. Alternately Latin lover (Rudolph Valentino) and violent gangster (Al Capone), the Italian male acquired added *machismo* with the rise of Benito Mussolini. Not unlike the meteoric career path of New York City Mayor Rudy Guiliani, Mussolini, abetted by American media, including Italian-language press such as Generoso Pope's *Il Progresso*, projected the persona of a strong leader who had saved Italy from communism, the Mafia, and chronic inefficiency. To be sure, a considerable number of Italian Americans, led by Carlo Tresca and Luigi Antonini, among others, campaigned against fascism, but many Americans admired this "sawdust Caesar." Witness, for example, Cole Porter's rapture in his hit song, "You're the tops— you're Mussolini."[30] Until 1940, John P. Diggins asserts, Mussolini's dominant image as redeemer attracted hordes of admirers. His heroic projection of masculine power, coupled with his reputation as sexual stud who quoted Dante as he fornicated, seems to have titillated those who should have known better, namely, the *intelligentsia*.[31] Italy's assault on Ethiopia in 1934 and Mussolini's pact with Hitler two years later generated disenchantment. His insistence that Italians abroad owed loyalty to their mother country raised knotty questions about dual loyalty. Italian Americans needed a homegrown hero to eclipse the megalomaniac on the balcony.

The greatest Italian player of his or any other era was of course Joe DiMaggio. Author Jack Moore clearly shows how DiMaggio's rise coincided with and contributed to Mussolini's decline. Moore cites a *Life* magazine article from May 1, 1939, that favored "The Yankee Clipper" (in radio broadcaster Arch McDonald's coined phrase) at the expense of "Il Duce," who had recently launched a pusillanimous attack on Albania. In this juxtaposition, DiMaggio emerged as a "safe ... symbol of Italian success" that counteracted anti–Italian feelings.[32] Neither ethnic stereotypes nor xenophobic reactions, however, dissipated fully. At the outset of American participation in World War II, 600,000 Italian aliens in the United States faced probable deportation by executive order, starting in January 1942, because of potential "Fifth Column" threats to national security. Citing the DiMaggio family as one dramatic case in point, attorney Chauncey Tramulto urged American government officials not to reclassify Italian Americans and cast them into legal limbo. Success crowned Tramulto's advocacy when President Roosevelt rescinded the order on October 12, 1942.[33]

Any doubt about dual loyalties was dispelled when prominent Italian athletes joined the war effort. The baseball inductees included Johnny Berardino, Al Brancato, Joe and Dom DiMaggio, Carl Furillo, Joe Garagiola, Cookie Lavagetto, Dario Lodigiani, John Lucadello, and Marius Russo, the last a basketball star as well as baseball star at Long Island University. In 1942, Italians could count 24 *landsleit* or *paisanos* among 285 major league players or 8.2 percent of the total. Either too young or too old (and/or 4F), some—including Ralph Branca, Tommy Brown, Dolph Camilli, Phil Cavaretta, Frank Crosetti, Dom Dallisandro, Vince DiMaggio, and Ernie Lombardi—stayed and played. A drop in the proportional representation of Italian players, Richard Renoff and Joseph A. Varacalli argue, resulted from the changing opportunity structure. The GI Bill encouraged the children of immigrants to pursue a college degree. While the percentage of ballplayers declined, the number of coaches increased to nearly 10 percent.[34]

Like other Italian youngsters, DiMaggio had to overcome his dad's strong opposition in order to play baseball. That bias against play in favor of work, as we have observed again and again, was characteristic of first-generation Italian patriarchs. The Yankees were lucky to acquire DiMaggio for an illustrious 13-year career that featured 9 World Series triumphs and

10 American League pennants. This magnificent Yankee from Olympus copped in three MVP awards: in 1939, 1941 (the year Ted "the Thumper" Williams hit .406), and 1947. A great fielder, baserunner, slugger, batter for average, team leader, DiMaggio could do it all—and did, including marriage, however brief, to Hollywood goddess Marilyn Monroe.[35] DiMaggio's brothers, Vince and Dom, played the outfield for the Pirates and Red Sox, respectively. Vince quipped, "Joe was the best hitter, Dom, the best fielder, and I was the best singer." Author Baldasarro points out how Joe served as a link between the Lazzeri generation and the one that followed from the 1950s on. Both Lazzeri and Joe DiMaggio most certainly "served as a source of ethnic pride" and fueled the engine that powered the American Dream.[36] Italian Americans flocked to the Yankee banner under the aegis of Jolting Joe DiMaggio. Thanks to this native from the sandlots of San Francisco and to other Italian ballplayers from the 1930s on, a new, positive image began to eclipse the old negatives embedded in the distorted past. DiMaggio might have eclipsed other Italian players, but they—Tony Cuccinello, brother Al Cuccinello, and Ernie Lombardi, for example—deserve mention as well. Despite leaden-foot speed, Lombardi, "The Shnozz" (because of his prominent nose), was a fine fielder and an outstanding hitter. Batting .306 over 17 seasons, Lombardi started with Brooklyn in 1931 and won batting titles twice: He hit .342 in 1938 and .330 in 1942. Fittingly, he wound up in the "Big Apple" with the Giants of New York. Happiness unfortunately eluded him as he was dogged with depression after he hung up his spikes.

Italian players such as Lombardi seemed to gravitate to New York City's three teams. Phil Rizzuto, Yogi Berra, Vic Raschi, and Billy Martin (ne Pesano) joined DiMaggio in pinstripes while Cookie Lavagetto, Ralph Branca, Carl Furillo, Vic Lombardi, Joe Pignitano, Gino Cimoli, and Roy Campanella (Italian Father) wore Dodger blue. Sal Maglie and Danny Gardella (two Mexican "jumping beans"), Ernie Lombardi, and Johnny Antonelli played across the river and under the trees of Coogan's Bluff. Later, Rocky Colavito, Ron Santo, Tony and Billy Conigliaro, Rico Petrocelli, Joe Torre, Ken Caminiti, Mike Piazza, and Paul Lo Duca added to this constellation but with less attention to their ethnicity than in pre–World War II America.[37]

Many of the best Italian American players picked up the "tools of ignorance," a rubric sometimes assigned to catching equipment. Backstops of note: Joe Garagiola, Joe Torre, Joe Girardi, Joe Pignitano (lots of Joes in this lineup), Roy Campanella, Mike Piazza, Yogi Berra, Rick Cerone, and Paul Lo Duca have given us excellent baseball and great quotations, especially Berra. Emerging from the Hill section of St. Louis that Gary Mormino so vividly evoked in his writing, "Yogi" Berra became one of the best and most popular man-children to play the game. Making his debut as a Yankee at the end of a disappointing 1946 season, Berra hit a home run in his first game. Yankee legend Bill Dickey taught the neophyte from Missouri how to catch. In his rookie year, 1947, Yogi hit .280 with 11 home runs, while alternating with Aaron Robinson behind the plate. When he hung up his spikes 18 years hence, Berra had amassed a .285 batting average. Along with 358 career home runs including 20 or more for 10 consecutive seasons, Berra drove in 100-plus runs five times, a rarity for a catcher, and copped the MVP award three times, in 1951, 1954, and 1955. In addition, he set several records in World Series competition: most appearances (14), most games (75), and most hits (71). Despite his powerful swing and his penchant for swatting at balls outside of the strike zone, Berra rarely struck out: only 415 K's over 19 years, or fewer than 22 times each year. Inept as a catcher initially, he became — along with Campanella — baseball's best. He handled 950 chances without an error from July 1957 to May 1959. As a player, Berra led the Yankees to 14 pennants and 10 championships.[38]

This gruff, earthy man also managed two teams, the Yanks and Mets, to pennants in two leagues, yet he lost both jobs shortly thereafter. A firing by the mercurial and dictatorial Yankee owner George Steinbrenner led to Berra's principled boycott of the Bronx Bombers for 14 seasons. Finally, Suzyn Waldman, the first female Yankee sportscaster and one of several Steinbrenner shills, engineered an apology from the "Boss" that brokered a peace and broke the silence. The imperious Yankee owner tendered a sizable contribution to Berra's Montclair–based baseball museum.

As the master of malaprop, Berra became something of an armchair philosopher, not unlike his "Huckleberry" friend and occasional business partner, Phil Rizzuto. Too numerous to catalogue here, his quotes have been elevated, thanks to the hype of fellow Hill native Joe Garagiola and teammate Rizzuto, to folkloric gems. [39]

> It's *déjà vu* all over again.
> Nobody goes there anymore; it's too crowded.
> If you come to a fork in the road, take it.
> Think! How the hell are you gonna think and hit at the same time?
> I really didn't say everything I said.
> It ain't over till it's over.

This last oft-quoted Berra line was validated by the Red Sox' unprecedented comeback against the Yankees in the 2004 American League Championship Series.

Berra's counterpart with the Dodgers, Roy Campanella, merits mention in this discourse by virtue of his Italian father. After eight years in the Negro Leagues sandwiched around two in Mexico where he developed into the finest defensive catcher in baseball, "Campy" joined the Brooklyn

Dodgers as a 27-year-old rookie. In 10 years with "Dem Bums" that were cut short by a devastating car accident, he hit .276 with 242 home runs, averaging more than 24 home runs per season. In 1953, he hit a then-record 40 home runs as a catcher. Like Berra, his Yankee counterpart, Campanella copped the MVP of his league three times: in 1951 (the same year as Berra), 1953, and 1955. His alleged confrontations with Jackie Robinson over the appropriate response to racism are still subject to debate. When Robinson insisted that they fight for equal accommodations with white players in St. Louis's Chase Hotel, Campy confessed, "I'm not a crusader." He preferred a slower, more peaceful path to progress. Robinson could not wait. In a 1954 television program, he challenged the Yankees to hire a black ballplayer.[40] With the exception of writers such as Roger Kahn, the press corps preferred Campanella to Robinson. Still, lingering questions go unanswered. Why did Campanella gravitate to the role of accommodation? Did fatalism on his Italian side render Campanella less militant and more passive? Why couldn't Campanella accept Robinson's moral urgency?

Neither passive nor indifferent to moral issues, Angelo Bartlett Giamatti represents the great ascent from Ellis Island to "Eli" Eden and baseball nirvana. His life was tragically shortened by a massive coronary in the wake of cigarette smoking. Giamatti, a Renaissance man, cut a wide swath through academe as well as through popular culture with equal panache. Like the mythical St. George, Giamatti slew the dragons of Italian stereotype. Born in Boston on April 4, 1938, the grandson of an immigrant laborer, the son of a college professor and a New England bluestocking, he grew up in Hadley, Massachusetts. His father, Valentin, a Yale graduate, taught literature at Mt. Holyoke College with a specialty in Dante. As a youth, Bart worshipped the Boston Red Sox. Bobby Doerr, more accessible than the majestic Ted Williams, became his idol. Giamatti attended Phillips Academy in Andover, then Yale, from which he graduated *magna cum laude* in 1960. Four years later, he earned a doctorate in comparative literature. After a two-year apprenticeship at Princeton, the prodigal son returned to New Haven. He rose rapidly on the academic ladder at Yale: a full professor at age 33; president at 40 on July 1, 1978.[41]

Administrative life tested the young lion. Labor disputes and fund raising proved less than pleasant. Striking workers carried placards that read, "Bart, Bart, Have a Heart! Boola, Boola, Where's our Moola?" Giamatti ended his tenure as Yale University's 19th president two years early after six grueling years of cost cutting and budget balancing. On June 9, 1986, he found a new vocation: president of the National League. Signed at $200,000 per year, he earned the same salary as the president of the United States. Ever the man on the move, Giamatti became baseball commissioner in 1989. At $350,000, he now earned three times that of a Yale University president.[42]

Some of the best and the brightest commentary on baseball can be found in his sparkling prose. "What's home?" He asked and answered.[43]

> Home is a longing for when you were happy because you were younger.... Leaving home and struggling to return is as ancient as Homer. Baseball is about going home and how hard it is to get there. Its wisdom says you can go home again but that you cannot stay. The journey must always start once more, the bat an oar over the shoulder, until there is an end to all this journeying.

As a youngster growing up in New Haven, Giamatti compiled an Italian American All Star team that featured Joe DiMaggio, brother Dom DiMaggio, and Al "Zeke" Zarilla in the outfield. Although he was primarily a shortstop, Frank Crosetti played third. At short, second, and first, the future baseball czar placed Phil Rizzuto, Tony Lazzeri, and Dolph Camilli. Ernie Lombardi was his catcher; Sal Maglie and Vic Raschi, the pitchers.[44]

Perhaps Giamatti's greatest contribution to the national pastime came with the banishment of Pete Rose. As baseball commissioner, he patterned himself after the first man in that office, Judge Kenesaw Mountain Landis, minus the racism. Giamatti dealt harshly with the compulsive and unrepentant gambler. Despite popular opposition to his controversial move against the man with the most career hits in Major League Baseball, Giamatti stood his ground, the high moral ground. After a six-month investigation and much deliberation, Giamatti announced his decision on August 24, 1989, on national television from the New York Hilton.[45]

> The banishment for life of Pete Rose from baseball is a sad end of a sorry episode. One of the game's greatest players has engaged in a variety of acts, which have stained the game, and he now must live with the consequences of these acts. Let it also be clear that no individual is superior to the game. I will be told I am an idealist. I hope so. I will continue to locate ideals I hold for myself and for my country in the national game, as well as in other of our national institutions. The matter of Mr. Rose is now closed.

As witnessed by Giamatti's elegant remarks, the stereotypical image of Italian Americans has changed dramatically thanks in no small measure to baseball. Not only are Italian players, officials, umpires, and managers revered, they are also viewed as sex symbols. Witness the "Italian Stallion" rubrics pinned on Lee Mazzilli, Rick Cerone, Johnny Berardino (remember the old St. Louis Brownie who became a big TV star?) and of course the always elegant Joe DiMaggio.

In the 2004 Word Series, two Italian managers, Tony La Russa and Terry Francona, matched wits. Indeed, in recent years the Italian image has been burnished by the efforts of managerial expertise in the World Series. In 1977, for example, the World Series brought two traditional archrivals — the Dodgers and Yankees — into high relief. At the helms were Tommy Lasorda and Billy Martin, Italian American baseball gurus. Both won championships in the 1970s and 1980s. Today, that baton has been passed to Tony La Russa (Italian on his father's side), who won the World Series in 1989, and Joe Torre, the man who tamed the beast in the Bronx, raging bull George Steinbrenner, and has won four World Series (1996, 1998–2000). On the basis of his record as a player, let alone manager, Torre deserves consideration for Hall of Fame honors. As a catcher, third baseman and first baseman, Torre banged out 2,342 hits and 225 home runs on his way to a .297 lifetime batting average. With the Cardinals in 1971 at third base (Torre started as a catcher with the Milwaukee Braves), he led the National League with a sparkling .363 batting average and 137 RBIs. Torre believes that his low power numbers and lack of postseason exposure have precluded his entry into baseball's shrine. He takes solace, however, that he is "a proud member of the Parade Grounds Hall of Fame [in Brooklyn] and the Italian American Hall of Fame."[46]

Friends, fans, and *paisanos*, the final words belong to A. Bartlett Giamatti, who combined an Italian sensibility with a tragic sense of life.[47]

[Baseball] breaks your heart. It is designed to break your heart. The game begins in the spring, when everything begins again, and it blossoms in the summer, filling the days and evenings. And then as soon as the fall rains come, it stops and lets you face the fall alone. You count on it, you rely on it to buffer the passage of time, to keep the memory of sunshine and high skies alive, and then, just when the days are all twilight, when you need it most, it stops.

And so do I. Keep your eyes on the ball and budding star Rocco Baldelli. *Mille grazie.*

Notes

1. Lawrence Baldassaro, "Before Joe D: Early Italian Americans in the Major Leagues," in *The American Game: Baseball & Ethnicity*, edited by Lawrence Baldassaro and Richard A. Johnson (Carbondale, IL: Southern Illinois UP, 2002), 92–115.

2. Duncan Clarke, *A New World: The History of Immigration into the United States* (San Diego: Thunder Bay Press, 2000), 175.

3. Charles A. Coletta, Jr., *Gangsterism, Guidos, and Grandmas: Italian Americans in Twentieth Century American Popular Culture* (May 2000), unpublished dissertation, 65.

4. James S. Olson, *The Ethnic Dimension in American History*, 2nd edition (New York: St. Martin's Press, 1994), 117–119.

5. Olson, 171–172.

6. Daniel Bell, *The End of Ideology* ... (New York: The Free Press, 1962), 127–174, While he understates the role of *Cosa Nostra,* Bell offers compelling, perhaps definitive, observations on American crime.

7. Olson, 173. For a definitive study of the New Orleans lynching, see Richard Gambino, *Vendetta* ... (Garden City: Doubleday, 1977).

8. Olson, 173; Jerre Mangione and Ben Morreale, *La Storia: Five Centuries of the Italian American Experience* (New York: Harper Collins, 1992), 290–301.

9. As quoted in William E. Leuchtenburg, *The Perils of Prosperity: 1914–32* (Chicago: University of Chicago Press, 1958), 82–83.

10. Carmelo Bazzano, "The Italian American Sporting Experience," in *Ethnicity and Sport in North American History and Culture*, edited by George Eisen and David K. Wiggins (Westport CT: Greenwood Press, 1994), 103–105.

11. Bazzano, 106–108.

12. Bazzano, 108–109.

13. As quoted in George DeGregorio, *Joe DiMaggio: An Informal Biography* (Princeton: Townhouse Publishing, 1981), 83.

14. DeGregorio, 110.

15. Richard Renoff and Joseph A. Varacalli, "Italian Americans and Baseball," *The Nassau Review*, 6:1 (1990): 107.

16. Baldassaro, 93–97.

17. Baldassaro, 97–98.

18. Baldassaro, 100–102.

19. Baldassaro, 102–106.

20. *The New York Times*, February 13, 2002, A29.

21. Mangione and Morreale, 373.

22. G. Edward White, *Creating the National Pastime: Baseball Transforms Itself, 1903–1953* (Princeton: Princeton UP, 1996), 251.

23. Frederick G. Lieb, "Baseball — The Nation's Melting Pot," *Baseball Magazine* 31 (August 1923): 393 as cited in Lawrence Baldassaro, "Introduction" in Baldassaro and Johnson, 3.

24. Lieb.

25. Charles C. Alexander, *Breaking the Slump: Baseball in the Depression Era* (New York: Columbia UP, 2002), 193.

26. White, 257.

27. As cited in Mangione and Morreale, 374. For greater detail, see Gary R. Mormino, "The Playing Fields of St. Louis: Italian Immigrants and Sports, 1925–1941," *Journal of Sports History* (1949): 72–85; Gary R. Mormino and George Pozzetta, *Immigrants on the Hill: Italian Americans in St. Louis, 1882–1982* (Champaign, IL: University of Illinois Press, 1986).

28. Renoff and Varacalli, 107–108.

29. Jack Moore, "Understanding Joe DiMaggio as an Italian American Hero," in *Italian Americans Celebrate Life, The Arts and Popular Culture*, edited by Paola A. Sensi Isolani and Anthony Julian Tamburri (American Italian Historical Association, 1990), 172.

30. Moore, 173.

31. John P. Diggins, *Mussolini and Fascism: The View from America* (Princeton: Princeton UP, 1972), 59–60.

32. Moore, 175.

33. Moore, 176; Diggins, 400.

34. Renoff and Varacalli, 108–109.

35. Donald Dewey and Nicholas Acocella, *The Biographical History of Baseball* (New York: Carroll & Graf, 1995), 113–115.

36. Baldassaro, 112–113.

37. *Ibid.*

38. Dewey and Acocella, 34–35; most of the statistics come from Joseph L. Reichler, ed., *The Baseball Encyclopedia*, 4th edition (New York: Macmillan, 1979), 736.

39. Geoffrey C. Ward and Ken Burns, *Baseball: An Illustrated History* (New York: Alfred A. Knopf, 1994), 314.

40. For Campanella's statistics see, Reichler, 31, 792.

41. Jerome Holtzman, *The Commissioners: Baseball's Midlife Crisis* (New York: Total Sports, 1998), 238–240.

42. Fay Vincent, *The Last Commissioner: A Baseball Valentine* (New York: Simon & Schuster, 2002), 79.

43. Holtzman, 236.

44. Mangione and Morreale, 376.

45. Holtzman, 253. James Reston, Jr., *Collision at Home Plate: The Lives of Pete Rose and Bart Giamatti* (New York: Harper Collins Edward Burlingame Books, 1991) has captured this dramatic encounter judiciously as well as elegantly.

46. Joe Torre with Tom Verducci, *Chasing the Dream: My Lifelong Journey to the World Series ...* (New York: Bantam Books, 1997), 98. Torre's offensive prowess is documented in Joseph L. Reichler, ed., *The Baseball Encyclopedia*, 4th edition (New York: Macmillan, 1979), 1458.

47. Ward and Burns, 453.

4

Ichiro, Godzilla, and the American Dream: Japanese Players in Major League Baseball

Yasue Kuwahara

On April 6, 2004, Kazuo Matsui marked his Major League Baseball debut with a home run, followed by two hits and two walks. Matsui's unexpected accomplishments on his first day as a New York Met were the biggest news item of the day to the Japanese news media. NHK 7 o'clock news, for instance, presented a five-minute package that consisted of the video showing Matsui's spectacular plays, coverage of the US media's reaction, an interview with Matsui and Art Howe, the manager of the Mets, and a live shot of New York City with a voiceover stating that soon New Yorkers would wake up to read about Matsui's great plays. This package was followed by the story about a pension plan reform bill pending in the diet. To an outsider, it might seem that NHK mixed up the order of news stories because, according to the traditional news pecking order, political and economic issues are given priority over sports news. But to the Japanese who follow their fellow countrymen in the majors, it was definitely more important on that day to know Matsui's athletic achievements than the pending bill. The NHK newscast thus attested to the current Japanese enthusiasm about Major League Baseball.

Ever since Hideo Nomo proved that a Japanese pitcher could be a valuable member of a major league team, a small but steady number of Japanese ballplayers have followed his footsteps by crossing the Pacific Ocean.

With this migration an increasing number of Japanese fans have turned their attention to American baseball. When Ichiro Suzuki, the first Japanese non-pitcher in the majors, excited Japanese fans by playing better than Americans, MLB firmly established its place in Japanese popular culture. In order to assess the implication of such enthusiasm for MLB among the Japanese, one must analyze the media coverage of players and games as well as commercial and fan Web sites. Today, for instance, Japan's sports newspapers have a section on MLB, and television news reports the results of MLB games, often before the Japanese games. NHK, Japan's public broadcasting corporation, televised 330 hours of MLB games in 2003.[1] Star players such as Ichiro and Hideki "Godzilla" Matsui are treated as heroes by the mass media. At least 20 books have been written on Ichiro. *Yomiuri Shimbun*, a daily paper, ran a weekly column on Hideki Matsui during the 2002 season that was eventually published in book form as *Matsui Ga Iku*. TBS, a television network, aired a special program, a talk show, with Ichiro and Matsui in January 2004. Well aware of a growing interest among the Japanese, MLB arranged the opening games between the Mets and the Chicago Cubs at the Tokyo Dome in 2000 and again between the Yankees and the Devil Rays four years later. An MLB office has been open in Tokyo since 2002.

Because the United States has been more or less perceived as the promised land by a majority of Japanese people since World War II, ballplayers who make it in the majors have achieved the American dream of success and thus are given a hero's status in Japanese popular culture. This is one reason for the enthusiasm for MLB. Another reason, which a closer examination reveals, is that the growing support for MLB is a criticism of Japanese baseball controlled by the old-fashioned management. Both players and fans who have shifted their attention to the American majors grew up in Japan, where traditional values were questioned and often replaced by new ones. It is difficult for them to accept the traditional style of Japanese baseball. Hence, enthusiasm for MLB reflects changing values in contemporary Japanese society.

From Little League players to professional players in foreign leagues, anyone who plays baseball naturally dreams about some day playing in America. Especially in the case of star players in foreign leagues, they think about testing their abilities in MLB to see how good they are compared to the best players in the world. This is certainly a reason for most Japanese players who have come across the Pacific to join MLB. Beginning with Hideo Nomo, Japanese pitchers who moved to the majors became the symbol of their country's achievement in the post–World War II world. A small Asian country finally had become competitive with the United States, which had served as a role model since the end of the war.

While they were undoubtedly proud of the players who made it, many Japanese still felt that only pitchers could play in the majors because their small physiques suggested less power and therefore a Japanese fielder would not have a chance. Thus, when Ichiro became the first Japanese fielder to play in MLB and was selected as the American League Rookie of the Year as well as the MVP, he was destined to become a superhero in Japan. The Japanese mass media sent reporters called "*Ichiro ban*" to cover their favorite player and the Mariners' games throughout the United States. Because Ichiro played in every game, it became a daily routine for many Japanese to read about his performance from the previous day and then leave for work or school. (Due to the 13-hour time difference, the game is played while they are sleeping).

Thanks to such intensive media coverage, it did not take long before the image of Ichiro as a cultural hero was established. This image often compares Ichiro to *samurai*, an internationally known symbol of traditional Japan. For instance, Takeshi Kato writes,

> Ichiro brings to his craft a new-samurai mentality rare in present-day Japan. Baseball has been his life since he was three. His constant preoccupation is with improving his ability. His politeness, simplicity and frugality are reminiscent of a traditional warrior's noblest virtues. For him, transferring to the majors is less a matter of personal ambition than an opportunity to mix with the best players and raise his own play to the highest level.[2]

Tim Larimer says,

> Although his persona is unassuming compared with the big egos and bigger mouths of some U.S. players, he carries himself with confidence that translates back home into attitude.... Here was someone his balding, angst-ridden, sake-swilling countrymen could toast.
> ...Ichiro is a most traditional Japanese man: quiet, polite, a testament to the single-minded work ethic admired by older generations.

He also quotes a Japanese office worker who says, "The way he hits is just like a samurai.... I'll bet he could split a mosquito with a sword."[3]

Ichiro's devotion to baseball is well known. Ichiro started baseball at an early age, joined a team in his hometown, went to a high school known for its baseball team, and played twice in the national high school tournament before he was drafted by the Orix Blue Waves. His life story is typical of those who make it in professional sports in Japan. It is also considered idealistic, for the Japanese believe that a person must focus on one sport exclusively in order to excel. What made Ichiro's story unique, on the other hand, is the presence of his father, Nobuyuki Suzuki. Realizing the potential in baseball his second son had, he literally dedicated his life to making his son's dream come true. Ichiro first got media attention when he established a new record with 210 hits in 130 games in 1994. Finding out about Nobuyuki, the media wrote about him as much as his son, for their relationship reminded them of a popular comic of the 1960s, *Kyojin No Hoshi* (*Hoshi of the Giants* or *The Star of the Giants*). The main character, Ittetsu Hoshi, single-mindedly trained his son, Hyuma, to become a member of the Tokyo Giants, then considered the best team in Japan. Ittetsu was a disciplinarian and chauvinist who never allowed Hyuma to give up. *Kyojin No Hoshi* appealed to the Japanese because they valued the single-minded devotion and perseverance depicted in the comic. While they did not always approve of Ittetsu's harsh training, they were happy when Hyuma made it to the Giants.

When the media made his relationship with Ichiro public, Nobuyuki had to assert repeatedly that he did not resemble Ittetsu at all in that he never forced Ichiro to become a professional ballplayer. All he did was help Ichiro achieve his goal in any way he could. He was not a disciplinarian but rather a supporter. Indeed, Nobuyuki is an extraordinary father. Nobuyuki and Ichiro started their daily baseball practice when Ichiro was in the third grade and never missed a day until the son joined a high school team. The father also massaged Ichiro's feet every night as long as Ichiro lived with him at home. Throughout Ichiro's high school years, Nobuyuki was always present at the team's practices and games just to observe his son and give moral support. To him Ichiro was more important than his work, so his wife kept the family business running throughout these years.[4] Nobuyuki's experience is atypical of Japanese men of his generation whose priority was work. Usually, they were often absent from home and could not develop close relationships with their children. Even today, it is considered the mother's role to educate and train children in Japan.

Raised by a father with nontraditional values, Ichiro was not confined by the traditional ways of Japanese society. For instance, despite overemphasis on education in postwar Japanese society, Ichiro said that he stopped studying once he entered high school because it was not possible to remain a good student and a good ballplayer at the same time.[5] Drafted by the Blue Waves, he refused to change his batting form as requested by the coach and thus failed to secure a regular position for the first few years. He is reluctant to talk to the mass media not because he has the quality of *samurai*, who considered being silent as virtuous, but rather because he does not trust the media. He remains loyal to himself instead of his team; he knows what he likes and what he wants to do. Ichiro did his best for the Blue Waves when he was a member, but he did not think about remaining on the same team, as is expected of all ballplayers. His goal was to become the best ballplayer, and in order to achieve this goal, he moved to the United States. Contrary to the image of Ichiro as a man of traditional values that the media

have painted, Ichiro is self-oriented and thus goes against the group ori-
entation and collectivism that prevails in the Japanese professional league.

Other Japanese players in the majors more or less share Ichiro's characteristics. They have played baseball all their lives. They endured hard
training in order to excel in their chosen sport. In this sense, they are traditional, but their personal values are different from those of the older generations. A new generation of ballplayers grew up after the 1970s, when the
high economic growth of postwar Japan began. As represented by *Shinjin-
rui* (*New Human Beings*) — those who possess nontraditional values — of the
1980s and in more recent years by the "freeter" — those who refuse full-time
work and support themselves by working several part-time jobs — the young
Japanese who did not experience the war nor postwar hardships do not
share their parents' traditional values, such as hard work, frugality, and
modesty, but instead are primarily concerned with consumption, leisure,
and individuality. Growing up in affluent Japan, their priority was not to
plan survival nor to reconstruct the country but to enjoy life and to achieve
individual goals. The new generation of ballplayers, therefore, cannot get
along with Japanese baseball, which operates based on traditional values.

Japanese professional baseball differs from its American counterpart
due to cultural differences. While the latter stresses home runs, for instance,
the former places emphasis on contact hitting, as Ichiro exemplifies. Based
on his two-year experience in Japan, former American player Hensley
Mulens characterizes Japanese baseball as "very passive, not aggressive."
Many players do not dive for balls or break up double plays because it is
not polite. Reflecting a cultural emphasis on group and unity, players are
expected to put the interest of the team before their own. According to Tom
O'Malley, who played in Japan for six years, the average Japanese ballplayer
is "very coachable, highly disciplined, and always willing to give 150%."[6]
Other American players who have experienced Japanese baseball agree with
O'Malley in that they had to learn to be a team player, to work hard, and
to keep their mouths shut in order to succeed in Japan.

This practice is often compared with the feudal system of pre-mod-
ern Japan, which demanded from *samurai* complete devotion and loyalty
to their lord. The lord in turn took care of *samurai* and their families. This
system was adopted by Japanese businesses after World War II and became
a common practice in postwar Japan. A majority of Japanese men stayed
with the same company that had hired them upon graduation from high
school or university until retirement. In baseball, too, it was assumed that
"a player would end his career in [sic] the team that had drafted him."[7] If
he stayed, the team would find him a post-retirement job — a managerial
or coaching position for a superior player and something else for lesser
players. It is no surprise, therefore, that players could not hire agents to

represent them in contract negotiations as recently as 2001. Players are mere employees whose loyalty to the team forces them to accept the contract blindly. Individual rights and needs of players are basically ignored in Japanese baseball.

Nomo was not the first Japanese to play in MLB. Masanori Murakami played with the San Francisco Giants as early as 1964 and opened the door for other players, albeit long afterwards. While Murakami came to the United States through the exchange system that his Japanese team, the Nankai Hawks, had with MLB, other players' departures from Japan were not always amicable. For instance, Yoshiharu Wakana was sent to the Mets' Triple-A team due to troubles he had on his Japanese team. Yutaka Enatsu gave Japanese baseball an ultimatum by saying that there was nothing left for him to do in Japan. Mac Suzuki left his high school team as a result of a fight and joined the Mariners. Others, including Kunikazu Ogawa, left Japan for the opportunities that MLB offered.[8] What is common among these players is their refusal to conform to the style of Japanese baseball. Current Japanese players in MLB are no exceptions. Both Nomo and Kazuhiro Sasaki left Japan as a result of contract disputes with the team management. Hideki Irabu, whom Ichiro regarded as the best pitcher in Japan, had to fight a bitter battle against his Japanese team's management when he joined the Yankees instead of the Padres, the organization for which his Japanese team wanted him to play. Tomokazu Ohka was cut from his team and came to the United States to try his luck.

Comparing Japanese and United States baseball, Sasaki, who was critical of the chauvinistic attitude of the Japanese management toward the players, stated,

> When we play our best, the fans are happy. Baseball is for the fans—that's the way they think in the majors. In Japan, it's the opposite: The owners figure they're doing the fans a great favor by making baseball available to them. That's how different Japan is from America.[9]

Sasaki appreciated all the arrangements the US teams made, including travel, training facilities, and locker rooms, to enable players to do their best in the field. What appeals most to the players dissatisfied with Japanese baseball is the respect and freedom given by MLB teams.

Once one knows the style of Japanese baseball, it makes sense that the mass media initially would be critical of the players who moved to MLB by characterizing them as mavericks. That had to change eventually, however, because baseball fans did not share that view. For instance, members of the media in general considered Nomo a defector because, they said, a Japanese ballplayer should play in Japan. But only a small number of them criticized "Godzilla" Matsui when the country's most popular ballplayer announced his decision to move to MLB years later. A majority of Japanese were delighted and looked forward to his playing among MLB players. Such changing attitudes indicate the existence of problems with Japanese baseball, which resulted in growing dissatisfaction among the fans.

The popularity of the Japanese baseball league has continuously gone down since the 1980s. The number of young boys who identify themselves as baseball fans, for instance, has gone down 66 percent during the last 23 years. According to a *Los Angeles Times* report, "TV ratings are down 15% and attendance for the Ichiro-less Orix Blue Waves is off 40%."[10] The *Japan Times* predicted that Japanese baseball would not "have any top players left in the country, and front pages on the sports pages, very few fans watching on TV, and even fewer fans in the stands."[11] One columnist compares MLB with Japanese baseball and lists the following as the majors' advantages:

> Games move fast and quickly.
> Commentators are more interesting and knowledgeable.
> Better attitude toward the fans.
> Going to the game in the stadium is more enjoyable.[12]

These points are repeated by others as well. Even Ichiro has expressed a growing concern with Japanese baseball. Despite the declining popularity of baseball and stadium attendance, his Japanese team's management had no intention of changing their old ways as long as they maintained crowds over 40,000.[13] This eventually became a reason for his departure.

Clearly, Japanese baseball must change its practices to get the fans back. What the management needs to understand is the changing values in contemporary Japan. Sasaki's recent decision to return to Japanese baseball illustrates this well. Sasaki, who had a less-than-satisfactory last season due to an injury, was fully expected to come back and play for the Mariners this year. Therefore, his decision surprised everyone. As he said during the press conference, the reason for his decision was his two children, who lived in Japan and asked their father not to leave.[14] It has been a common practice in Japan for a father to live away from the family to pursue his career. Sometimes the family does not want to move with him because they do not want to change schools or leave friends behind. Because the father is expected to stay with the same company according to the traditional practice, he alone moves to a new location. Sasaki's decision clearly puts his family before his career and goes against the common practice.

As Japanese culture shifts its values, Japanese baseball fans hope returning players can change the game in their native country. Sasaki's decision seems to have been received well by the Japanese public partly because they could sympathize with him. They too have begun to value their family more than their work. Another reason is the fan's desire to see, in person, a player who performed well in the majors. They are happy to have their hero back. Even Tsuyoshi Shinjo, who had to return to Japan because of being cut from the Mets, is getting a hero's welcome. The fans perhaps expect these players to change Japanese baseball so as to meet their needs, which include a later start time for games (the current 6 p.m. start time is too early for the average office worker), lower admission prices (currently $15–50), and fewer interruptions with seemingly unnecessary meetings during the game. Many Japanese also want "management to accommodate them on a more personal level," such as opportunities for interaction with players, which hardly exist today.[15]

It is understandable that the teams are concerned about sending players to the majors because this might make Japanese baseball another farm for the majors and thereby alter a highly structured system that has both conformed to traditional values and benefited the owners. Currently, the teams require nine years of play before granting players free agency, but regardless of Japanese baseball's concern, more and more players will move across the Pacific, and the fans will increasingly watch the MLB games. Both players and fans have new values and cannot accept the old-fashioned baseball in their own country.

Notes

1. Shozo, "*Akuma No Shinario* (Devil's scenario)," January 25, 2004, <http.//www.bluewave.nu/ichiro51/cgi/bbs.cgi?mode=past> (March 2, 2004).

2. Takeshi Kato," Japan in the Majors," *Japan Quarterly* (April–June 2001): 32+.

3. Tim Larimer, "Asian Heroes—Ichiro Suzuki and Hidetoshi Nakata," *Timeasia*, <http://www.time.com/time/asia/features/heroes.nakata.html> (October 30, 2002).

4. See Nobuyuki Suzuki, *Musuko Ichiro* (*My Son Ichiro*) (Tokyo: Futami Shobo, 2001).

5. Narumi Komatsu, *Ichiro on Ichiro*, Interview Special Edition Tokyo: Shinchosha Co. Ltd., 2002, 174.

6. Captain Japan, " Japanese Baseball's Search for Line Drivers," Sake-Drenched Postcards, September 25, 2001 <http://www.bigempire.com/sake/newark.html> (February 3, 2004).

7. Kato, 38.

8. Osamu Nagatani, *Ichiro Shori No Houteisiki* (*Ichiro's Formula for Victory*) (Tokyo: Mikasa Shobo, 2000), 197–198.

9. Kato, 39.

10. Captain Japan, "Japanese Baseball: For Love of the Lame?" Sake-Drenched Postcards, August 1, 2001 <http://www.bigempire.com/sake/jbaseball.html> (February 3, 2004).

11. Captain Japan, "Japanese Baseball."

12. "Matsui Senshu (Kyojin) No Meja Iseki" ("Giants' Matui's Move to the Majors") *Shukan MLB*, August 25, 2002, <http://neko89.site.ne.jp/oldatc02.html> (May 26, 2004).

13. Komatsu, 131.

14. Tsutomu Hirai, "Sasaki Saitan 2–1 Kara Yokohama Kyampu" "Sasaki May Join the Yokohama Camp as Early as 2/1") Nikkan Sports, January 21, 2004 < http://infoweb.nikkansports.com/ns/baseball/p-bb-tp0-040121-0011.html> (May 28, 2004)

15. Captain Japan, "Japanese Baseball."

III. GOLF

5

Tiger Woods: Golf's Modern Catalyst for Change

Donna J. Barbie

Mine was a golfing family. We talked it and watched it. We sat around on Sundays, and we each picked our guy. Mom and Dad rooted for Arnold Palmer, my brother Dana was a Jack Nicklaus fan, and I was enchanted by Gary Player's accent and black attire. Prodded by my father and inspired by that celebrity trio, Dana took up golf. He was big, even in junior high, and rather dorky. People teased him — a lot. When he was in high school, before he won the state championship, Dana lettered in golf. The "studs" scoffed. While golf might be a game, it certainly was *not* a sport. He was *not* an athlete. Despite Dana's gift with a club, his accomplishments earned him little respect at school, that is, until he became a heavyweight wrestler. Now a true athlete, he was part of the jock club. Glowing with approbation, Dana displayed his wrestling letter on his jacket, but no more proudly than the first he earned in golf.

Since then, attitudes have changed tremendously. While some "studs" might continue to think golf is for wimps incapable of proving themselves on fields of combat, general perceptions have modified. More people now see golf as a sport requiring real athleticism. Many young men and women are choosing golf first, not migrating to it after battering their bodies in other endeavors. Growing participation in junior and senior high golf teams has translated to stiffer competition for college scholarships. Media commentators have pointed out the most obvious change — exponential increases in professional prize moneys.

A nexus of factors has driven these changes. Widespread television coverage beginning in the 1960s, for example, transformed a number of professionals, including Arnold Palmer and Jack Nicklaus, into celebrities. Entrepreneurs developed reasonably priced and accessible courses. Many Americans found leisure time to devote to the game, and the links became an extension of the corporate boardroom. Technology, moreover, continues to spur the development of better, more efficient equipment, so even duffers can send the ball out there a long way.

Throughout these decades, a number of professional golfers have also influenced the sport. No modern personality, however, has had as significant an impact as Eldrick "Tiger" Woods. Some might argue this contention, especially since he no longer dominates the field every week. Although he squeaked by Vijay Singh to be named player of the year in 2003, Woods won no majors, and by the beginning of the 2004 season, he was obviously struggling. However, he was also among only six athletes named in *Time's* list of the world's 100 most influential people of 2004. Several contributors to AOL's sports discussion board balked. One user wrote, "Tiger lost it ... it's over. He's about done now." Coming to Woods's defense on the same board, "Alfadog2002" claimed that an apt selection is "the individual who has had the greatest impact on the sport as it is viewed by the overall population and throughout the global community."[1] As this commentary implies, Woods's influence is not limited to his ability to win tournaments.

Woods, as "Boot-Pong" proclaims in Askmen's message board, "is great for games of golf."[2] This fan makes clear that Woods's allure is not based solely upon his play and certainly extends beyond American culture. Woods is an international phenomenon whose ethnicity, physicality, and charisma have been catalysts for important changes in the sport. Despite his relatively short career, his presence and play have altered media coverage, challenged and motivated other players on the tour, increased the number and kinds of fans watching televised events and flocking to tournaments, and inspired diverse people to play.

Despite its claim as a "melting pot," American culture remains extremely race-conscious. Woods learned this early. When he was a child, unknown assailants pelted his parents' house with rotten fruit and stones, an act thought to be inspired by miscegenation. Once when he was on the practice range, a bunch of oafs decided to hit balls into neighboring homes for "kicks." Course managers automatically accused Woods.[3] Because he is a person of color and because he engages in a sport previously restricted to white men, Woods's ethnicity has been an important factor in his emergence as a player.

According to *Golf Digest*, the 1990s began with public exposure of golf's "dirty little secret." The media learned that Shaol Creek, a course hosting a PGA Championship, had no black members. An anonymous member of the board stated that it was "just not done in Birmingham." As these blithe words imply, barring black players from access was deeply embedded in the culture. The rectitude of exclusion was manifest. Fourteen-year-old Woods was aghast at this revelation, but it also inspired him to win a junior tournament the next day.[4] By the end of the decade, the young man had matured, displaying skills that changed many people's perceptions of the relationship of ethnicity and golf.

The evolution began at Augusta National, a former plantation and epitome of the Old South. In the late 1970s, I attended America's most aristocratic tournament, the Masters, at Augusta, awash in dogwoods, azaleas, and wisteria, and I witnessed ethnic exclusivity. My colleague belonged to the National, or to be more accurate, her family had belonged for decades. Because she had clubhouse privileges, we walked right past the multitudes and stepped into the realm of rich folk. Black men silently served food and beverages. Clubhouse caddies were black. As my friend confirmed, no person of color held membership. Since then, an African American has become a member, perhaps in part because of Woods's 1997 Masters victory. As *Golf Digest* claims, he won in "an explosion of brilliance" and began to "transform golf from an elitist game into an egalitarian one."[5]

Neither a political activist nor a crusader, Woods underplays his ethnicity. Although many perceive Woods as black, in actuality, his is a multiplicity of heritages. He is the son of a Thai mother and an African American father whose birthright includes Native American ancestry. Woods has commented in several interviews that he does not want to be the best black player, but aspires to be the best *player* ever. Obviously feeling some pressure to address the issue, he submitted a media statement. He wrote, " My parents have taught me to always be proud of my ethnic background. The critical and fundamental point is that ethnic background … should NOT make a difference. I don't consider myself a great black hope. Now, with your cooperation, I hope I can just be a golfer and a human being."[6] The phrase "with your cooperation" is especially noteworthy as it implies endless questions and tedious inquiries. For Woods, ethnicity is a fact, not the focus of his work.

Although Woods views himself as a golfer, many see race. Woods's former swing coach Butch Harmon claims that he has often heard people yell racial slurs at the young man.[7] This occurred during the 2001 Bay Hill Invitational. Just as Woods was setting up to tap in a putt, someone in the crowd yelled a racial epithet. The commentators responded with audible gasps, and then foundered, sputtering, "Yes," and "ah, well." Woods just turned and stared at the offender. Then he drilled the ball.

Some despise Woods because of race, but his ethnicity has also been part of his magnetism. As Hank Aaron says, his first Masters win "was inspiring in ways that I never would have imagined growing up." Alert to the historical "moment," black people watched, even those who knew little about the sport. Aaron further notes, "His winning meant the same things to us that Jackie Robinson meant in baseball and Joe Louis meant in boxing. He lifted us up and showed us what we could do."[8] Although hyperbolic, Dick Gregory contends that the victory took on the same "aura" as "watching Nelson Mandela come out of jail."[9] African Americans have not been Woods's only admirers, however. In *Raising the Bar*, a work recounting Woods's early career, Tim Rosaforte describes a scene at a Manhattan laundry. People of various ethnicities and ages gathered around a black-and-white television, and Woods was one of them, "a new hero being born."[10] Neither rich nor elite, they loved Woods because of his talent *and* his ethnic difference.

I have attended a considerable number of Disney Classic and Bay Hill Invitational tournaments, and Woods has competed in both. Without a doubt, he is a crowd magnet, drawing diverse fans. At one Disney Classic, for instance, I sat near the midpoint on a hole. A number of spectators were getting into position, because Woods was on his way. Among them were an African American woman and her two children: a boy, about five years old, and a girl, about four. The kids busied themselves with matchbox trucks and cars a little way off. Their mother was watchful but let them play. Woods's group was next. Gathering the children, the woman steered them to the ropes, right next to me. She said to them, "Okay, this is *it*. This is something I want you to remember your whole life!" They sat quietly, waiting for the event, for the "giant" man to pass. The little girl's eyes widened as Woods came into view. Then she exclaimed, " Momma—he looks like *us*!" The mother smiled, looked at her children and said, "Yeah, I know."

According to Rosaforte, Woods was very pleased with the gallery at that tournament. He pointed at a bevy of young people and proclaimed that they were the future of the sport.[11] While the two children I observed might well be part of that future, Woods has not left it to chance. At the turn of the millennium, the National Golf Foundation revealed that only 5 percent of American golfers were minorities, adding that multiple barriers have discouraged economically disadvantaged children.[12] "Golf had never been a black child's game," Hank Aaron says, because courses were exclusive and golf could not "be played for $1.50–2.00."[13] Established in 1996, The Tiger Woods Foundation aims to ensure that youngsters reach their fullest potential by funding clinics and exhibitions directed to underrepresented groups and offering grants and scholarships. These include The William and Marcella Powell Scholarship commemorating the first African Americans to design, own, and operate a golf course in the United States; The Alfred

Holmes Memorial Scholarship honoring the man who helped to desegregate Atlanta's public golf courses; and National Minority Golf Scholarships. Since its inception, the foundation has touched thousands of children across America.

Responding to a question posed during a 2001 foundation clinic in New Orleans, Woods stated, "Golf needs to be more inclusive."[14] For this to transpire, however, minorities must want in. Serving as a vital role model, Woods has begun to create that desire. In April 2004, for example, he provided one-to-one instruction to soldiers' children at Fort Bragg. Aaron claims that foundation programs are working, as more African American youths are on golf courses than he has ever seen.[15] Although most of these children will not become professional golfers, churning out future Tigers is not the fundamental purpose of the programs. Instead, they aspire to instill skills and ethical behaviors through participation and play. Exhibitions and clinics create desire to play while simultaneously opening access to diverse populations. Shaping golf to look like America might be Woods's greatest challenge, but it might also be his most lasting legacy. As Rosaforte argues, the "Tiger Effect" is about to "hit shore," in waves of minority players. [16]

In addition to his ethnicity, Woods's physicality has also caught the world's attention. Unlike so many players of past decades, Woods conditions his 6'2" body. He is fanatical about physical training, working out daily to maintain his mental and physical edge. Claiming that the most important lesson he has learned off the course is taking care of himself, Woods engages in a fitness program that incorporates diet and exercise, especially weight lifting.[17] Woods's regimen began while he was a student at Stanford and increased when Butch Harmon became his swing coach. At that point, Woods put on 20 pounds, all muscle.

Anyone who has seen him, even on television, knows that Woods works out. The nearly total coverage of professional golf attire does not disguise his wedge-shaped body and incredibly muscled shoulders and arms. Gallery members are palpably aware of his physicality, very often commenting when they see him in person for the first time. As he approached a tee at the 2001 Bay Hill Invitational, for example, I overheard two young women marveling at his conditioning, especially the size of his arms. They had no doubt that he is an athlete.

Many fellow players have commented about Woods's athleticism. Gary Player claims that Woods is far stronger and more supple than Greg Norman was in his prime. Buddy Marucci, who came in second to Woods in a U.S. Amateur, writes, "Tiger is the best athlete that golf has seen. He's lean, he's strong."[18] Although Woods's workouts remain secret, his fitness level is well known. In April 2004, for instance, news agencies widely publicized his trip to Fort Bragg, where he engaged in four days of Special Forces boot camp training. Woods remarked that he enjoyed the three- to four-mile "sing along" runs. Verifying his vigor and resilience, Woods added that these outings were more slowly paced that his typical workouts.

He has certainly "raised the bar" in golfers' fitness, and many players are taking a lesson by losing weight and working out for strength and flexibility. Mark O'Meara, for instance, reported in 2002 that he had begun a program of his own, but he also admitted he was not as committed as Woods. But then he asked, "Who is?"[19] Although John Daly and others claim they will never become fitness converts, many players are reaping the rewards of Tigeresque workout routines. Darren Clarke accomplished perhaps the most stunning physical transformation between the 2003 and 2004 seasons. Renowned on tour for imbibing and cigar smoking, Clarke wrote on his official Web site that he is "already beginning to feel the benefits" of taking on a personal fitness trainer.[20] While he reported 17 dropped pounds, sports commentators claim the total is well over 20. During a 2004 interview, a noticeably leaner Clarke stated that he became concerned about fitness the previous year. Although he led the 2003 Masters after the first round, he admits that his game suffered when his stamina flagged. As he said, "trudging" up and down Augusta's hills after substantial rains left him exhausted. Now, he claims, fitness has eliminated endurance problems. As an additional benefit, Clarke's swing has improved because he has far less "belly to swing around." Even Phil Mickelson, who appeared resistant to such regimens in the past, now works out with zeal, traveling with a trainer. Better fitness no doubt aided Mickelson in winning the 2004 Masters, his first major victory. During the tournament broadcast, several commentators conversed about Woods's struggles, especially off the tee. Ian Baker-Finch suggested that Woods might have overbuilt his body. Too much weight lifting seems to be interfering with his swing he argued. Despite this speculation, Woods's physical conditioning, coupled with talent, has translated into incredible performance, and the seeming parade of fitness-conscious players continues.

However important, ethnic distinctiveness and extraordinary fitness alone do not account for Woods's immense popularity. Other players, even exceptionally talented ones, have excelled and some, such as Vijay Singh, maintain an admirable, even daunting, work ethic. But very few have possessed Woods's flair and crowd appeal. The man has charisma. He has captured the public imagination. Generating tremendous interest in the sport during his first few years on tour, Woods continues, even during periods of lackluster performance, to maintain broad appeal. "Woods creates electricity whenever he plays," writes Ron Sirak, "his presence doubling and tripling galleries."[21] Promotion gurus rely on this. In February 2001, for instance, a radio advertisement for the Bay Hill Invitational used his celebrity to sell the tournament. Even though Woods's West Coast swing had been somewhat uninspired that year, the announcer cajoled listeners to "come and see Tiger Woods." There was no mention of any other player. Advertisers know that Woods rouses people, bringing in spectators like no one else. As one fan, "Jaeger," says on the Askmen Message Board, "He must be seen live to be appreciated.... Truly amazing talent." [22]

Without doubt, Woods's play is a spectacle, and witnessing the display is worth enduring the press of massive crowds. In fact, experiencing the galleries is an important aspect of any tournament. I arrived at the 2000 Bay Hill Invitational, for example, when host Arnold Palmer was teeing off. The group of 50 or so middle-aged spectators was low-key, watching golf's elder statesman with respect and awe. This is nothing, however, like the invigorated hordes that follow Woods, regardless of his tournament standing. Each day, even those who are not part of Woods's gallery, constantly talk about him. They monitor his progress on the course, strategizing how to intersect with him. Such was the case at the 2000 Disney Classic. Spectators swarmed one food court on the front nine, waiting under canopies in the heat. Not there simply to eat or drink, they wanted to glimpse Woods play. One little boy, no more than three, wandered around waving a huge orange plastic golf club while his grandparents sat in the shade. He strolled up to me and boldly announced, "I am going to see TIGER!" I am not positive he really understood who Woods was, but he was excited.

When Woods was leading the 2001 Bay Hill and had a late tee time on Sunday, early arrivals watched other players, not in throngs, but in clusters. Moving from trio to trio, fans clapped appreciatively, but without great enthusiasm. About noontime, I overheard a conversation between a father and his teenage son. Obviously tired and dragging, the father finally agreed, "Okay, Okay, we'll stay to see Tiger for a while, and then we go home." They were watching John Daly, who barely made the cut to play the weekend. He was the only player who drew a substantial gallery that morning, and included among them was a former student of mine. As the student reported, he and his buddies planned to stay with Daly for a time because he is exciting and fun, not like some "stiffs," such as Davis Love III or Vijay Singh. The student quickly added, however, they would jump over to the first hole as soon as Woods was ready to tee off. They loved this guy, he said.

Ironically, this situation was inverted in 2004. Despite aspirations for a Bay Hill "five-peat," Woods played poorly on Friday and Saturday. Teeing off early on Sunday, he was obviously not in contention. Woods's gallery was nonetheless as massive as ever and very enthusiastic. They cheered and gasped and applauded their way around the course. Daly, on the other hand, was in contention, teeing off just after Woods made the turn. Although many view Daly as Woods's primary competition for gallery attention, very few spectators deserted Woods that day. They continued to follow Woods, perhaps anticipating a late rally.

Some critics have bemoaned Woods's galleries, disparaging their ignorance and oafish behaviors. I have not witnessed such displays. These huge crowds of admirers seem to be waiting for the guy to do something special, and Woods strives to give them exactly what they want. The 2001 Bay Hill Invitational is a perfect example. I was sitting on the par five sixth hole. Encircling a big lake, this monster can be deadly. Like on the previous day, the wind was strong, full into the players' faces on the tee shot. The first 12 players I saw used an identical strategy. Trying to avoid penalties, they "bit off" less water on the tee to land the ball safely in the fairway. Their second shots were irons, again avoiding the lake and laying up short of the green. Most were on the green in three; some had a chance for birdie. They used their heads, thought it through, and stuck with reasonable course management.

Then Woods arrived with multitudes in tow. Although I was too far from the tee to see exactly who was hitting, it was soon obvious. Woods's drive was 40 yards ahead of the others. Already in place as his fans approached and not about to surrender my spot despite a little shoving, I was in perfect position to see his second shot. Murmurs of "Is he going to go for it?" ran through the crowd. He grabbed a wood but seemed hesitant. When he put the club in the bag and chose an iron, a man beside me whispered, "Rats, he's going to lay up too. Wind is just too strong." Then Woods stopped, went back to his bag, and retrieved the wood. The gallery applauded. He had not even hit the shot, but they were thrilled with his gumption, his confidence, and his dynamism. Here is a player with heart. Woods hit the ball, hard, landing it on the green. The crowd loved it. As one fan said to his friend, "You gotta admit; he's exciting!"

During the final round of the 2004 Bay Hill Invitational, Woods's ball was in a similar position, and the wind was not nearly so strong. Using a wood, he went for it, and the gallery was again audibly excited. This time, however, he hit into the hazard. A groan swept through the crowd. One member of the gallery asserted, "Well, at least he tried." He might have too much confidence in his own abilities at times, but his fans appreciate his willingness to be "out there," to risk it all.

Although Woods always draws huge crowds, the number of people who attend tournaments is miniscule in comparison to those who watch golf on television. Woods's charisma obviously translates very well even through that medium. ESPN reports that nearly 3 million homes (the network's highest ratings for a golf telecast) tuned in to watch Woods win the 2000 Canadian Open.[23] Although drawing an audience to cheer a victory seems no challenge, Woods attracts viewers even when he is not scoring well. The Golf Channel, for example, played and replayed his less than stellar round on one Thursday afternoon in 2000 even though top contenders were still playing. When quizzed about this, spokesman Dan Higgins said they tried to "deliver what the viewer wants." Several players were angry, but Higgins also reported that they received few complaints from fans.[24]

This "Tiger coverage" issue has been the center of an on going conversation between my mother and me. A televised golf aficionado, she wants to see as much play from as many players as possible. After Woods had been missing from several PGA events early in the 2002 season, however, she said, "I *don't* want Tiger to win every tournament. And I *hate* to admit it, but it's just not the same when he's not playing. The spark of excitement, that potential 'explosion' is just missing."

That promise of the extraordinary is exactly what has drawn new fans to view the action. About 53 million watched the 2000 U.S. Open, for example, indicating that people who were not regular golf fans witnessed the event. NBC Sports President Dick Ebersol says Woods is among the few athletes attracting viewers who have not played that particular sport. "People want to watch history," he says. "And Tiger is history."[25] Commentaries posted on various Web sites support this contention. Evangeline Brackett writes, "He's Secretariat, and while I am not a golfer (yet?), I find it inexplicably exciting to see him play."[26] Even my mom somewhat begrudgingly reports that Thelma, a bowling friend who has *never* watched golf, "glues herself to the set when Tiger is playing."

Thelma, who is in her 70s, will probably never play golf, but Woods has stirred many others to learn. In a 2000 poll sponsored by *Golf Magazine*, 59 percent of respondents cited talent as Woods's greatest asset, but 27 percent claimed it was his potential to inspire others to play; 30 percent reported that they knew someone who began to play because of Woods.[27] Aldrick Washington, for example, is a golf convert. Born and raised in a poor family, he played football in high school. He was never interested in golf, especially not on television. After Woods captivated him with a spectacular Masters performance, Washington became a confessed fanatic. He has even transformed his backyard into a putting green, sand trap, and chipping station. Tim Rosaforte, senior writer for *Golf World* and former president of the Golf Writers Association of America, says this African American man "represents the changing face of golf."[28]

Although commentators and fans might disagree about Woods's continued ability to dominate the tour, most concur that he has been a positive catalyst, a boon for the game of golf. As fan "Coolness Factor" notes on Askmen's message board, "Tiger Woods changed things. Like it or not, he turned the world of golf on its head."[29] Even before his record-setting

2000 season, Payne Stewart acknowledged his impact, claiming that the young man was "the greatest thing that's happened to the tour in a long time."[30] Perhaps Stewart was referring to how other players have improved their own performances in response to Woods's work ethic.

Other reasoning might have prompted Stewart's comments, however. As Tommy Roy, executive producer of NBC Sports and new player, asserts, "This kid has made golf cool."[31] "Coolness Factor" concurs, asserting that Woods turned the game into "*the* trendy activity."[32] Ron Sirak, executive editor of *Golf World* and contributing writer to *Golf Digest*, offers another point. He contends that Woods's "most immediate contribution" to the game has been convincing sports fans that golfers are athletes, something that has never been easy for a golfer. In 2003, Woods posted a commentary about this issue on his official Web site. As he claims, "I always got made fun of. They'd say, Golf is a wussy sport ... nonathletic ... takes no skill to play." He adds that he knew otherwise. He has passed that understanding to the world. Sirak claims, "With his power and aggressive style, Woods has convinced people that golf is not just for out-of-shape, badly dressed old men."[33]

Various qualities and capacities, including Woods's ethnicity, physicality, and charisma, have conjoined to produce significant changes in the sport of golf. I just wish they would have occurred earlier. Although wrestling garnered my brother some respect in high school, Dana's true sport and passion has always been golf. If he had been born 30 years later, he certainly would have encountered stiffer competition on the links, but he would not have had to endure cauliflower ears and suffer from mat burns to be deemed an athlete.

Notes

1. America Online News, Sports Discussion Board, http://www.aol.com.

2. Askmen Message Board, http://www.askmen.com/message_boards/index.html, (hereafter cited as Askmen).

3. Tim Rosaforte, *Raising the Bar: The Championship Years of Tiger Woods* (New York: St. Martins, 2000), 37.

4. "Newsmaker of the Decade — 1990s: Tiger Woods," *Golf Digest*, January 15, 2000, http://www.golfdigest.com.

5. *Ibid.*

6. Tiger Woods, "On Race," The Original Tiger Woods Web Page, http://www.geocities.com/mairj2344/tigerrace.html.

7. Butch Harmon, "Tiger's Main Man: Butch Harmon on What It's Like to Teach Golf's Best Players (and Some of Its Worst)." *Golf Digest*, March 2001, 156.

8. Hank Aaron, "Tiger Woods," in "50 Greatest Golfers of All Time and What They Taught Us," *Golf Digest*, July 2000, 114.

9. Rosaforte, *Raising the Bar*, 43.

10. *Ibid.*, 32.

11. *Ibid.*, 90.

12. Official Web site for Tiger Woods Foundation, http://www.twfound.org/home/.

13. Aaron, 114.

14. Tiger Woods Foundation.

15. Aaron, 114.

16. Rosaforte, *Raising the Bar*, 42–43.

17. Tiger Woods, "The Lessons I've Learned and What You Can Learn from Them," *Golf Digest*, Sept. 2000, 74.

18. *Ibid.*, 305.

19. "Woods and O'Meara: Friends talk golf — and life," *Golf Digest*, Dec. 12, 2000, http://www.golfdigest.com.

20. Darren Clarke, Official Web Ssite, http://www.darrenclarke.co.uk.

21. Ron Sirak, "Tiger Lives for Only One Person's Expectations— His Own," Tiger Woods Official Web Site, http://www.tigerwoods.com.

22. Askmen.

23. Michael Anthony, "Golf Tip: The Tiger Woods Appeal," *Golf Digest*, Sept. 24, 2000, http://www.golfdigest.com.

24. "Do You Suffer from Tiger Overkill: All Woods All the Time?" *Golf Digest*, Oct. 12, 2000, http://www.golfdigest.com.

25. Tim Rosaforte, "The Power of Tiger: Tiger Continues to Put Golf on the Front Page." *Golf Digest*, June 22, 2000, http://www.golfdigest.com.

26. Abuzz Message Board, http://www.abuzz.com.

27. "We Want to Know What You Think about Tiger Woods" *Golf Magazine*, Jan. 27, 2000, http://www.golfonline.com.

28. Rosaforte, *Raising the Bar*, 4.

29. Askmen.

30. "Tiger Woods Anecdotes and Quotes," Unofficial Tiger Woods Home Page, http://world.std.com/~rgu/tigerwoods/quotes.html.

31. Raosforte, *Raising the Bar*, 7.

32. Askmen.

33. Ron Sirak, "Honor for Woods is a breakthrough for golf," Tiger Woods Official Web Site, http://www.TigerWoods.com.

6

The Masters on Trial: Culture Wars Over Women Members at Augusta National Golf Club

Tom Cook

On June 12, 2002, Dr. Martha Burk of the National Council of Women's Organizations (NCWO) sent a 69-word letter to chairman William "Hootie" Johnson of Augusta National Golf Club (ANGC). The letter noted that no woman has been invited to join ANGC since it was founded in 1932 and encouraged ANGC to review its policies and practices with a view to opening its membership to women before the 2003 Masters Championship.

On July 8, 2002, Johnson sent a terse three-sentence letter to Burk affirming the distinctly private character of ANGC and suggesting that any further communication between them would not be productive. If this were all Johnson had done, the issue might have developed quite differently, with much less public controversy. But the next day he also issued a bombastic 932-word press release from which the *New York Times* on July 10 quoted several key passages, including a statement by Johnson that any future change by ANGC would be on its own timetable and not "at the point of a bayonet."[1]

This was the beginning of a very public political quarrel that might not be fully resolved for quite some time. At this point a symbolic interactionist might say that Johnson labeled himself and created a self-fulfilling prophecy, destining himself to seek heroic redemption through adversarial action. He had previously been seen in Southern corporate and political circles as a moderate and mannerly progressive, but henceforth many people who didn't know his former reputation would perceive him as a bigoted and bull-headed Bubba. Like Johnson, Burk was not very well known nationally before the Augusta membership controversy. But Johnson's diatribe made both of their names household words. Ironically Burk's childhood nickname was Hootie, so it could be called a case of Hootie vs. Hootie.[2] She was a Texan, age 61, he a South Carolinian, age 72.

When the news of Johnson's press release hit the media, one of the first things that happened was that the opinions of the general public and the professional golfing community were solicited. In those early days the general public supported ANGC in a survey by *USA Today* on its Web site, usatoday.com, by a margin of about 3 to 1, and a much higher percent of pro golfers who chose to speak to the media, both male and female, supported the club. Arnold Palmer, the "King of Golf" and a multiple Masters winner, supported the club. Golf legend Nancy Lopez, the "Arnold Palmer" of women's golf, also favored the club, but then-current female world No. 1 Annika Sorenstam (winner of 13 tournaments worldwide in 2002) was one of a few who took the side of the NCWO. Much later, Sorenstam added fuel to the fire by stating that she would relish the opportunity to compete against the men on the regular PGA Tour, as precocious eighth grader Michelle Wie was already preparing to do. It looked like Sorenstam would get several sponsors' exemptions from PGA Tour events in 2003, and Wie would compete several times against her LPGA elders before even having a chance to try out for her local high school team. There was even a slim chance Wie could qualify for a future Masters invitation by winning the National Public Links Championship, an event previously entered only by males but with no specific prohibition of females. As Bob Dylan would say, the times they are a-changin'. The Year of the Woman in golf was unfolding.

It so happened that the British Open was being played shortly after Johnson's press release. Much media attention was given to the responses of male world No. 1 Tiger Woods to questions about the issue posed to him at the British Open. His carefully worded answers were ungenerously perceived as being too favorable to ANGC's rights as a private club. Some noted that Woods was not only the two-time defending champion of the Masters, aiming for an unprecedented three straight title, but also that ANGC had made substantial contributions to the Tiger Woods Foundation promoting golf among minority youth.

Seemingly rather unimpressed with the fine line Woods was trying to walk, the *New York Times* then got into the act and published a series of articles critical of ANGC and/or Woods. The *Times* campaign culminated in a November 18 editorial suggesting that Woods, as the top golfer and a minority group member, had a special moral obligation to confront ANGC on this issue by boycotting the Masters if necessary. [3] This idea was supported only by the most radical advocates of change at Augusta. Most of the golfing community said the *Times* should give Woods a break. *Times* reporter Dave Anderson agreed with this viewpoint in a December 8, 2002, article and reveal that a previous version of his article had been squelched by the editors. [4] After Anderson's article, the *Times* was quieter on the issue of Woods's special obligations to gender equity. Already they had published a November 21 letter to the editor from Julian Bond of the NAACP stating that gender equity was an important social goal but that no individual should bear a disproportionate political burden on its account. [5]

Woods tried several times to clarify his position and polish his image as a role model. On his Web site, tigerwoods.com, he said in effect that both sides were right. He hoped ANGC would admit women, but they could not be forced to do so, and he wished Burk and Johnson could just sit down and talk about it. Burk welcomed the change in Woods's tone but said she hoped he'd take his advocacy of her cause to the next level. This seemed pretty unlikely, as did any sort of friendly chat between the two Hooties. For the next several months this remained the position of Woods on this issue despite persistent media efforts to draw him out and pin him down. Clearly he was tiring of the issue and wished it would go away. What he really wanted was to win another Masters and choose his own political battles to fight.

Johnson's main action in the early going was to get the sponsors of the Masters off the hook politically by stating that the ANGC would cover the entire multimillion-dollar cost of TV on CBS, with which the Masters has had a long series of annual TV contracts. CBS showed no indication of wanting out of this relationship. Later Johnson hired a women's polling service to survey the general public and was pleased to report that the data favored the club by majorities of about 2 to 1 on most of the survey questions. [6]

Meanwhile, Burk was not idle. She published a list of all the members of ANGC, including their corporate affiliations. She made a number of public statements and appearances, and later in the fall she set up a Web site, augustadiscriminates.org. This Web site included a Corporate Hall of Hypocrisy, with the Professional Golf Association (PGA) listed as the top hypocrite. This is because the PGA has a formal anti-discrimination policy and will not hold PGA Tour events at discriminatorily exclusive clubs, yet it still counts the Masters as a major championship and counts the winnings as official PGA money despite the fact that the Masters is a private invitational event. Burk sees no difference between this issue and the 1990 controversy that forced Shoal Creek Country Club in Alabama to quickly change its policies and promise to admit a black member if it wanted to host the PGA Championship that year. She therefore wants the PGA to completely disaffiliate itself from the Masters until ANGC admits a woman. Loss of major championship status could be the leverage to turn the tide.

About the time Johnson released his poll data, Burk began to acquire some louder voices on her side. The Ladies Professional Golf Association (LPGA) released a strong statement encouraging ANGC to open its membership to women "for the good of the game of golf."[7] Several prominent women golf pros supported their organization's leaders in this statement, and only a few more chose to speak out on the other side. Two prominent members of ANGC withdrew their memberships. They were Thomas Wyman, a former CBS executive, and John Snow, a nominee for the cabinet position of treasury secretary. A third ANGC member, the already politically embattled Lloyd Ward of the U.S Olympic Committee, was under criticism for not giving up his membership, partly despite or because of the fact that he was one of the few black members of ANGC.

That's where matters stood at the end of 2002. It was clear the issue would not go away and neither side would back down without a fight. So it appeared that the Masters would soon be contested under considerable rhetorical and political duress. Potential demonstrators, including the Reverend Jesse Jackson were preparing to invade Augusta in April with placards and slogans.

Anticipating the likely arrival of protestors and demonstrators, the city of Augusta in January 2003 discussed amending its public demonstration ordinance. The newly proposed law would require groups of 5 or more protestors to apply for a permit from the sheriff 30 days before the event, and the sheriff would have 10 days to approve or deny the application. Sheriff Ronnie Strength was quoted as saying public safety would supersede free speech, and public property near ANGC would be out of bounds for demonstrations. There were two tie votes on the amendments with local officials divided 5–5 along racial lines. [8]

Also anticipating the impending political fireworks, *Golf Digest* took a well-designed phone survey with a random sample of 800 golfers and non-golfers shortly before the new year and published the results in their February issue. The general public was about twice as likely as the golfers to support the NCWO on a variety of relevant issues surveyed. On most of the questions, the majority of both golfers and non-golfers said that the controversy had not changed their previous opinions on either the subject or the disputants. Only 8 percent of golfers and 22 percent of the others thought Woods should boycott the Masters. [9]

To start formulating her protest strategy, Burk took a low-key trip to Augusta in February, scouting out the site for the first time with some of her political advisors. The official purpose of the Georgia trip was to promote the WNBA, but there was little doubt about the real objective. Sheriff Strength had clearly not been engaging in idle speculation about the likelihood of political demonstrations and protests. A week after Burk's trip, the Augusta City Council passed its new protest ordinance by a 6–5 vote with the former tie broken by Mayor Bob Young, who is white. Burk then announced that she would not be intimidated by this limitation on her First Amendment rights.[10]

On a more cheerful note, Annika Sorenstam finally accepted an invitation from a PGA event, scheduled in May shortly after the Masters at the famed Colonial course in Fort Worth, Texas, noted for its tight fairways and small greens. A majority of those who replied to an electronic *USA Today* survey on USATODAY.com expected her to make the cut, but few expected her to win or contend. Without the Augusta flap, it was quite unlikely so many PGA tournament sites (about 10 to date) would have wanted to recruit Sorenstam to play. Very likely the PGA encouraged its local sponsors to invite her to play at their events in order to demonstrate its lack of prejudice despite its ongoing relationship with ANGC and the Masters. In any case it was probably good business. Female entrants might soon become just as good a draw as Woods in some PGA tournaments, whose attendance and viewership decline markedly if he is absent.

Despite Sorenstam's previous public support of the LPGA's officially declared position vs. the ANGC and her subsequent offhand comment that she would gladly accept on offer of membership at ANGC, she repeatedly said she was not making a political statement by competing against the men. Instead she viewed it as a personal test of her golf game, like a fifth major championship in her season. Sorenstam was hardly the first LPGA star to challenge the men, but she was probably the one with the best chance to do it successfully. As long ago as 1945, the legendary Babe Didrickson Zaharias had entered the Los Angeles Open and made the 36-hole cut, but did not finish in the money. [11]

As if to add humor to the fray, little-known Phoenix pro Brian Kontak announced his intention to enter the 2003 U.S. Women's Open. Eligibility rules clearly stipulate that contestants must be female, but Kontak said he had a secret plan to get around this. Perhaps he was contemplating surgery. [12]

On the heels of Sorenstam's decision to play at Fort Worth, the Senior PGA was just starting the 2003 season. Six-time Masters winner Jack Nicklaus was asked about the ANGC membership issue and politely stated that his record speaks for itself. As a leading golf course designer, he has always insisted on nondiscriminatory membership policies. But like Woods, Nicklaus said he didn't expect the ANGC to ask his opinion. The difference is that unlike Woods, an honorary member, Nicklaus and Palmer are regular members of ANGC with voting rights. Surprisingly, there has been little public pressure on either of them to speak out or resign, compared with the intense pressure the *New York Times* and others placed on Woods to boycott the Masters. This tends to confirm Burk's contention that too many rich old white guys get a free ride.

As February was coming to a close and the Masters was just six weeks away, the action began to pick up on the political front. A coalition of women's groups at Harvard University protested the membership in ANGC of several leading persons affiliated with the university or its corporation and encouraged the university to reaffirm its public commitment to diversity. Jesse Jackson confirmed the intention of his Rainbow/PUSH group to support the NCWO in its protests at Augusta. Mayor Young of Augusta affirmed his support of Burk's First Amendment rights while echoing Sheriff Strength in his stated concern for public safety. Meanwhile, some strange political bedfellows began to emerge. A Ku Klux Klan group applied to the sheriff for a permit to demonstrate on behalf of ANGC, as did two other newly formed local groups called Women Against Martha Burk (WAMB) and People Against Ridiculous Protests (PARP). The ANGC tried to disavow the KKK's support but could not get it to back off. Meanwhile another pro–ANGC group headed by unemployed Tampa resident Todd Manzi applied for a permit to have as many simultaneous demonstrators as Burk's group in whatever locations NCWO was allowed to use. Manzi also started two anti–Burk Web sites at TheBurkStopsHere.com and ItTakesBalls.com. With friends like these, who needs enemies like Martha Burk?

Some of ANGC's other supporters couldn't wait until the Masters to start publicly exercising their First Amendment rights. At a hotel where Burk was speaking March 8 in the Washington DC suburb of McLean, Virginia, 10 members of a men's rights group called the National Coalition of Free Men waited two hours for her to leave so they could chant "Just Say No to Burk." Without comment she calmly took out a camera and photographed them but later said she admired their pluck. Two days later she announced that she had written a letter to CBS president Les Moonves requesting a meeting to persuade him to cancel his commitment to televise the Masters for the 47th consecutive year. A CBS spokesperson immediately confirmed the network's intent to go ahead with the broadcast.

On March 12 Burk's plans received a setback when her request for a permit to have 24 protesters at the front gate and 200 more across the street on Saturday April 12 was modified by Sheriff Strength on alleged public safety grounds. She in turn rejected the sheriff's plan, which would restrict all protesters with permits to a less conspicuous ANGC-owned location in a field about a half mile away, and within hours the Georgia chapter of the

ACLU filed a federal lawsuit on behalf of NCWO and Rainbow/PUSH challenging the constitutionality of the City of Augusta's recently amended protest ordinance. It was inevitable that lawyers would eventually get into the act, and now a courtroom showdown loomed.[13]

At this point the only protest permit that had been granted was to Augusta restaurant owner and WAMB founder Allison Greene, who proposed to hold a lighthearted pre-tournament cookout near her Boll Weevil Café to show support for ANGC. But the sheriff said a "host of groups" had applied for permits and he was expecting more. His apparent plan was to direct them all away from the main gate of the club, a public place, toward the alternative location, which was on private property. Whatever the outcome of the lawsuit, Burk promised that she and her supporters would be at Augusta in one form or another.

As the ACLU's court case was pending, Burk stepped up her rhetoric against CBS. Anticipating a resolution against CBS from NCWO, she said at a press conference that broadcasting the Masters during wartime demeaned the 250,000 American women in uniform who know what it's like to fight for equal opportunity. This comment probably didn't win Burk very many new fans. [14]

A key event in the week before the Masters was the federal court hearing in front of longtime Circuit Court Judge Dudley Bowen, appointed in 1979 by then–President Jimmy Carter, perhaps the most prominent Georgian to publicly support Burk. The hearing occurred on Wednesday, April 2 (adroitly averting April Fools' Day by just a day). Bowen had a solid reputation for being conservative but fair. By the following Monday, the beginning of Masters week, he still had not announced his ruling, with the NCWO's protest scheduled for the coming weekend. Burk proceeded to coordinate her plans to bus protesters to Augusta from as far away as Washington, DC. Other buses would leave from nearby Atlanta and Athens. On the first day of official Masters play, two days before her scheduled Saturday protest, Burk planned to hold a press conference in Atlanta. While in Georgia for the court hearing, Burk appeared on the Atlanta-based sports talk show "Listen Up," confronting an argumentative foe in host Charles Barkley and revealing herself to be just as quick with a quip as the former Auburn and NBA star. In *Newsday* the following weekend, Burk was quoted as saying her side had already won.[15]

During the same week a number of members of Congress, including presidential candidate Dick Gephardt, introduced a resolution against high-ranking federal employees belonging to organizations that discriminate on the basis of race or gender. It was noted that a number of key federal officials were implicated by this, including some who belong to all-male clubs in the DC area such as Burning Tree and at least one who belongs to ANGC.

Burk was one of those who addressed Congress on behalf of the resolution.[16]

As the tournament began, many contestants interviewed by the media declared their intent to treat it as "golf as usual," but of course they could not. Some golf traditionalists, such as Davis Love III, popular winner of the Players Championship a week earlier, openly decried the "zoo" or "circus" environment. Odds-on pre-tournament favorite Tiger Woods, a winner in three of his first five events in 2003, lives in a constant media bubble. So he merely said it would be great if they could just play golf but that's not the reality. There were almost as many media references to Burk and Johnson as there were to Woods, and it might have been a welcome reprieve for Woods not to be the only one on the spot.

With AGNC footing the considerable bill, CBS confirmed its plan to show continuous coverage of commercial-free golf, giving little or no attention to politics. Meanwhile, it was almost impossible for anyone else to ignore the political dimension. Despite the rain several dozen people showed up for Allison Greene's pro–ANGC cookout on Sunday, April 6, and some of them added their names to her anti–Burk petition, which by then had been signed by more than 1,300 women. Starting on Monday, April 7, West Virginia businessman Tim Taylor and his partner Vincent Vaughan began selling "I Support Hootie" buttons for $5 each outside the main gate of ANGC, saying they'd give the profits to charity. At this point they were the only ones who had permits for that prime location.[17]

At least half a dozen groups were planning to demonstrate at the alternative location, and some of them were still hoping to thwart the plans of Sheriff Strength to keep them there. Altogether the sheriff estimated that as many as 1,000 demonstrators were expected during the week, including both pro–ANGC and anti–ANGC factions. To dramatize his alleged public safety concerns, the sheriff announced plans to have a spacious paddy wagon and a large posse of extra police officers available in full riot gear. Burk must have gloated inside when she learned this. With the possible exceptions of Ma Barker or Mother Jones, no graying American grandmother had ever before provoked such a massive police presence to deter her dangerous acts. In retrospect, the sheriff's overreaction almost matched Johnson's.

On Tuesday April 8 Burk received a shock when Judge Bowen ruled in favor of the sheriff on the ACLU's lawsuit. So the NCWO would have to use the alternative site a half mile away. The judge's main reasons for this in his 17-page opinion were that the sheriff treated all protestors and demonstrators alike in the eight protestors' permits he issued, (not counting the vendor's permit issued to Taylor), and all groups would at least be allowed to demonstrate somewhere in the vicinity of ANGC. Burk said the judge was apparently more concerned about the interests of the city and the club than he was about the First Amendment, and with only four days remaining before the targeted Saturday protest, she immediately appealed the ruling to the 11th Circuit Court of Appeals.[18]

On Wednesday, April 9, Hootie Johnson broke a long silence with the media by holding a pre–Masters press conference. At least 36 of the 44 questions he was asked were mainly about the ANGC membership issue, and despite his declared intent to avoid politics, he answered a number of them while sidestepping others. With a phalanx of 60 green-jacketed members standing nearby to support him, he reiterated the club's position on making its own membership decisions without external interference. It appeared that his own position was firmer than it had been at any time since Burk's letter 10 months before. When asked how long ANGC might keep paying for the TV coverage, Johnson unflinchingly said, "Indefinitely." He even criticized Woods, whose position had seemed to move a small rhetorical step toward Burk, in his own pre-tournament press conference on Tuesday. Without waiting for any political questions Woods had said that everyone present knew he favored women becoming members of ANGC. This defused most of the hard questions. Former Masters winner Gary Player, an elder statesman of golf, welcomed the up-front statement, saying it enhanced Woods's status as a great role model for the game. Burk was pleased too. But Johnson was not, commenting that he wouldn't tell Woods how to play golf if Woods wouldn't tell him how to run a private club. The gratuitous putdown of Woods did not sit well with the media.[19]

In the rest of his Tuesday press conference, Woods was much more successful than Johnson in his effort to focus on golf rather than politics. Although he still said the club had a legal right to choose its own members, the media seemed to have gained some grudging respect for the cautiously assertive moral position Woods was now taking in the knowledge that most of his pro golf peers felt otherwise, and some reporters even praised his directness or his diplomacy while critics of the club saved their harshest comments for Johnson. Although Johnson had fewer overt defenders than Burk in the media, both of them had plenty of public detractors for their perceived obstinacy. Articles with a "Who cares?" or "So what?" tone were quite frequent as Masters week unfolded. Yet even these neutral or mildly negative articles provided more media exposure for the issue, hardly a political failure for Burk. A new member survey of NCWO-affiliated organizations revealed solid support for her position, despite limited support from women in general or women golfers in particular. The anti-corporate symbolism of Burk's message was catching on better with people who understood it in political or socioeconomic terms than with those who thought her protest was mostly about golf. But she was still preaching mostly to the choir. And it had not helped her cause that she and Johnson were easily lumped together as two equally stubborn foes who somehow deserved each other. Their personas were taking priority over the issues, and Burk risked being painted with the same broad brush that Johnson had used to label himself.

On Thursday, April 10, Mother Nature spoke. The Masters was scheduled to begin, but heavy rains intervened, and play was postponed until Friday. Meanwhile, a three-judge panel of the Federal Circuit Court of Appeals refused to review Judge Bowen's ruling. This effectively put the legal victory almost in the hands of Sheriff Strength. As a last resort, Burk could still try to get injunctive relief from any federal judge in the 11th Circuit, and with the rain falling, she might have had some extra time to do so. It was like an unexpected Mulligan, but tournament officials were hoping to get back on schedule by playing 36 holes Friday. At her Thursday press conference in Atlanta, flanked by feminist and civil rights leaders, including Martin Luther King III, Burk said her next round of efforts would be to get more ANGC members to resign or speak out if they did not agree with Johnson. By teleconference Jesse Jackson confirmed his support and said people who agreed with them should boycott products of companies whose CEOs belonged to ANGC. The next day Burk went one step further and announced plans to target the 37 sponsors of all the regular events on the PGA Tour by writing letters to them and adding their names to her Corporate Hall of Hypocrisy. But instead of the word "boycott," she used the phrase "consumer education." Although he would not be present at Augusta, Jackson did not rule out civil disobedience or arrest as protest tactics for his Rainbow/PUSH group if the courts and the sheriff would not change their minds about the protest site. Burk, on the other hand, had clearly said she would not break the law.[20]

Individual protesters and groups of fewer than five were not required to get permits, so it was not clear if this would become a loophole in the sheriff's plan to move all the protesters away from the main gate. In addition to groups mentioned above, others planning to be present included the Brotherhood Organization for a New Destiny, an anti–Jackson group from Los Angeles, and Golfers for a Real Cause, who were raising money for breast cancer research. On Friday Sheriff Strength continued to overplay his hand by meeting with representatives of a number of groups to warn them not to go near the front gate or stray from the protest site in small groups if they wanted to avoid arrest. The comments of the captain in charge of the security effort made it clear that he felt overprepared for the task ahead.[21]

By mid-morning Saturday, the golf had finally caught up with the weather interruptions. Woods barely made the 36-hole cut after getting up early to finish his second round. At the midpoint of the competition, Canadian lefty Mike Weir was 4 strokes ahead of his nearest pursuer and 11 strokes ahead of Woods, who then rallied with a 66 in the afternoon to get back on the leader board. Meanwhile, as they gathered for a political rally at the muddy protest site, several dozen Burk supporters were overwhelmed by more than 100 police cars and over 100 police. Reporters, hecklers, and pro–ANGC advocates collectively outnumbered anti–ANGC demonstrators, even accepting Burk's rather generous estimate of her own crowd. Few others were present. For props there were an inflatable pig and a cardboard Klansman. For comic relief there were an Elvis impersonator and a tuxedo-clad man whose placard merely said, "Formal Protest." There was no judicial injunction, and no protestors risked approaching the main gate. Burk spoke briefly but emphatically and emphasized the political importance of ANGC as a symbol of male domination and corporate arrogance. Her punch line was that protests by women with placards would precede protests by women with their pocketbooks. Despite Johnson's increased obstinacy, Burk did not propose to return to the 2004 Masters and even suggested that this might not be needed with her new pocketbook strategy. A number of others spoke too. About 20 of Burk's supporters were from Jackson's group. The unruly hordes of protestors feared by Sheriff Strength simply did not materialize. A rumor was afoot that ANGC supporters had reduced the anti–ANGC turnout by purchasing tickets on Augusta-bound buses at $75 per ticket. Most media accounts of Saturday's events made it seem fairly low-key, perhaps even anti-climactic.[22]

In the short run the impact of Burk's protest did not match its big buildup, and she did not achieve her specific objective by her stated deadline. One of the biggest unknowns in this case is whether ANGC would have opened its membership rolls to women if they had not been pressured to do so. Some people close to Johnson say he was about ready for this, perhaps even soon enough to meet Burk's deadline of the 2003 Masters had the deadline been set by himself and not by others. When given a specific deadline by an external agency, Johnson behaved remarkably similarly to the way Saddam Hussein behaved in 1991 and again in 2003. It's a macho thing and a cultural thing for both of them. So Burk's crusade might have been the spur to Johnson's Jihad, and otherwise his more moderate tendencies might have emerged as they had during the era of racial unrest.

Of course we'll never know the answer to this cultural conundrum. Counterfactual conditionals must remain perpetual mysteries to be resolved only by counterfactual speculations. If the answer to this one is "yes," the case is ironic if not tragic, like a three-putt bogey after a good opening drive. But if the answer is "no," the NCWO can probably congratulate itself for saving par from the bunker by making a memorable symbolic case against the obstinate enforcement of obsolete attitudes, while attempting to open some important doors for women in a social environment dominated by male corporate power. They competed for air time with Tiger Woods and the war in Iraq, and thanks largely to Johnson, they achieved much more than a mere 15 minutes of fame. But like Johnson and Sheriff Strength, did Burk overplay her hand? Was her strategy commensurate with her goals?

One way to ask whether Burk's protest was worthwhile or anticlimactic would be to consult the recently deceased John Rawls, the "Tiger Woods" of America philosophy in the 20th century. When he died in November 2002 at age 81, Rawls, in his long and honorable career as a political philosopher at Harvard, had come to epitomize the rational voice of American democracy almost as much as historic superstars such as Franklin, Jefferson, or Madison. His *Theory of Justice*, published in 1971, was viewed by his many admirers as the set of philosophical principles the country's founders should have had in mind had they only been as profound and articulate as Rawls. After three decades the ideas of Rawls have now become as firmly embedded in American popular culture as any academic philosopher's since William James or John Dewey.

The two key principles of justice that Rawls emphasized were the principle of equal liberty and the principle of positions equally open to all persons. Furthermore, he would tolerate social or economic inequalities only if they were to everyone's advantage, especially that of the least advantaged members of society. It is quite evident that powerful, exclusive organizations such as ANGC violate the spirit of Rawls's philosophy of justice even if they do not violate the letter of the law.

What then should people try to do about it? If society's institutions were only more perfect, they would probably be self-corrective, but indeed they far too often are not. They must at least as often be corrected by the people themselves, and this is just as much part of a healthy democracy as the institutions the people are trying to correct.

Rawls briefly analyzes this sort of situation in his 1969 essay on civil disobedience.[23] He says that a first step in removing injustice is always to use standard democratic processes while working through existing institutions to give them a fair chance to correct themselves. This is exactly what happened when the PGA quickly corrected its own policies and practices a decade ago over the issue of holding official competitions at racially exclusive clubs. The issue was dealt with remarkably smoothly, and such clubs will never again host PGA-sponsored events.

Why then does the PGA not step in and set Johnson straight on gender bias? As noted previously, it's a complex issue because the PGA does not officially sponsor the Masters, although it accepts Masters dollars as official PGA winnings. There even used to be another PGA event the same week as the Masters. But Burk still puts the PGA above ANGC in her Corporate Hall of Hypocrisy, and perhaps rightfully so. Unlike ANGC, the PGA does have a very clear nondiscrimination policy in writing for all to see, yet it winks at ANGC and does nothing.

In this case working through established institutional channels (by writing to Johnson and lobbying via the conventional media) got Burk next to nowhere. So Rawls, an unabashed though somewhat theoretical feminist, would likely consider other political methodologies, such as demonstrations, protests, or even civil disobedience if the right theoretical criteria could be met. First, there would have to be a clearcut violation of the fundamental principles of justice. I think Rawls would readily agree that this is a clearcut violation because blatant gender bias is at least as serious as blatant racial bias in Rawls's scheme of things. Second, it would have to be a last resort. This was not the case until Johnson's position hardened, and Burk's letter might have unwittingly caused this to happen. But his confrontational "point of a bayonet" rhetoric and his boorish pre–Masters press conference would lead one to believe that once the lines were drawn, more vigorous measures would be needed. Third, it should be an unjust situation that, if rectified, would help do away with other social injustices. Some have said that it hardly matters to the poor non-golfing women of America whether a few rich women get into a private golf club. Others have said that the symbolic opening of this door is all that's needed to open many other doors. It might depend on who the first women members are at Augusta. Not every famous woman has the capacity to be the Rosa Parks or the Billie Jean King of this issue. Sandra Day O'Connor and Nancy Lopez are likely choices. Annika Sorenstam might be a better one. Fourth and finally, Rawls would insist that the protester's strategy should be rational and reasonably designed to advance the protester's aims. Here's where the greatest questions might arise. Burk's detractors portray her as a mere media hound, with little genuine concern for the outcome of her protest. This is certainly unfair to Burk, just as some of her friends have probably been unfair to Johnson. There's no question of her rationality and her commitment to the goals of her quest. What might still be questioned, however, is the reasonableness of her means/ends analysis. Rawls is clearly opposed to purely symbolic windmill-tilting protests, and perhaps especially to those that make one's goals harder to reach by making one's opponents more stubborn. Perhaps Burk has good reasons to believe that Johnson's days are numbered as the autocratic leader of ANGC and that other leaders or more democratic institutional structures might soon take his place. If so, her strategy is clearly reasonable. But if not, even her erstwhile ally John Rawls might be forced to say that she pushed too hard too soon when a more patient strategy might have been more effective. The inflatable pig was probably a bad idea when Johnson was already doing such a good job of stereotyping himself.

This of course would depend largely on whether the main goals of Burk's protest were really about golf or ANGC at all. In Burk's highly strategic mind, ANGC might be only a rhetorical fulcrum to draw attention to women's issues in general and especially to women's economic issues. To help her keep doing that in the future, it might even be to Burk's ultimate political advantage for Johnson to have become a more visible and stubborn symbol of her opposition than he was the previous summer. If people like Johnson and Sheriff Strength had not existed, Burk might have had to invent them. One day they might be seen as the Orval Faubus and Bull Connors of Burk's campaign, and this might become a case of losing the battle in order to win the war. The *New York Times* tentatively suggested this point of view in its post-mortem on the above events.[24]

Only time will tell. As a lifelong golfer and former women's golf coach, I have some of the same mixed feelings about this controversy that have emerged in several media surveys. I want the game I love to represent more progressive cultural values than it currently does, and I am well aware that its recent history, especially in the United States, has often perverted the tradition of democracy that once prevailed in the good old days when golf was played on public meadows by Scottish shepherds using crooked sticks and sheep dung.

I watched the 2003 Masters more avidly than ever, with no thought of boycotting the sedate CBS coverage. It was very nice not to have so many commercials. However, a small voice in the back of my brain was softly saying, "Go, Martha, go!" (By the way, the winner of the 2003 Masters was Mike Weir in a playoff with Len Mattiace.)

Six weeks later I watched equally avidly as Annika Sorenstam tried to make the 36-hole cut at the PGA event in Fort Worth. On the first day she hit the ball brilliantly, easily outplaying her male partners from tee to green, but couldn't make her birdie putts, carding a one-over-par 71. On the second day she scrambled valiantly for her pars but didn't hit enough greens, settling for a 74 and missing the cut by four strokes. Except for a few PGA tour members who expressed some sour grapes about her invitation to the event, almost everyone was extremely impressed by her competitiveness and especially by the grace with which she handled the intense pressure brought about by the extreme media hype. Live spectators and TV viewers approached major championship numbers for early-round action. Tiger Woods took the week off but consistently supported Sorenstam in a number of media interviews and made several encouraging phone calls to her. In a post-round interview Sorenstam announced that this would be her only foray on the PGA Tour. Afterward Martha Burk congratulated her on a memorable performance but reminded anyone who was still interested that several executives of sponsor Bank of America were members of ANGC who were profiting hypocritically from Sorenstam's performance.[25] This was the first time the golf world had heard very much from Burk in more than a month, but it was a pointed reminder that fans of the sport might expect to hear from her later.

There were no protests at the 2004 Masters, and there were no commercials on the CBS coverage. That summer, Burk's civil rights lawsuit against Augusta city officials was settled for $120,000. [26] Shortly afterward Hootie Johnson announced that corporate sponsors would return to the CBS coverage in 2005, prompting speculation that all the fireworks were about to begin again.[27]

Notes

1. Brown in *New York Times*, July 10, 2002.
2. Nordlinger in *National Review*, January 27, 2003.
3. *New York Times* editorial, November 18, 2002.
4. *New York Times*, December 8, 2002.
5. *New York Times*, November 21, 2002.
6. Logan in *Philadelphia Inquirer*, November 14, 2002.
7. Brown in *New York Times*, November 21, 2002.
8. Carvell and Markiewicz in *Atlanta Journal-Constitution*, February 4, 2002.
9. *Golf Digest*, February 2003.
10. Associated Press Online, February 19, 2003.
11. Herrmann in *Newsday*, February 13, 2003.
12. Green in *Charlotte Observer*, February 24, 2003.
13. Associated Press Online, March 11, 2003.
14. Emling in *Atlanta Journal-Constitution*, March 27, 2003.
15. Howard in *Newsday*, April 6, 2003.
16. Mihoces in *USA Today*, April 1, 2003.
17. Brown in *New York Times*, April 7, 2003.
18. Newberry in Associated Press Online, April 8, 2003.
19. Ostler in *San Francisco Chronicle*, April 10, 2003.
20. Pucin in *Los Angeles Times*, April 11, 2003.
21. Price-Brown in *Newsday*, April 11, 2003.
22. *Atlanta Journal-Constitution*, April 13, 2003.
23. Cf. Freeman, *John Rawls, Collected Papers*. (Cambridge: Harvard University Press, 1999.)
24. Pennington in *New York Times*, April 14, 2003.
25. Bonk in *Los Angeles Times*, May 24, 2003.
26. O'Keeffe in *New York Daily News*, August 1, 2004.
27. Stewart in *Los Angeles Times*, August 28, 2004.

IV. FOOTBALL

7

"On the Threshold of Broad and Rich Football Pastures": Integrated College Football at UCLA, 1938–1941

Lane Demas

On the morning of December 9, 1939, the UCLA football team prepared for the most important game in school history. That day's contest versus cross-town rival USC marked the end of a tumultuous regular season, the pinnacle college football match-up of 1939 and a game that would draw more than 100,000 spectators to Los Angeles's Memorial Coliseum, at that point the largest audience ever to watch a football game in American history. Yet some who felt the excitement, anticipation, and fear did so for very different — and more important — reasons. Poised within the sea of 60 UCLA Bruins, their faces obscured by leather helmets and their nameless jerseys sporting only "UCLA," stood five African American student athletes. For these five, the exhausting 1939 season had represented a turning point in collegiate racial integration, and the significance of the impending contest with USC weighed even more heavily on the shoulders of the black Bruins than those of their teammates.

During the 1938–1941 period, a group of black students made UCLA's football squad the most racially integrated major college team America had ever seen. While only a maximum of five African Americans ever played on the Bruin team at any one time, their collective impact led to disparate reactions on the Los Angeles campus itself, among mainstream media outlets and African-American sportswriters, and in the Jim Crow South. Three players, Kenneth Washington, Woodrow Strode, and Jackie Robinson, held prominent starting positions, each playing both offense and defense. Washington was highly regarded as the best football player in UCLA's history, graduating in 1940 after contributing to the team's most successful season ever. Excelling in four sports, football, basketball, baseball, and track, Jackie Robinson played two seasons at UCLA, transferring in 1939 from Pasadena Junior College. Although he left in 1941 without graduating, Robinson's short career at UCLA is perhaps the most impressive in collegiate athletic history. Woody Strode was a successful starting end for the Bruin football squad and also earned considerable success throwing the shot put. His large, athletic frame and good looks eventually helped land him in movie roles throughout the '60s and '70s. Washington, Robinson, and Strode formed the core of the team, often nicknamed the "Sepia Trio" by the mainstream media. Washington and Strode went on to become the first African American football players to join the National Football League, while Robinson's first season as a Brooklyn Dodger has joined the Montgomery bus boycott, *Brown v. Topeka,* and the March on Washington as a seminal event in the history of American civil rights. Although not a consistent starter, African American end Ray Bartlett also made significant contributions to the UCLA squad, while teammate Johnny Wynne played sparingly as a lineman.

The Bruins reached the height of their success during the 1939 season, when all five African American teammates helped lead the squad to an unbeaten 6-0-3 record and a final game versus USC, with the winner going to the Rose Bowl to face the University of Tennessee. UCLA's on-field success garnered high national rankings and publicity, while their popularity within the African American community has led Michael Oriard to label them "Black America's team."[1] Using the excitement of UCLA's 1939 Rose Bowl campaign as a framework, one can explore the possibility of using collegiate football as an analytic tool for examining issues of race in the American 20th century. An examination of the diverse public reactions to the 1938–1941 Bruins illuminates how African Americans, cultural critics, mainstream sportswriters, and southern institutions all symbolically appropriated the UCLA football team in vastly different ways, attempting to comprehend the liminality of college football within the traditional binary frameworks of "race figures," "color lines," and Jim Crow segregation.

Unfortunately, scholarly attention devoted to race and sports in the American 20th century has been largely dominated by biographical portraits of the "race hero." Perhaps this is why historians have focused so much on professional and individualized athletics instead of amateur, team-oriented sports. Specific attention has been paid to boxing and baseball, the first of which is an obvious cultural spectacle of violence played out between two figures, the other a team sport that nevertheless emphasizes individual contribution and statistical achievement. This line of analysis yields a canon of "race hero" biographies—Jack Johnson, Joe Louis, Jackie Robinson, Muhammad Ali—even John L. Sullivan and Rocky Marciano have been treated largely as race (or ethnic) figures.[2] All of these scholarly treatments are valuable, yet they should be seen as only a starting point.

The study of collegiate football represents the antithesis of this approach. It is an amateur sport (at least in theory), free of the corporate imaging necessary in constructing a race hero. Instead, it is dominated by the supposed anonymity of the student athlete, a sea of faceless helmets scattered across the field. "There was no Jackie Robinson in football," Oriard writes in his book *King Football*.[3] Indeed, there never was a single "color line" or integrating figure in college football, but rather a tediously slow, arduous, and non-linear process—one that spanned nearly 80 years and countless players. From William Henry Lewis—who integrated Harvard football in 1892—to the stubborn integration of the Mississippi, LSU, and Georgia football programs in 1972, scholars have referred to the men who integrated college football as a "collective Jackie Robinson," a movement toward integration that more closely resembled the broader African American struggle for civil rights during the 20th century.

Yet while history yields no "Jackie Robinson of football," it is nevertheless true that a group of African American students helped lead one of the country's most popular college football programs seven years before Robinson would take the field as a Brooklyn Dodger. Thus, an examination of integrated football at UCLA during this period represents a logical point of departure from the older scholarship of the "Great Black Hope" ideal, precisely because Washington, Strode, and Robinson emerged from the amateur ranks of the Bruins and went on to join the pantheon of "race figures" who broke color barriers at the professional level.

"Sideline-Stepping Sepias"

While UCLA was not the first major team to allow African American participants, it was the first to feature a group of black players in prominent positions. According to one newspaper's count, during the 1939 season some 38 black players "peppered" white teams throughout the country.[4] Most of these, however, were lone individuals who rarely saw playing time. Moreover, because they were not integral to their team's success, the few black players on white teams could also be benched by coaches without stirring much animosity, a useful tool whenever a Northern squad faced off against a Southern school with strict segregation policies.

It was very rare to find a prominent team with a national following that was willing to accept African American participants. Many of the celebrated teams of the period were clear segregationist powerhouses— Tennessee, Alabama, Duke, and others—yet even Northern football shrines such as Notre Dame remained all white. On the West Coast, however, the king of football was undoubtedly the University of Southern California, a school that had not featured a black player for some time. Woody Strode recalled, "Back then it was always USC; they were the machine. USC and Notre Dame had the best teams every year. But USC and Notre Dame didn't give the black athletes a chance to play at that time."[5] Actually, during the '20s two African American students played on Trojan squads, although they rarely participated. It was even rumored that a "scandal involving a white woman" had led to the hardening of coach Howard Jones's prejudice and the end of black football at USC.[6] Strode and his teammates thus chose to attend a smaller school, one with a burgeoning new campus (about five buildings) west of its prominent commuter campus in downtown Los Angeles. "I ended up at UCLA," Strode wrote, " … which I barely knew existed." The school was "looking to compete in athletics on a national level" and willing to give African American athletes its full support.[7] Within four years, the Bruins were not only national contenders on the field, but also major fodder for a growing public dialogue surrounding the role of race in American sport and society.

Most of the UCLA student body agreed that the Bruin football team "oozed class from the moment they trotted on the greensward."[8] Student publications, most notably the *Daily Bruin*, celebrated the success of Kenny Washington throughout his career and made him one of the most popular students on campus. Upon his final game versus USC in 1939, Washington received an extended standing ovation from the student body. The 1938 Bruin yearbook hailed Washington as "our hero," while student sportswriters concurred with opposing coaches that he was the best athlete in UCLA's history, his abilities surpassing even the mythical talent of Red Grange.[9] When Jackie Robinson joined the club in 1939, the only debate among student sportswriters was whether Robinson and Washington would be awarded the All-American honors they deserved.[10]

The 1939 squad opened with a difficult game against Texas Christian University, the highest-ranked team in the country the previous year. As heavy underdogs, the Bruins shocked the Horned Frogs 6–2 at Memorial Coliseum. The following week, Robinson helped spark his new team in a 14–7 upset over the University of Washington in Seattle. "Our Bruins have just finished astounding the football world for the second week in a row," exclaimed one student sportswriter who traveled with the team. "Saturday's ball game was just a little too much Washington (Kenny), Robinson, and UCLA and not enough Washington (University)."[11] Under first-year coach Babe Horrell, black America's football team had started the 1939 season in surprising fashion, overcoming two difficult opponents. Throughout the period, however, the Bruin footballers garnered the support of UCLA's student body in both success and defeat. Student publications announced with pride whenever Washington or Robinson appeared in national publications or were interviewed for radio, a rarity for black athletes, especially collegians.[12] In addition, students cheered the team en masse at Memorial Coliseum and jammed auditoriums to watch film footage from road games.[13]

Most important, student sportswriters recognized the broader significance of the team's African American players and were the first to decry prejudice toward the Bruins. Although the *Daily Bruin* sports department did not appear to have any African American students on staff, its editor and columnists were among the more progressive students on campus, especially when it came to issues of racial prejudice. When many writers around the country left Washington off their All-American lists, *Daily Bruin* columnist Milt Cohen responded with a plea to "pick again, boys" and correct the slight against UCLA. "It's with a distinct sour taste in our mouth that we read the lists of All-American selections that are now pouring out of all sections of the country," Cohen wrote, "We don't care what they do with any other ball player in the nation — but we don't like the way they're treating our Kenny Washington."[14] In an even greater slight, Robinson was later left off the first team of the All-Division basketball selections in 1941 despite leading the conference in scoring. Bruin sportswriters pinned the act on the prejudice of UC-Berkeley coach Nibs Price, who neglected to list Robinson on any team. "This obviously prejudiced attitude of Price led to the placing of the entire Stanford team in the honored positions, moving Robinson down to the second team," lamented one student. "This in itself is no cause for protest, but the fact that Price didn't even mention Jack on three teams strikes a new low in sportsmanship."[15]

Such student support for UCLA's black athletes helped reinforce the institution's reputation for being a racially open campus. "Whatever racial pressure was coming down in the City of Los Angeles, the pressure was not on me in Westwood," Strode said. "We had the whole melting pot ... and I worked hard because there was always the overriding feeling that UCLA really wanted me."[16] The Associated Students of UCLA (ASUCLA), precursor to the athletic department, routinely offered players loans and financial support, including Robinson and Washington.[17] Yet the greatest example of institutional support for the African American players came in the wake of Robinson's arrest in October of 1938. While cruising with teammate Ray Bartlett after a softball game in Brookside Park, Robinson became involved in an altercation after a white motorist "said something about niggers" at an intersection.[18] While it was Bartlett who initially confronted the man, police arrived to find "between 40 and 50 members of the Negro race," all of whom quickly dispersed with the exception of Robinson.[19] Charged with hindering traffic and resisting arrest, Robinson immediately received quick help from powerful Bruin loyalists and coach Babe Horrell. The university refunded Robinson his court costs and fines, hired a "prominent sports attorney," and requested to the judge that "the Negro football player be not disturbed during the football season."[20]

While reaction to Robinson's arrest exemplified UCLA's commitment to an integrated campus and support for African American athletes, it also revealed the nebulous status of its black students, one that called into question whether racial acceptance depended on a certain level of athletic achievement. White teammate Don McPherson said, "Sometimes Jackie had a little bit of a chip on his shoulder."[21] Robinson ultimately never felt the kind of acceptance at UCLA that his other black teammates experienced, although he wrote a series of personal letters upon his graduation that expressed some positive sentiments. "It really is something to know you have friends like the ones I made while attending UCLA," he wrote.[22] Nevertheless, Robinson was absent from his senior football banquet and left the university without graduating, writing back mainly to request help in obtaining employment.[23] Even Strode recalled that his first introduction to the "Southern mentality" occurred while on the freshman squad in 1936, when he and Washington heard, "There are some players on the varsity saying they don't want to play with any niggers."[24] After one particularly brutal confrontation on the scrimmage field, a lineman nicknamed "Slats"—a "blond-haired, blue-eyed farm boy from Oklahoma"—called Strode a "black son of a bitch." Strode said, "The bulldog came out of me. I climbed on top of Slats and started punching. The coaches stood around and watched for a little while. Finally they said, 'That's enough, Woody!' and they came and pulled me off. Slats and I became good friends after that."[25]

Even as the black Bruin players enjoyed the support of the student body and a progressive institution, they functioned within a community that was still struggling with issues of racial prejudice. Tom Bradley, president of the University Negro Club and future mayor of Los Angeles, routinely joined the University Religious Conference in addressing issues of discrimination on campus.[26] "We had no minorities in our fraternity at that time," William Forbes, a prominent undergraduate said. "I think the main reason would be that there were not that many minorities in Los Angeles at that time."[27] The few minority students on campus were expected to steer away from most social events, and the Bruins' African American footballers recognized the unwritten boundaries that existed. "The Communist party used to have mixed dances for us with white girls," Strode said. "I saw through that even as a teenager…. They were still hanging us by the neck.

Well, I wasn't about to go through that, not for a piece of ass. Kenny Washington and I used to kid each other about that. If I saw Kenny looking at a white girl, I'd yell out, "To the Trees!"[28]

Even student support for the Bruin team betrayed the hidden structures that permeated racial prejudice throughout the period. Most notably, students usually praised the black players with racially tinged terminology that emphasized the differences between the African American student athletes and the rest of the campus. Along with nicknames like "Kingfish Kenny" and "Jackrabbit Jackie," student sportswriters routinely invoked such cringe-worthy allusions as "sideline-stepping sepia" and "dusky flash" when lauding the Bruin players.[29] The 1941 yearbook featured Kenny Washington in a section entitled "Outstanding Men," placing his face alongside such prominent campus figures as Bob Park, the sweater-toting head of the Rally Committee and "A Man's Man." Yet Washington was also described as "a boy"— albeit one with "ability, personality, and gameness."[30] Such terminology was hardly unique to the *Daily Bruin*, as many of the most progressive sportswriters and publications nationwide continued characterizing athletes with racial nicknames and descriptions. Racially biased language was not reserved for African American minorities either, for any contest involving the Stanford Indians inevitably involved somebody being "scalped" or "massacred."[31] In fact, some of the biggest slights came from the black players' own teammates—for Robinson, Washington, and Strode mysteriously were never named as team captains, a distinction voted on by the entire team.

Despite these shortcomings, African American players at UCLA enjoyed an unprecedented college experience at UCLA that was simply unavailable at other white universities. "We were out there knocking down people like we thought we were white," Strode wrote.[32] Yet the 1939 Bruins were not only knocking down people, they were knocking down opponents as well as any team in the entire country. After its impressive 2–0 start, the squad continued its unexpected success, forging a 14–14 tie with the Stanford Indians before rattling off three straight wins over Montana, Oregon, and California. With an unbeaten record of 5-0-1, the Bruins were now ranked 19th nationally and serious contenders for their first Pacific Coast Conference championship. In addition, the squad was beginning to draw an increasing amount of attention from around the Los Angeles area and America's most prominent sportswriters.

"Suppose UCLA Wins"

While the Bruins enjoyed the support of UCLA's 9,600 students, they were also becoming a hot topic of discussion throughout Southern California, as local sportswriters welcomed the addition of a second powerful team to the Southland. "Football is the great equalizer," Paul Zimmerman of the *Los Angeles Times* wrote. "You have to throw racial prejudice out the window when a couple of gentlemen like Jackie Robinson and Kenny Washington do the things they do."[33] The annual cross-town meeting with powerhouse USC was shaping up to be a classic, while the most celebrated football game on the planet, the Rose Bowl, awaited the PCC champion. "The Bruins are capable of giving any team in the United States up to and including Tennessee a very busy afternoon," exclaimed Charles Paddock in the *Pasadena Star-News*.[34] Unbeaten, untied, and unscored upon in two years, the University of Tennessee's football squad was the most dominant team in the country in 1939, which most likely meant a trip to Pasadena, assuming the Volunteers could defeat Auburn in their final regular-season game.

Meanwhile, the city of Los Angeles continued to laud the resurgent Bruins and the "presence of the Chocolate Bombers."[35] Like UCLA's student writers, Los Angeles sportswriters recognized the significance of the Bruin's black players and came to their defense on the national stage. When it was revealed that Kenny Washington was leading the nation in rushing yards, the *Los Angeles Times* proclaimed that Washington had "put to shame those All-America pickers who inexplicably failed to include the great Negro halfback on their 'must' list."[36] Paddock agreed, writing in the *Star-News*, "Anyone who picks an All-America team and leaves [Washington] off needs to have his head examined."[37]

Yet while the local media in Los Angeles echoed the support of the Bruin students, it also grappled with the image of UCLA's African American players in light of the city's racial tensions. The *Los Angeles Times* reported that Robinson was arrested after "the youth assertedly resisted the officer's attempts to disperse a group of Negroes threatening a white man," then later ran a report that the "negro grid star" failed to appear in court.[38] Los Angeles did not pretend to be the idyllic melting pot that UCLA's campus claimed itself to be, nor were the surrounding Pasadena and Westwood communities free of overt racial animosity. While Paddock, Zimmerman, and other sportswriters crusaded for UCLA's black players on the national stage, Pasadena was locked in a legal battle with the NAACP over the integration of its Brookside Park public swimming pool.[39] And earlier in the year, the NAACP had also expressed outrage over an alleged beating of Robinson's younger brother Edgar by Pasadena police, an incident one black newspaper called, "The latest instance of flagrant discrimination and brutal treatment of colored citizens in Pasadena...."[40] Thus, as Los Angeles still grappled with issues of overt racial prejudice, its sports fans were ironically called to rally behind the city's "negro backfield aces."[41]

The Bruin football team was also receiving marked attention through-out the nation, although its talented players had been recognized before. As a sophomore in 1937, Washington made headlines by launching a 62-yard forward pass to teammate Hal Hirshon against USC, unheard of in the game at that time. The *New York Times* called it "the longest authentic completed touchdown aerials executed in college football."[42] As the 1939 season wore on, however, the nation's sportswriters began to realize that the Bruin team could end up being a true contender on the national stage. After starting out 5-0-1, UCLA forged another tie against non-conference Santa Clara. The following week, the Bruins were losing 13–7 against Oregon State before Washington set off a thrilling last-second touchdown that tied the game. The Bruin's weakest link, their kicking game, failed to convert the winning point. Nevertheless, a sound victory over Washington State the next week made UCLA the ninth-ranked team in the country with only one game remaining. With the Bruins' record now at 6-0-3, the *New York Times* announced, "The undefeated Uclans remain on the edge of the Rose Bowl picture."[43] UCLA was not only an exciting team for national fans to watch, it was also developing a penchant for big plays and last-second heroics. As one of only two unbeaten teams in the West, the Bruins would now have an opportunity to play for the prestigious Rose Bowl—against coach Howard Jones and the USC machine.

As the Bruins continued their surprising season on the field, main-stream sportswriters began to foresee the potential for a troubling off-field confrontation regarding race. "[I]f the Bruins should receive the Pacific Coast Conference invitation, the boys who invite the visiting team from another section might find themselves in a very embarrassing position," Paddock wrote in the *Pasadena Star-News*, "for to date the outstanding eleven in the Nation is Tennessee."[44] The prospect of a matchup between the Bruins and the Volunteers on the game's most important stage, the Rose Bowl, meant that Tennessee's strict policies regarding segregation on the field would be put to the test before a huge national audience. As Tennessee prepared to ensure its nomination by defeating Auburn, Allison Danzig of the *New York Times* traveled with the team and pondered such prospects. "There is an angle to the situation … that seems to have escaped general attention or which is being ignored," Danzig wrote, alluding to the fact that many sportswriters chose to turn a deaf ear to issues of race and segregation on the collegiate football field:

> There is a possibility that Kenny Washington, Jack Robinson, Woodrow Strode, and associates will … win the Rose Bowl assignment from the Trojans…. The statement was made here definitely tonight by parties in a position to know that Tennessee will not play in the Rose Bowl if UCLA, with its three colored stars, is the host team.[45]

The prospect of an integrated Rose Bowl forced sportswriters to grapple with the standard methods by which national collegiate football had dealt with regional prejudice and Jim Crow. Some, such as Bob Foote of the *Pasadena Star-News*, felt that a Rose Bowl involving the African American Bruins would pose no threat to the convoluted system meant to pacify schools from around the country. "There is at present a very satisfactory custom in effect between Northern and Southern schools which have conflicting ideas on who should play on college football teams," Foote wrote. "It is just 'When in Rome do as the Romans do.'"[46] While Foote proclaimed that such an idea would convince Tennessee and "apply very well to the Rose Bowl," other sportswriters, such as Allison Danzig, were not so sure.[47] Danzig wrote from Knoxville that Clemson or Duke would be less likely to "raise the Negro question," contending that Tennessee officials found themselves in a tight spot because of a pending lawsuit against the state that was trying to force the university to "admit a number of Negro applicants for matriculation."[48]

As the implications of the USC-UCLA showdown loomed large, the mainstream press was beginning to realize the significance of the Bruins as a "black team." Simply placing its African American players on the bench to avoid controversy was out of the question, for a black student touched the ball on nearly every play UCLA ran. "Coach Babe Horrell most of the time has had a 4-man instead of an 11-man team," Paddock wrote in the *Star-News*—and those four players were each African American.[49] As the USC-UCLA game inched its way closer, Paddock asserted that it was "very doubtful if the authorities at Tennessee would allow the team to play against UCLA ... unless it was definitely understood that the opponent in question would only use white players."[50] Yet it was long recognized by African American fans that such a proposition was out of the question when it came to UCLA. Only now, as the Bruins reached the height of their national prominence, did the mainstream media begin to realize what black sportswriters and the African American community had long found so appealing—UCLA was a black team. "Take away the Negro stars from the UCLA team," Paddock wrote, "and you would not have a team."[51]

"We Will Do the Rest"

African American sportswriters had varying reactions to integrated college football and its meanings for the advancement of basic civil rights. In the Los Angeles area, black newspapers were the first to foresee the importance of collegiate integration at UCLA beyond the region. In particular, J. Cullen Fentress of the *California Eagle* emphasized coverage of black athletes at UCLA, clearly supporting the Bruins over USC throughout the period. During the 1939 Rose Bowl campaign, Fentress wrote, "If they [UCLA] do get into the Rose Bowl, it will be one of the best things that ever happened to Pacific Coast Conference Football. And that goes for the Nation as well for we have long had the opinion that sports ... is the most logical medium through which to effect world peace and all it implies."[52] In light of the perceived threat from global fascism that penetrated newspapers throughout the period, many African American sportswriters juxtaposed the plight of black athletes with the supposed American political ideals of democracy and equality. Fentress was no different, exclaiming, "If for no other reason, we should like to see UCLA ... get the Bowl bid, and prove to this nation that its peoples can play together in the most approved manner as sportsmen, upholding as they do so the democratic principles as outlined by the signers of the Declaration of Independence."[53]

By 1939, such assertions had proved invaluable in garnering mainstream support for Joe Louis and America's black olympians. Americans were forced to make symbolic decisions when Louis faced the German Max Schmeling or the Italian Primo Carnera, and likewise when Jesse Owens raced under the eye of Hitler at the Berlin Olympics in 1936. However, collegiate football has always been a uniquely American spectacle, and as black athletes struggled to penetrate mainstream football teams, African American sportswriters could not so easily appeal to American patriotic sentiments. According to the *Eagle*, the African American collegian nevertheless found himself "on the threshold of broad and rich football pastures," and the newspaper's sports pages overflowed with the anticipation and optimism brought on by the five black Bruin players, "the largest number ever to play on a major university team."[54]

Unlike the *Eagle*, other African American newspapers did not have the benefit of a "black team" close to home. Prominent black newspapers such as the *Chicago Defender* and the *New York Amsterdam News* focused their attention primarily on recognizing the lone individuals who had managed to infiltrate Northern teams. The *Amsterdam News* lauded the "astounding" 38 African American football players who were listed on Northern lineups in 1939.[55] With a sense of optimism, sportswriters celebrated when Northwestern's black reserve Jimmy Smith quietly entered a home game against Oklahoma — and was promptly booed by the visiting Sooner contingency. Charlie Thomas of Boston University and Charlie Anderson at Ohio State also received attention for their roles on all-white teams. Yet all of these players routinely succumbed to an unwritten rule not to face Jim Crow teams from the South. As members of large and powerful college squads, the few black individuals who participated in football felt pressure to "take one for the team" and remain on the sidelines rather than stir up controversy. "I didn't really mind not playing," said Lou Montgomery, a

Boston College back who was asked to sit out games against Florida and Auburn. Montgomery explained to the *Amsterdam News* that his coach was "in a difficult spot" and had decided that "it was best not to sacrifice his valuable player to the mercies of the Florida boys."[56]

Unlike the Bruins with the *Eagle*, the trials of individual black football players sometimes met with skepticism from those in the black press. "Do Colored Athletes Help Cause of Jim Crow at Big White Universities?" asked one *Amsterdam News* headline.[57] Sportswriter Neil Dodson said the answer was clear. "White coaches have a subtle form of convincing colored players to stay on the bench," Dodson wrote. "Negro athletes, caught between their desire to play and the knowledge that they are being discriminated against, usually succumb to the first." Dodson went on to actually criticize "the average young athlete" who "brushes aside or refuses to face the fact that accepting discrimination is putting it a step ahead, entrenching it deeper." [58]

Considering the black press had its share of prominent race heroes to support, many had difficulty in appropriating anonymous "average young athletes" as symbols for broader statements regarding civil rights. Joe Louis, for example, was ubiquitous throughout both the white and black press, a rehearsed spokesman for his race who had managed to construct a powerful yet unassuming image, one that tended to pacify white anxieties. Obviously, there was no "benching" Louis either, nor did he ever have to share the spotlight with white teammates or participate within the structure of a team sport. In contrast stood the specter of black college football players, one that could generate the very fear and anxiety that Louis sought to avoid. In the mind of Jim Crow, a young group of powerful, unruly, and anonymous black men created the very same kind of tension that had led to Robinson's arrest in Pasadena. Therefore, the emergence of UCLA in 1938 at once gave black sportswriters their wish while simultaneously confronting them with serious questions about the standard "Joe Louis" approach to sports integration and the pursuit of civil rights. African American sports editors thus recognized better than anyone the significance of the integrated Bruins. "We have yet to find another single coach in the history of football that has had the guts to play three of our race at one time and have five on the squad," Fay Young wrote in the *Chicago Defender*, adding, "The three continued to start in the game even against southern teams."[59]

While celebrating UCLA's remarkable success, the black press attempted to alleviate these underlying tensions by cultivating a positive, unassuming team image and emphasizing Kenny Washington as a sort of spokesman. While a senior in 1939, Washington was the focus of a fierce campaign mounted by African American sportswriters, an attempt to get the Bruin runner on the Associated Press All-American team and immediately drafted into the National Football League. Washington was lauded for his "level-headedness," while readers were reassured that "no amount of favorable publicity, however great, would affect the demeanor of this young man."[60] The black press ultimately played a significant part in convincing UCLA to hire Washington as coach of the freshman team upon his graduation in 1940, an unprecedented decision. "We believe that Kenny is an inspiration to all youth.... He knows the game at which he is so adept," an *Eagle* editorial explained. "We take this opportunity to suggest that it would be entirely fitting and proper that he become a member of the coaching staff at the Westwood institution."[61] UCLA's decision to hire Washington reverberated across the country the following year, when in New York the *Amsterdam News* gave the former Bruin its highest support — not while Washington was playing for the Rose Bowl, but as "the first Negro in history to coach a major white eleven."[62]

Thus, while the excitement and appeal of the Bruins came from their status as a "black team," African American sportswriters who were used to trumpeting the charisma of Joe Louis and Jesse Owens still felt the need to portray the Bruin five as a cohesive unit. When the six most prominent African American students at UCLA (the five football players and Tom Bradley) were invited to attend an unprecedented banquet with local business leaders, it was Washington who took the podium and "spoke for his mates," telling the crowd, "There is so much to be said I hardly know where to begin, but I am certain I express the sentiments of the rest of the fellows when I say that we certainly appreciate this manifestation of interest in us. We want action and the opportunity to put our foot in the door. We will do the rest."[63]

Yet while Washington appeared for a time to be spokesman for the black Bruins, it was impossible to construct any one player as "the image" of black football at UCLA, especially after Washington's graduation in 1940. Robinson, Strode, Bartlett, Wynne, and Washington were each unique individuals, unable to be characterized as individual race heroes in the same way as professionals like Joe Louis, public personas who were able to triumph across "color lines." The black press and the African American community thus celebrated the emergence of a team, for no longer were black football players lone individuals to be rejected, cut, or conveniently benched in accordance with essentialist logic. "If we drew 100,000 people to the Coliseum," Strode said, "40,000 of them would be black; that was just about every black person in the city of Los Angeles."[64] Black individualism struck at the very heart of Jim Crow, and instead of avoiding controversy on the bench, America's black team would now be introduced directly to college football's heartland — the deep South.

"Empty Stockings"

The Bruins had actually run up against three segregated teams during the period, arranging matchups in Los Angeles versus Texas Christian, Texas A&M, and Southern Methodist University. While records indicate that ASUCLA spoke with at least one of the teams regarding a possible game in Texas, the possibility of the black Bruins participating in a game played on Jim Crow turf remained slim.[65] "We couldn't play in Texas because we had black guys on our team," Don McPherson said of his African American teammates. "They couldn't stay in the hotels or eat in the restaurants, so we didn't travel there."[66] Yet even black sportswriters praised the Southern schools for making the trek west and not calling for the Bruins to change their lineup. When defending national champion Texas Christian was stunned by the 1939 Bruins on opening night in the Coliseum, Fay Young of the *Chicago Defender* lauded coach Dutch Meyers for not asking "any coach to place a team on the field in his home city minus one or more stars because those stars were not white."[67] As a result, Young proclaimed that Meyers and the Horned Frogs had "lost, but lost fairly."[68]

However, even though schools like Texas Christian agreed to play the Bruins in Los Angeles, it did not mean that more covert tensions did not exist beneath institutional rhetoric. One example in particular typified the irony behind Texas Christian's "progressiveness." Coach Meyers, his players, and Texas Christian students had nothing but praise for the Bruin team, dishing out accolades in particular to "UCLA's colored twins."[69] After the team had been humbled 6–2, however, one student reporter for Texas Christian recorded the following events on the train ride home:

> Poss Clark [lineman] and Red Palmer [student manager] ... conspired to scare the negro porter. Poss told the porter Red had running fits and bit people and in the meantime Red had filled his mouth with Alka Seltzer, which produced a plentiful supply of froth, and started after the Negro. The porter was scared so bad that the boys had to get a new man to make up their beds. Afterwards Dutch [head coach Dutch Meyers] tried to sign him up to play football, because anyone who could run that fast would never be touched.[70]

The story speaks volumes on the role of public "color lines" and their nebulous meanings behind the scenes. By acquiescing to the African American Bruins earlier in the day, Meyers had just participated in making a significant social statement that many, including the *Chicago Defender*, had designated as a symbolic barometer for the condition of civil rights throughout the country. Yet the coach and his players still operated within a social system that saw African Americans as expendable rail porters, a system that could entertain the prospect of signing a black football player only within a context of mockery and facetiousness. Nevertheless, Texas Christian players and student sportswriters were willing to face UCLA's black squad in Los Angeles and offer uncompromising coverage of their defeat at the hands of African American players. Many were left wondering if the Volunteers of Tennessee would be willing to do the same.

On December 9, 1939, more than half the seats at Knoxville's Shields-Watkins Stadium remained empty as the mythical Volunteers rolled to victory over the University of Auburn. Apparently, nearly 20,000 students and fans were so sure of a Tennessee win that they decided to stay home and save their money to help pay for a trip to Pasadena.[71] Bob Wilson of the *Knoxville News-Sentinel* wrote that it was a "foregone conclusion" the Volunteers would be offered a place in the Rose Bowl. "Tennessee athletic officials have a 'definite understanding' with both Southern Cal and UCLA officials" Wilson wrote. The only suspense now was to sit back and watch for the results of the UCLA-USC game.[72] Many sportswriters were not convinced, nor were Tennessee officials, coaches, and players. When Allison Danzig of the *New York Times* asked Tennessee coach Bob "Major" Neyland what stand the Volunteers would take if UCLA were the host team, the coach "side-stepped the issue by turning aside to speak to friends."[73]

This was the lens through which Tennessee fans sat down to await the results from the USC-UCLA game and the status of the West's "black team." It was little wonder, then, that as Allison Danzig, Bob Wilson, coach Major Neyland, and a host of other writers and Tennessee officials gathered at the Farragut Hotel in Knoxville, "shouts went up" whenever news came that the USC Trojans were moving the ball against the Bruin defense. "It was evident that everybody in the room was pulling for Southern Cal to win or get a tie," Wilson wrote in the *News-Sentinel*. Despite the mixed reaction to black players from southern coaches and institutions— the eerie silence of coach Neyland, the heartless flattery of coach Meyers, the outright refusal of most to participate — the fact remained that the African American Bruins, poised on the threshold of broad and rich football pastures at UCLA, were also poised to create one of the largest racial scandals American sport fans had ever witnessed.

"Two Yards from Heaven"

By all accounts, the 1939 UCLA-USC game was a classic. More than 103,000 fans jammed the Coliseum and watched as both teams battled for "60 sensational minutes."[74] USC nearly scored early in the game, but quarterback Grenville Lansdell fumbled on the one-yard line and Woody Strode dived on the ball in the end zone to avert a Trojan touchdown. For the next three quarters, "the two undefeated teams tore into each other like unacquainted wildcats," yet no one could muster a score.[75] Locked in a scoreless tie, the Bruins launched one last drive in the game's waning minutes. The crowd erupted as Washington, Robinson, Strode, and Bartlett each led UCLA down the field. Fatigue began to set in for both squads, and "the tired Trojans couldn't stop the Bruins."[76] With first down and goal on the Trojan's two-yard line, the Bruins ran three straight unsuccessful plays. Facing fourth down and goal, the players huddled and decided to take a vote. Some wanted to have Robinson attempt a game-winning field goal, others wanted one last chance for a touchdown. In democratic fashion— white and black— each player raised his hand to vote. The result was 6–5 in favor of running one last play. The crowd stood breathless as Washington dropped back to pass and heaved the ball over the goal line. Before Washington's ball had reached its intended target, Trojan halfback Bob Robertson leaped into its path and swatted it to the ground. The game was over, and the USC Trojans had managed to forge a 0–0 tie, thereby ensuring a spot in the Rose Bowl.

The next morning, coach Major Neyland of Tennessee accepted an invitation from the USC Trojans to play in the Rose Bowl "with pleasure."[77] Meanwhile, the African American *New York Amsterdam News* announced what black Americans around the country already knew. "And Rose Bowl Remains White as a New Lily" read the headline, and black sportswriters around the country lamented that a "1939 'Civil War'" had been "averted."[78] Although the tie meant that the Bruin season was finished and "plenty of folk both in the North and South could sleep without nightmares," the fact remained that the UCLA team had accomplished an incredible feat while making a symbolic social statement— and America had listened. More than 400,000 spectators watched the 1939 UCLA Bruins, the most of any team in the nation, and millions had followed UCLA's story on radio and in newsprint.[79]

While the team's Senior Banquet program announced that the Bruins had fallen "two yards from heaven," UCLA's African American players had nearly created a national confrontation over race that could have dwarfed Robinson's Dodger debut seven years later.[80] It was a confrontation that many would have feared and others cherished. Either way, by both cheering and jeering the Bruins throughout 1938–1941, Americans were participating in a cultural spectacle that held deeper meanings for all. Such pressure fell on the broad shoulders of young black college students, who struggled to keep up with their course work and fit into campus life— not to professional athletes, properly groomed race heroes, or eloquent cultural critics. While the story of Robinson's first season as a Dodger or Joe Louis's triumphant knockouts appeal to a particular historicization— namely, our desire to create clear color lines in order to break them — history yields a much richer story. As America's black football team proved, the integration of college football was a nebulous and non-linear movement, one that better exemplifies the true struggle behind the story of civil rights in the American 20th century.

Notes

1. Michael Oriard, *King Football: Sport and Spectacle in the Golden Age of Radio and Newsreels, Movies and Magazines, the Weekly & the Daily Press* (Chapel Hill, NC: The University of North Carolina Press, 2001), 308.

2. Chris Mead, *Champion — Joe Louis, Black Hero in White America* (New York: Charles Scribner's Sons, 1985). Jules Tygiel, *Baseball's Great Experiment: Jackie Robinson and His Legacy* (New York: Oxford University Press, 1997). Russell Sullivan, *Rocky Marciano: The Rock of His Times* (Chicago: University of Illinois Press, 2002). Randy Roberts, *Papa Jack: Jack Johnson and the Era of White Hopes* (New York: Macmillan Inc., 1983). Michael Isenberg, *John L. Sullivan and His America* (Chicago: University of Illinois Press, 1994).

3. Oriard, *King Football*, 10.

4. Dan Burley, "Up Football's Glory Road," *New York Amsterdam News* (December 9, 1939), 18.

5. Woodrow Strode, *Goal Dust: An Autobiography* (New York: Madison Books, 1990), 26.

6. Strode, 29.

7. Strode, 26.

8. John Rothwell, *UCLA Magazine* (November 1939), 10.

9. *Southern Campus* (Volume 19, 1938), 215. Jerry Levie, "Ken Over Grange!" *California Daily Bruin* (October 23, 1939), 3.

10. John Rothwell, "Jack Robinson Registers in Extension," *California Daily Bruin* (February 16, 1939), 1.

11. Milt Cohen, "Robinson Sparkplug of Rally," *California Daily Bruin* (October 9, 1939), 1.

12. "Kenny Honored Over Air Friday," *California Daily Bruin* (December 3, 1939), 4.

13. *UCLA Magazine* (December 1940), 7.

14. Cohen, "Here's Our Angle," *California Daily Bruin* (December 1, 1939), 3.

15. Sam Sale, "Prejudice 'Rumored' to Have Played Major Role in Selections," *California Daily Bruin* (March 5, 1941), 3.

16. Strode, 35.

17. "Minutes of the ASUCLA Board of Control, June 1935–June 1939" (March 3, 1939), 84. "Minutes of the ASUCLA Board of Control, June 1940–June 1941" (August 8, 1940), 82.

18. Arnold Rampersad, *Jackie Robinson: A Biography* (New York: Alfred A. Knopf, 1997), 65.

19. *Pasadena Star-News* (September 6, 1939), cited in Rampersad, 65.

20. *Pasadena Star-News* (October 18, 1939), cited in Rampersad, 66.

21. B.J. Violet, "Teammates Recall Jackie Robinson's Legacy," *UCLA Today*.

22. Jackie Robinson to John Jackson (May 7, 1941), UCLA University Archives, Prints/Reference Collection Biographical Files, Series 745.

23. Jackie Robinson to John Jackson (November 6, 1941), UCLA University Archives, Prints/Reference Collection Biographical Files, Series 745.

24. Strode, 64.

25. Strode, 65.

26. "Prejudices Discussed," *California Daily Bruin* (October 30, 1939), 1.

27. William Forbes Oral History (300–341), UCLA Oral History Project, 68–69.

28. Strode, 21.

29. "Frogs Okay," *California Daily Bruin* (September 29, 1939), 7.

30. *Southern Campus* (Volume 22, 1941), 396.

31. "Stanford Scalps Bruins 12 Times," *The Goal Post* (October 31, 1942), 6.

32. Strode, 64.

33. Paul Zimmerman, "Sport Post-Scripts," *Los Angeles Times* (October 9, 1939), A11.

34. Charles Paddock, "Spikes," *Pasadena Star-News* (November 3, 1939), 20.

35. *Ibid.*

36. Al Wolf, "Today's Game Full of Angels," *Los Angeles Times* (December 9, 1939), A9.

37. Paddock, "Spikes," *Pasadena Star-News,* (December 7, 1939), 20.

38. "Pasadena Grid Player Arrested," *Los Angeles Times* (September 7, 1939), 14. "Negro Grid Star Forfeits Bond," *Los Angeles Times* (October 19, 1939), A12.

39. Rampersad, 64.

40. "Brother of Jack Robinson Beaten by Pasadena Police," *California Eagle* (January 12, 1939), 1.

41. "UCLA Defeats Huskies," *New York Times* (October 8, 1939), 90.

42. "Pass Traveled 62 Yards," *New York Times* (December 6, 1937), 20

43. "Rally by UCLA Ties Oregon State," *New York Times* (November 26, 1939), 82.

44. Paddock, "Spikes," *Pasadena Star-News* (November 6, 1939), 14.

45. Allison Danzig, "Tennessee Hopes to Insure Rose Bowl Nomination by Beating Auburn Today," *New York Times* (December 9, 1939), 20.

46. Bob Foote, "Foote-Loose in Sports," *Pasadena Star-News* (December 6, 1939), 20.

47. *Ibid.*

48. Danzig, "Tennessee Hopes to Insure Rose Bowl Nomination by Beating Auburn Today," *New York Times* (December 9, 1939), 20.

49. Paddock, "Spikes," *Pasadena Star-News* (November 6, 1939), 14.

50. *Ibid.*

51. *Ibid.*

52. J. Cullen Fentress, "Down in Front," *California Eagle* (November 9, 1939), 3B.

53. *Ibid.*

54. Fentress, "Down in Front," *California Eagle* (August 14, 1939), 3B. "61 Huskies to Answer Grid Call at UCLA," *California Eagle* (September 7, 1939), 3B.

55. Burley, "Up Football's Glory Road," *New York Amsterdam News* (December 9, 1939), 18.

56. "Lou Montgomery, Backfield Ace of Boston College, Isn't at All Upset over Being Benched Twice in Dixie Tilts," *New York Amsterdam News* (November 11, 1939), 18.

57. Neil Dodson, "Do Colored Athletes Help Cause of Jim Crow at Big White Universities?" *New York Amsterdam News* (October 21, 1939), 19.

58. *Ibid.*

59. Fay Young, "The Stuff Is Here," *Chicago Defender* (December 16, 1939), 26.

60. Fentress, "Down in Front," *California Eagle* (November 16, 1939), 2B.

61. *California Eagle* (December 31, 1939), 8A.

62. "Chalks Up Another First," *New York Amsterdam News* (December 7, 1940).

63. "UCLA Grid Stars and Coaches Entertained by Business Leaders," *California Eagle* (November 16, 1939), 2B.

64. Strode, 62.

65. The 1942 ASUCLA Board of Control meeting minutes note that the "possibility of playing TCU [Texas Christian University] in Forth Worth" was discussed with the "TCU grad manager." "Minutes of the ASUCLA Board of Control, June 1941–June 1942," (May 11, 1942), 162.

66. Violet, "Teammates Recall Jackie Robinson's Legacy," *UCLA Today.*

67. Young, "The Stuff Is Here," *Chicago Defender* (November 4, 1939), 24.

68. *Ibid.*

69. Keith Guthrie, "Horned Frog Tracks," *The Skiff* (Texas Christian University: October 6, 1939), 3.

70. *Ibid.*

71. Danzig, "Tennessee Hopes to Insure Rose Bowl Nomination by Beating Auburn Today," *New York Times* (December 9, 1939), 20.

72. Bob Wilson, "Path to Rose Bowl Cleared for Vols," *Knoxville News-Sentinel* (December 6, 1939), 1.

73. Danzig, "Tennessee Hopes to Insure Rose Bowl Nomination by Beating Auburn Today," *New York Times* (December 9, 1939), 20.

74. Paul Zimmerman, "Bruins, Troy Tie: SC, Vols in Bowl," *Los Angeles Times* (December 10, 1939), 1.

75. "So. California Ties UCLA; Will Play Tennessee in Bowl," *New York Times* (December 10, 1939), 103.

76. *Ibid.*

77. Zimmerman, "Bruins, Troy Tie: SC, Vols in Bowl," *Los Angeles Times* (December 10, 1939), 1.

78. Daniel, "And Rose Bowl Remains White as a New Lily," *New York Amsterdam News* (December 16, 1939).

79. *Ibid.*

80. "1939 UCLA 21st Annual Football Senior Banquet Program," (January 18, 1940), UCLA Special Collections #227, "Department of Intercollegiate Athletics (1921–1987)," Box 2.

8

Holy War on the Football Field: Religion and the Florida State University Indian Mascot Controversy

Arthur J. Remillard

America's late 19th century saw entertainment spectacles such as Buffalo Bill's Wild West Show feeding a growing Euro-American fascination with the American Indian. From these circus like events, audiences began constructing a limited image of Indianness. Many performers, such as Sitting Bull, were from Lakota and Sioux reservations, thus leading onlookers to conflate the entirety of Indian culture with these traditions. Buffalo Bill's version of the Indian also became valuable for a generation searching for new models of manliness. Starting in the 1920s, Ralph Hubbard introduced Plains Indian culture to the Boy Scouts of America in his attempt to emphasize a primitive form of manhood that valued strength and durability — gender traits that he feared the youth of modern America desperately lacked. America's post–World War II era galvanized Buffalo Bill's Indian on the silver screen with a plethora of Wild West films. These movies created a radical dialectic where Indians were typically either horse-mounted warriors terrorizing the American West or trustworthy sidekicks like the Lone Ranger's laconic partner, Tonto.[1] These films made Indians into fictionalized typecasts from another time and place who all shared a common culture and identity. For the majority of Americans, Hollywood's Indian was their only encounter with Native culture.

Institutes of higher learning contributed to the cultural trend of adopting reductive versions of Indianness. The University of Wisconsin at Lacrosse first introduced the idea, naming themselves the "Indians" in 1909, and many others followed suit in the 1920s, '30s, and '40s. In contemporary America, however, the use of Indian mascots by professional and university athletic teams has come under heavy criticism from Indian and non–Indian advocates. The opposition has argued that such images unnecessarily demean and stereotype Indian culture in ways that would be unacceptable if applied to any other minority/religious/ethic group.[2]

Finding merit in such arguments, the United States Commission on Civil Rights released a statement in 2001 calling for "an end to the use of Native American images and team names by non–Native schools." The Commission concluded that public institutions employing Indian mascots both "teach all students that stereotyping of minority groups is acceptable," and "block genuine understanding of contemporary Native people as fellow Americans."[3] Adding a legislative voice, on March 3, 2003, Congressman Frank Pallone, Jr., a Democrat from New Jersey, introduced a bill entitled "Native Act to Transform Imagery in Various Environments." Pallone labeled Indian mascots "offensive" and counter to the ideals and goals of American education. His bill proposed a solution that would "provide funding for the establishment of an incentive program for schools to eliminate the use of names and symbols that are offensive to Native American people."[4] Professional, civic, and educational groups have also added a voice to the debate. The Modern Language Association, the National Education Association, the NAACP, the Presbyterian Church, U.S.A., and the United Methodist Church all have issued statements decrying the use of Indian mascots.

Responding to the criticisms, a host of colleges and universities, such as Adams State, Eastern Michigan, Dartmouth, Marquette, and Stanford, have retired their respective Indian mascots. The Florida State University "Seminoles" have yet to do the same. Instead, the university claims that its use of Seminole culture has sustained a level of validity that other schools have not. FSU supporters generally eschew the potentially pejorative label "mascot" when speaking of the Seminole. Former university president Sandy D'Alemberte insisted that the Seminole is not a mascot, but rather a "symbol" of pride and honor. D'Alemberte's assertion effectively encapsulates FSU's argument. The Seminole is a symbol that fans revere because it represents the finest attributes of both the tribe and the university's athletic team. As such, FSU states that by uniting the two, they honor both with a similar level of integrity. A second critical step for the university has been to show how it has gone to great lengths to consult with the actual Seminole tribe and gain its approval. Such endorsements from key Seminole leaders have prompted many supporters to conclude that there is no controversy. Instead, they insist the protests are the misguided actions of a few agents of political correctness.

Indian scholars C. Richard King and Charles Fruehling Springwood have argued, however, that FSU's mascot ultimately stereotypes the Seminole culture and thereby promotes racially insensitive images of Indianness. While insisting the practice surrounding the mascot "is much more than kids having fun," the authors do not grant FSU immunity. Instead, King and Springwood attempt to show how the mascot "vividly illustrates popular prejudices about Indians" by keeping alive images from an Indian past wrought with oppression — a history that Hollywood's Indian has only helped enable.[5] For these scholars, the mascot debate is far from being a trifling issue. Instead, it represents a continuation of the lengthy and misguided history of America's unwillingness to take Indian culture seriously. A historical and cultural survey shows that the university's mascot has more in common with Buffalo Bill's Wild West Show than the actual Seminole culture. FSU's Seminole rides a horse and throws a spear, yet the Seminoles of Florida had no horses to ride nor spears to throw. Still, the university maintains its claim that it accurately depicts this Indian culture.

Certainly, finding a new mascot 20 years ago would have saved the university a great deal of time and energy. As this debate continues, therefore, a question arises: Why has FSU gone to such great lengths to maintain its mascot? One must take steps toward answering this question by examining the religious conflict that lurks amid the debate. The opposition argues that the mascot degrades its cultural and religious heritage by misusing objects and traditions on the field of play. For FSU, the Seminole personifies the virtues of a football team that they revere with deification and dedication. For FSU supporters, concerns for accuracy and honor are a means to an end. By claiming reverence toward Seminole culture, even though their mascot has numerous inaccuracies, supporters justify to themselves the right to retain their Seminole. The mascot controversy is a holy war on the football field between the popular religion of football and the cultural-based faith of the Seminoles.

The Popular Religion of Football

Indian monikers were common when Florida State University held a student vote in 1947 to determine their mascot. The students faced six options on the ballot: the Statesmen, Rebels, Tarpons, Fighting Warriors, Crackers, and Seminoles. With 381 votes, the Seminole became the new mascot in "commemoration of the tribe of Indians whose descendants still live in the Florida Everglades."[6] Since its adoption, the former tribal leader Osceola has been a key image in the mix of Seminole mascots. The controversial Osceola show, which includes a flaming spear, galloping horse, and 80,000 screaming football fans, began on September 16, 1978, during a home game against Oklahoma State. Florida State won the game, and the show has since become a collegiate legend. Sportswriter Richard Billingsley called the pregame ritual "one of the most recognizable, revered, and respected traditions of all time." Moreover, he credited FSU for "maintain[ing] their mascot with dignity, respect, and the goodwill and wishes of the Seminole Tribe."[7]

Many of FSU's fans who agree with Billingsley often talk about the Seminole using religious language. Systematically explaining the virtues of each symbol, one fan stated, "To us, the 'war path' is our journey to make the best possible life we can for ourselves." "[Osceola's horse "Renegade"] is not simply a horse, but rather the educational system on which we are attempting to ride, so that we can move with greater speed and stability towards our own personal futures." Finally, Osceola "is the courage within each of us. He represents our ability to lead, have confidence, and to not settle, but rather to go for our goals, and with hope, attain what we desire."[8] Such sentiments are common among FSU's legions of followers who have a great sense of pride for their mascot.

Supporters also find virtue in the warring acumen of the Seminoles and regularly draw parallels between the Seminole wars of the mid–19th century and the tenaciousness of their football team. "FSU selected the Seminoles," one fan noted, "because they wanted to reflect in their teams the 'never say die' spirit of the Florida Seminole and the bravery and cohesiveness of that tribe" who faced near-certain death at the hands of Federal troops.[9] The virtues heralded by this fan echo the quest for primitive manhood sought by Hubbard and the Boy Scouts. Osceola is a model of courage, bravery, and determination — all virtues born from warfare. Just as Hubbard wanted to reinforce a model of manhood that derived from a nostalgic image of pre-industrial America, FSU fans look to the warring history of early Florida. Thus, for FSU supporters, critics who claim the mascot is demeaning simply are not aware of its privileged place amid the sacred ground of FSU's athletic legacy.

For Florida State football fans, the Seminole represents all that is true and good about their athletic heritage. In his 1992 book, *Saint Bobby and the Barbarians,* journalist Ben Brown presented an account of FSU's 1991 championship season.[10] It was no mistake that Brown labeled FSU's head coach Bobby Bowden a "Saint." For the fans of the team, Bowden is the transcendent figure who brought a struggling team to national prominence. For supporters, the Seminole mascot is a symbol that combines Bowden, FSU football, and their meteoric rise to success. As such, the Seminole is coveted, cherished, and loved just as much as "Saint Bobby" is. As the

Indian opposition began leveling attacks against this symbol, therefore, fans rose quickly to its defense and struggled to retain a profoundly important part of their popular religious faith.

"White Man's Hollywood"

The Indian opposition has a difficult battle. It must convince an unwilling population that FSU's religious devotion to the Seminole mascot does not honor, but instead perpetuates a history of misunderstanding. Humor has helped its cause. At a protest over similar problems in Illinois, poster boards displayed pithy phrases such as, "Imagine the Pope dancing at halftime," and "How would you like Jesus on a butt cushion?"[11] Arguably, one of the most notorious examples of humorous comparison comes from Wade Churchill's article "Crimes against Humanity." Churchill first tentatively accepts that Indian mascots represent "good clean fun," but then imagines what other minority mascots might look like. After proposing team names like the "Galveston 'Greasers'" and "San Diego 'Spics,'" Churchill turns his focus to faith. "Have a religious belief? Let's all go for the gusto and gear up the Milwaukee 'Mackerel Snappers' and Hollywood 'Holy Rollers.' The Fighting Irish of Notre Dame can be rechristened the 'Drunken Irish' or 'Papist Pigs.'" Churchill's point is both sarcastic and clear. Indians are small in number and their religious world has long been the subject of abuse, misunderstanding and mistreatment. America's mainline religions would not stand for the trivialization of their faith on the football field — especially by people who failed to understand the essence of such a religion. Churchill simply asks that institutions like Florida State respect Indian culture and religion as they would any of America's mainline faiths.[12]

A central concern for the Indian opposition is the viability of their religious heritage. While mascots might not employ obvious religious symbols, it is worth noting that Indian religion often coexists with practically every element of Indian life. "If you pull on the thread of 'Native American religion,'" Joel Martin wrote, "you end up pulling yourself into the study of Native American culture, art, history, economics, music, dance, politics, and almost everything else."[13] For the opposition, schools like FSU that use, misuse, and mock Indian traditions, objects, and people, subsequently extend such insults to Indian religion. As a result, a concern for the vitality of their sacred symbols feeds the opposition's concern.

There are a number of specific instances where FSU has misused Indian religious symbols. The opposition often criticizes "the tomahawk chop," a unified, chopping hand-motion performed by fans at FSU games. For many Indians, the tomahawk is a weapon and tool, but it is also "a ceremonial object, a decorative item, and a symbol of leadership."[14] When Florida State fans perform the tomahawk chop, the university's marching band, the Marching Chiefs, plays an accompanying drum beat and brass anthem reminiscent of a 1950s Western film. Commenting on FSU's tomahawk chop, one protester said it represents "white man's Hollywood, not respect for tradition."[15] Michael Haney, an Oklahoma Seminole opposed to FSU's mascot, explained that the traditional Seminole drumbeat represents the sound of a beating heart. [16] By equating Seminole Indianness with this generic Indianness, Haney contended, FSU sends the message that all Indians are the same.

While the tomahawk chop has no origin in Seminole culture, FSU fans continue the practice and still claim that they honor the tribe. FSU officials insist that while the university strives for authenticity, sometimes the fans can go too far. To this point, former FSU president Dale Lick wrote:

> Some traditions we cannot control. For instance, in the early 1980's, when our band, the Marching Chiefs, began the now-famous arm motion while singing the "War Chant," who knew that a few years later the gesture would be picked up by other team's fans and named the "tomahawk chop?" It's a term we did not choose and officially do not use.

Lick further explained how the university has maintained contact with Florida's Seminole tribe to "ensure the dignity and propriety of the various Seminole symbols we use."[17] Lick's argument is quite perplexing for the Indian opposition. In spite of Lick's assertion, the university's athletic Web site lists the "War Chant" as one of FSU's traditions and, in a written statement, outlines its history and national influence.[18] This, of course, leads the opposition to wonder how the university defines official and unofficial traditions. For the opposition, the "War Chant" lacks the dignity that Lick says the university wishes to uphold. While Lick defers blame for the practice to the fans and the Marching Chiefs, the opposition demands to know where the duties of the university stop and the actions of fans begin.

This kind of crowd generated trivialization of Indian culture appears elsewhere in FSU's use of the Seminole mascot. During the Second Seminole War, the "scalp dance" was a cultural ritual that celebrated victories such as the 1835 Dade Massacre, when Seminoles killed a number of their Federal enemies.[19] White perceptions of Indianness have made scalping a symbol of savageness, incivility, primitive immorality, and bloodthirstiness. In spite of the various negative connotations behind scalping, FSU uses it as common rally cry. The Florida State fight song cries, "Scalp 'em, Seminoles!" and declares that the team is "on the warpath." [20] Additionally, Bobby Bowden regularly applies the salutation "Scalp 'Em" to his autographs. The effects of this behavior can create a variety of misunderstandings of Indian culture and practice. Recalling his visit with his son to a

Florida State game, Joe Quentone, a member of the Kiowa tribe, spoke of the frenetic atmosphere of game day. As students rushed through the stands sporting tomahawks, war paint, loincloths, and feathers, he overheard a nearby fan say to a young boy, "Those are real Indians down there. You'd better be good, or they'll come up and scalp you!"[21] For the opposition, experiences like Quentone's demonstrate that, as the fans sing the fight song and wave their spears, the dignity of the Seminole tumbles further into the homogenous pit of Hollywood Indianness.[22]

Responding to a journalist who suggested that FSU should retire the Indian moniker, a fan wrote, "FEAR THE SPEAR" at the bottom of a vitriolic e-mail.[23] The journalist quipped, "I wonder if that's the kind of image the Seminole tribe wants portrayed?"[24] While perhaps saying this as a sardonic aside, his question raises another key point made by the opposition. Even if FSU did use Seminole culture accurately and honorably, there are no guarantees that fans would not subject the mascot to abuse. Furthermore, by having an Indian mascot, FSU also makes Seminole culture available for further devaluation by fans from rival universities. On January 3, 1999, the *Knoxville News-Sentinel* printed a cartoon for the Fiesta Bowl football game between Tennessee and FSU. This cartoon shows a train hitting an Indian who is saying "Paleface speak with forked-tongue! This land is ours as long as grass grows and river flows ... oof!" The caption at the bottom of the cartoon reads, "Don't worry, Folks.... He's not a full-blooded Indian.... He's just a Semi-Nole!" Finally, a sign behind the train reads, "New and improved Trail of Tears."[25]

The newspaper did print a perfunctory apology saying that it had no malevolent intentions. "Certainly there was no intent to belittle anyone. The cartoon was aimed at a worthy foe in the spirit of athletic rivalry, as were previous cartoons this past season featured in game-day editions."[26] Like Lick and others at FSU, the editor employed the tactics of deferment by blaming the "spirit of athletic rivalry" and downplaying what the opposition saw as a very real case of racial insensitivity. King and Springwood used this very example as evidence showing that "Florida State University itself is guilty of propagating precisely the kind of environment in which Native Americans are likely to be 'playfully' victimized."[27]

For the opposition, just as tomahawk chops and "scalp 'em" slogans diminish Seminole religion, so does FSU's use of Osceola. Background on the Seminoles and Osceola helps explain the origins of this criticism. In the early 18th century, the Seminoles broke from the Creeks and later migrated to northern Florida. These small hunting-and-gathering clans made material profits by trading manufactured goods with local non–Indians. After the Second Seminole War in 1842, 3,612 of the Indians were "removed" and settled in present-day Oklahoma, while 350 to 500 remained in south

Florida.[28] For the opposition, Florida State's Seminole has little in common with these Florida and Oklahoma Seminoles. FSU's Seminole comes principally from the image of Osceola — a key Indian leader during the Second Seminole War killed by Federal troops in 1838. Osceola's pregame show imagines him atop his appaloosa horse with spear in hand. The regalia worn by the actor are, by most accounts, accurate; the university enlisted Seminole representatives for this task. Nevertheless, the Seminoles had neither appaloosa horses nor spears — both critical elements in their nationally renowned pregame show. An American Indian Movement flier mocks FSU's Osceola, saying that he is "a Lakota who got lost in an Apache dressing room riding a Nez Percé horse."[29]

In spite of such inaccuracies, on October 10, 2003, FSU unveiled "Unconquered," a hulking bronze statue of FSU's horse-mounted, spear-wielding Osceola in front of its football stadium. Stephen Reilly, a Tallahassee native, initiated the project and said the monument "celebrates the human spirit that refuses to be defeated." Echoing FSU's mantra, Reilly further stated that the finished product "symbolizes the unconquered spirit of the Seminole people of the nineteenth century."[30] For the opposition, the statue further perpetuates the inaccuracies of Seminole transportation and weaponry while also reducing the history of the tribe to a war in the mid–19th century. The Seminoles' status as warriors was not a cultural tradition; they were instead a society that tended to avoid war. The "Unconquered" statue does not show a tribe that valued peace, but rather, one forever locked in bitter warfare. By casting a man as the central figure, the statue also diminishes the prominent position for women within a Seminole culture that maintained its Creek-based matrilineal social structure.

Even more troubling for the opposition is FSU's logo. These disembodied screaming heads of Osceola are a common sight on team uniforms, fan apparel, and Florida license plates. The opposition's criticism on this matter originates from Osceola's untimely end. Following the tribal leader's death, Dr. Frederick Weedon removed Osceola's head and placed it on display in the window of his St. Augustine drugstore. The head eventually made its way to the Medical College of New York, where an 1865 fire presumably consumed it.[31] For the opposition, the logo is a macabre trophy that stands as a reminder of a past that despicably turned one of its own into a public spectacle. Like the newspaper cartoon, the logo is part of ongoing campaign of abuse against the sacred people and practices of the Seminoles.

Indian Approval

On January 30, 2003, FSU dedicated a bronze statue entitled "Integration" with the intention of paying tribute to three black students who were among the first admitted to the university in the 1960s. One of the figures, FSU's 1970 homecoming queen, Doby Flowers, stands with an Indian-style feathered headdress. Protesting the statue on April 10, 2004, one speaker noted that, in fact, Seminole women did not wear such headdresses in the first place. Sheridan Murphy, a Lakota Sioux, acknowledged that the purpose of the statue was a worthy one but said, "When you apologize for racism with racism, it negates the whole thing."[32] Responding to such protests, Lee Hinkle, FSU's vice president for University Relations, said that the headdress was part of the homecoming custom until the 1970s. Hinkle explained that the university did discuss the headdress but said, "Ultimately, the decision was made to include the headdress in the sculpture to accurately capture that moment in 1970." In spite of its historical inaccuracy, Hinkle restated the university's position that "the leadership of the Seminole Tribe of Florida has indicated it is supportive of the sculpture as it stands."[33]

FSU's most effective means for deflecting the criticisms of the opposition has been the assent of Seminole officials. The March 4, 2002, issue of *Sports Illustrated* cited a survey conducted by the Peter Harris Research Group that asked a diverse sample of 352 Indians living both on and off reservations whether they disapproved of Indian mascots. The results showed 81 percent of the respondents affirming that colleges and high schools should keep their Indian mascots, and 83 percent saying professional teams should do the same. Most of those surveyed thought that Indian mascots had an endearing quality. Much like Notre Dame's fans for their "Fighting Irish," respondents considered the mascots harmless, spirited, and entertaining, rather than demeaning. Furthermore, a majority were not offended by the Redskins mascot of Washington DC's professional football team — a logo that is arguably the most insulting to those opposing Indian mascots.[34]

In some respects, the Florida Seminoles seem to share this sentiment — a point that FSU supporters are not shy about sharing. In a rebuttal to critics within his own professional organization, FSU dean of Arts and Science Donald Foss quoted James E. Billie, the former chairman of the Florida Seminole tribe, as declaring, "I am proud of all those who are by birth or choosing a Seminole!"[35] Foss also cited Jerry Haney, chairman of the Oklahoma Seminoles, as saying, "I think that the Seminole/Florida State relationship has been a big shot in the arm for us. I think just about everybody out here is supportive of the Florida State Seminoles."[36] On July 2001, however, Haney signed an official statement from the Council of the Five Civilized Tribes "to eliminate the stereotypical use of American Indian names and images as mascots in sports and other events."[37] Nevertheless, writing a similar response, former FSU president Sandy D'Alemberte referred to Miss Seminole Nation of 1995–96 who thanked the university for "promoting our tribe" as she affirmed Billie's assertion: "We're behind it — we're supporting it."[38] Also coming to the defense of the mascot, Florida State Senator Jim King quoted Jim Shore, the official lawyer for the Florida Seminoles, as saying, "We're not offended, why should they [protesters] be offended?"[39]

Indian assent has been the most difficult hurdle for the opposition to maneuver. Statistics and statements on the issue combine to offer a sense that the opposition is small and misdirected. Indeed, the *Sports Illustrated* poll offered convincing numerical evidence to show that Indians remain generally apathetic toward the mascot issue. The opposition argues that this poll, just like the entire issue of Indian assent, is misleading. C. Richard King and Ellen J. Staurowsky noted the various limitations of the study and went on to cite statistics from an August 8, 2001, poll conducted by *Indian Country Today*. In this study 81 percent of the Indian respondents "indicated use of American Indian names, symbols and mascots are predominantly offensive and deeply disparaging to Native Americans." Furthermore, 75 percent maintained that the use of Indian mascots by non–Indian schools "should be seen as a violation of anti-discrimination laws" and 73 percent believed such situations created hostile learning environments for Indians attending such schools.[40]

On the specific issue of the Seminole's assent, the Indian opposition argues that the statements do not reflect the entire body of the Seminole nation. During the April 2003 Florida legislative session, Max Osceola, the current chairman of the Florida Seminoles, marched into the capitol proudly wearing an FSU jacket. During the session, Osceola affirmed that his Seminoles saw nothing derogatory in the mascot and supported "the ongoing use of the Seminoles by FSU."[41] Responding to this sort of event, David Narcomey, a Seminole and member of the Florida American Indian Movement, said while he constantly hears of the Florida tribe's approval of the mascot, the tribe as a whole has "never approved of it, or been officially approached about it."[42] Narcomey noted that neither the Florida nor the Oklahoma tribe has ever had a referendum on the issue. The assent of Max Osceola or James Billie, Narcomey concluded, does not necessarily indicate that the entire tribe supports FSU. Narcomey further explained that Billie in particular had more concern for money than culture when he was chief and that this legacy has continued with Osceola.[43] Seminole casinos generate a great deal of revenue for the tribe. In their effort to sustain the legality and prosperity of the casinos, Narcomey said, tribal leaders have endeavored to maintain agreeable relationships with Florida lawmakers— many of whom are FSU alumni. No doubt, the Seminole tribe recorded copious profits under Billie. In 1997, casino revenues from Seminole reservations reached approximately $120 million.[44]

In spite of the Oklahoma Seminoles' ambiguity, hazy statistics, and the misleading nature of Indian assent, statements of approval coming from tribal leaders have been invaluable for supporters. In their minds, such statements serve as ultimate rebuttals to any criticism. For the opposition, however, the approvals of Seminole leaders fail to account for the Indians outside of tribal power structures.

Fending off Political Correctness

In March of 1999, Florida Republican State Senator and FSU graduate Jim King added an amendment to House Bill 1735 that proposed making "Chief Osceola riding atop an appaloosa horse named 'Renegade'" the legal mascot of FSU. "For those of us who are of the garnet and gold persuasion, it is time, in fact it is long past time, for us to defend the heritage that is Florida State University," King said.[45] If passed, any attempt to change the mascot would need the assent of a Florida legislature that includes many FSU graduates and loyal followers of the football team. The Senate voted 38–0 in favor of King's proposal, and with FSU graduate John Thrasher controlling the House, the bill appeared as if it would pass there also. With only two days remaining in the legislative session, however, the House ran short on time and subsequently killed the bill.[46]

If there is any question as to the importance of the Seminole mascot, one ought to consider the alacrity with which fans such as King defend it. Not only did an elected official propose a law to protect it, but also the measure passed unanimously. With the multitude of issues that a state senator could concern himself with, he chose to fixate on this one — a measure to ensure the protection of his alma mater's athletic heritage. King's statement about defending FSU's "heritage" is perhaps more profound than he had intended. FSU's mascot is the Seminole, and King made it clear that the Seminole belonged to no one but the university. Furthermore, King's effort was an attempt to rescue FSU's sacred mascot from the clutches of political correctness. Many supporters consider the efforts to ban the mascot to be the work of untamed liberals whose lone goal is to agitate the majority in the never-ending quest for linguistic sensitivity.

Following King, columnist Charlie Barnes firmly asserted that the Seminole is an honored symbol rather than a mascot. For Barnes, the Indianness captured in FSU's Seminole is "noble, courageous and fierce." Those opposing the Seminole mascot, Barnes declared, are "sanctimonious actors from the fever swamps of America's political guerilla [sic] theater." He concluded by saying that supporters need to remain vigilant and, sounding much like Senator King, "refuse to relinquish our honored tradition."[47]

Despite the impassioned plea of Barnes, supporters have yet to quell the voices of dissent. On November 13, 2002, Florida State University's Student Senate passed a resolution to hold a town-hall meeting to discuss possibly retiring the Seminole mascot.[48] The mere mentioning of the issue in the university's student newspaper drew quick and vehement responses from supporters. While the standard appeals to figures such as James Billie and Max Osceola proliferated, many also argued that bigger problems faced Indians— such as alcoholism, gambling, and poverty. The entertaining responses tended to assail the culture of political correctness referred to by Barnes. Writing a mock letter to the Student Senate, one respondent stated, "Quit trying to make a name for yourself by jumping on a politically correct position that is against what a majority of your constituency wants." Another employed the "love it or leave it" motif: "If you hippies hate the name so much why don't you transfer to another state school that is more sympathetic to smelly, Birkenstock wearing, pot smoking, tree-hugging, vegans, like the University of Florida." There were also those who echoed Senator King's assertion that the Seminole belongs to FSU. One fan told those in the opposition, "Get a date, get some friends, have a drink, do whatever it takes to lighten up, but don't mess around with fifty plus years of tradition that have significant meaning to hundreds of thousands of FSU alumni, students, and friends."[49]

The impassioned defenses of FSU's football culture bespeaks of the devotion supporters direct toward their team. Clearly, supporters hold FSU football and the symbols that surround it close to their hearts. Fighting this, the opposition argues that FSU perpetuates Hollywood's versions of Indianness yet still says it genuinely honors Seminole culture. FSU's well-intentioned attempts to have amicable relations with the Seminole tribe mean little to an opposition that sees blatant discrepancies in an Osceola who gallops off into a sunset on a horse that he never road waving a spear that he never threw. FSU's mascot is safe so long as presidents defend it, politicians propose laws to protect it, and fans quickly deride the detractors.

Conclusion

The arguments over an Indian mascot at FSU involve a discussion of symbols— their purpose, meaning, and function. Anthropologist Clifford Geertz maintains that through symbols, people contact the religious.[50] Symbols are, in other words, conduits of the divine. Critics of this thesis might accept only half of the argument, questioning the claim that football is religious. Clearly, churches and football stadiums serve entirely different purposes, and Indian symbols, such as feathers and tomahawks, have religious value due to their functions in various ritual practices. But why is this latter point so easy to determine? Is it because Indians say that these symbols are religious? Indeed, someone's word does have value for determining what is and is not religious, but it should not put an end to the discussion. Otherwise, we might construct too narrow a definition of religion, or we might call something religious that is without sacred value.

Religious scholar Joseph Price calls American sports "a form of popular religion."[51] As Price explains, sports are not institutional religious bodies in the traditional sense, but they do offer fans opportunities to reconnect with the transcendent. Many FSU supporters find transcendent value in the embodied virtues of the Seminole mascot. The Seminole mascot is, therefore, a highly cherished part of FSU's popular religious faith. Virtue is the religious center of the Seminole mascot, and the manner by which FSU supporters virulently defend their symbol serves to demonstrate its importance. To them, the Seminole mascot is more than a novelty; it is a way of experiencing the world.

While faith in sport can often have positive outcomes, it can also have a blinding effect. The overwhelming religious fervor demonstrated by FSU supporters has fought to silence the opposition rather than truly considering its criticisms. The university uses words like "honor" and "accuracy," but the concern for Seminole culture is secondary to the retention of their sacred mascot. FSU does not respond to criticisms as much as it redirects the blame to outside sources or refers to statements from Seminole officials. Such tactics of deferral have allowed it to justify keeping the Seminole mascot, but they have not answered the criticisms fully.

Nevertheless, understanding this debate in religious terms makes it difficult to trivialize either side's claim. FSU supporters often complain that Indians should spend more time worrying about their reservations. Likewise, the Indian opposition cannot understand why people fight so hard to retain an athletic mascot. Each side claims exclusive rights to the symbol. Before any steps toward a resolution can occur, both must come to recognize the religious roots that the other brings to the debate, and perhaps then they can begin to resolve this conflict.

Notes

1. Carol Spindel, *Dancing at Halftime* (New York, New York University Press, 2000) 30, 35, 87–93, 114; See also Robert Berkhofer, *The White Man's Indian* (New York: Alfred A. Knopf, Inc., 1978).

2. "Indian opposition" or "the opposition" refers to all persons arguing to retire the Seminole symbol. Likewise, "FSU supporters" or "supporters" refers to all persons arguing to maintain the Seminole symbol.

3. The United States Commission on Civil Rights, "Commission Statement on the Use of Native American Images and Nicknames as Sports Symbols," issued April 13, 2001 [cited April 2002, available from http://www.aics.org/mascot/civilrights.html].

4. Mark LeBeau, "Bill to Eliminate Indian Mascots," *NAIIP News Path*, October 1, 2002 [cited

May 2004, available from http://www.yvwiiusdinvnohii.net/News2002/0210/LeBeau021001Mas-cotBill.htm].

5. C. Richard King and Charles Fruehling Springwood, "The Best Offense ... : Dissociation, Desire, and the Defense of the Florida State University Seminoles," *Team Spirits: The Native American Mascot Controversy*, edited by C. Richard King and Charles Fruehling Springwood (Lincoln, NE: University of Nebraska Press, 2001) 152, 153.

6. "FSU Team Now the Seminoles." *The Daily Democrat,* November 9, 1947.

7. Richard Billingsley, "Bowden's Dynasty May Never Be Equaled," ESPN.com [cited July 2002, available from http://espn.go.com/ncf/verge/s/fsuhistory.html].

8. Quoted from: John Donovan, "What's in a Name?" *CNN/SI The Inside Game,* May 17, 1999 [cited July 2002, available from http://sportsillustrated.cnn.com/inside_game/john_donovan/news/1999/05/17/donovan_column/].

9. E-mail to author, August 17, 2002.

10. Ben Brown, *Saint Bobby and the Barbarians* (New York: Doubleday, 1992).

11. Spindel, *Dancing at Halftime*, 10.

12. Ward Churchill, "Crimes against Humanity," *Sport in Contemporary Society*, edited by D. Stanley Eitzen (New York: Worth Publishers, 2001) 115–117, 121.

13. Joel Martin, *The Land Looks after Us: A History of Native American Religion* (New York: Oxford University Press, 2001) x.

14. "Tomahawk," *Encyclopedia of North American Indians*, edited by Frederick E. Hoxie (New York: Houghton Mifflin Company, 1996) 638.

15. Readers' responses to "Senate Acts on Mascot Issue," FSUNews.com, November 2002 [cited April 2003, available from http://www.fsunews.com/vnews/display.v/ART/2002/11/18/3dd84f7b0ca53].

16. Quoted from: Jay Rosenstein, "In Whose Honor? American Indian Mascots in Sports," (Ho-ho-kus, NJ: New Day Films, 1996).

17. Dale W. Lick, "Seminoles—Heroic Symbol at Florida," *Florida State Seminoles Official Athletic Web Site,* [cited July 2002, available from http://seminoles.ocsn.com/Trads/fsu-trads-seminoles.html].

18. "The War Chant," *Florida State Seminoles Official Athletic Web Site*, [cited May 2004, available from http://seminoles.collegesports.com/trads/fsu-trads-chant.html].

19. James W. Covington, *The Seminoles of Florida* (Gainesville: University Press of Florida, 1993), 79–80.

20. "FSU Fight Song," *Nolezone*.com [cited May 2004, available from http://www.nolezone.com/news/FSUFightSong.htm].

21. C. Richard King and Charles Fruehling Springwood, "Playing Indian: Why Native American Mascots Must End," *NAIIP News*, November 9, 2001 [cited July 2002, available from http://www.thepeoplespaths.net/Articles2001/Springwood-King011109 Mascots.htm].

22. King and Fruehling Springwood, "The Best Offense," 131.

23. Quoted from: John Donovan, "What's in a Name?"

24. *Ibid.*

25. *Knoxville News-Sentinel*, January 3, 1999.

26. *Knoxville News-Sentinel*, January 13, 1999.

27. King and Springwood, "The Best Offense," 130.

28. Richard Sattler, "Seminole," *Encyclopedia of North American Indians*, edited by Frederick E. Hoxie (New York: Houghton Mifflin Company, 1996) 576–578. Edwin C. McReynolds, *The Seminoles* (Norman: University of Oklahoma Press, 1957).

29. Quoted from: Alliniece T. Andino, "Indian Mascots Still Stir Emotions," Jacksonville.com, October 27, 2001 [cited July 2002, available from http://www.jacksonville.com/tu-online/stories/102801/met_7670344.html].

30. Quoted from: "Unconquered Statue," FSU Athletics, October 15, 2003 [cited May 2004, available from http://seminoles.collegesports.com/genrel/101503aac.html].

31. Patricia A. Wickman, *Osceola's Legacy* (Tuscaloosa: University of Alabama Press, 1991) 144–153.

32. Rocky Scott, "Groups Protest Headdress of New Florida State University Statue," *Eastern Echo*, April 14, 2004 [cited May 2004, available from http://www.easternecho.com/cgi-bin/story.cgi?1588].

33. Wilhelm Murg, "Florida State University's Dubious Tribute," Indian Country Today Online [cited May 2004, available from http://www.indiancountry.com/?1077727219&style=printable].

34. S.L. Price, "Indian Wars," *Sports Illustrated,* March 4, 2002.

35. Quoted from: Donald J. Foss, "Native American Mascots," APA Monitor Online, September 1999 [cited July 2002, available from http://www.apa.org/monitor/sep99/letters.html].

36. *Ibid.*

37. "Five Civilized Tribes Vote against Mascot," *NAIIP News,* July 2002, [cited July 2002, available from http://www.yvwiiusdinvnohii.net/Articles2001/FCTIC010726AgainstMascot.htm].

38. Quoted from: Sandy D'Alemberte, "We Honor the Seminole Legend," *Florida State Times,* February/March 1996.

39. "Alumnus Politician Wants to Put Seminole Mascot in State Law," *Tampa Bay Online,* April, 29 1999 [cited July 2002, available from http://tampabayonline.net/news/legiloot.htm].

40. C. Richard King and Ellen J. Staurowsky, "Response to the Indian Wars," *Sports Illustrated,* March 4, 2002.

41. Quoted from: Lucy Morgan, "Legislators, Seminoles Gather for FSU Day," St. Petersburg Times Online [cited April 2003, available from http://www.sptimes.com/2003/04/03/State/Legislators__Seminole.shtml].

42. Quoted from: Justin Rucki, "Senate Acts on Mascot Issue," FSUNews.com [cited May 2003, available from http://www.fsunews.com/vnews/display.v/ART/2002/11/18/3dd84f7b0ca53].

43. Phone interview with author, July 21, 2002.

44. Jeff Testerman, "Chief of Seminoles Speaks at Eckerd," *Saint Petersburg Times,* October 13, 1998.

45. Quoted from: "Senate Votes to Put FSU Nickname into Law," *Jacksonville Online,* May 1999 [cited July 2002, available from http://tampabayonline.net/news/legi100t.htm].

46. "Senate Votes to Put Seminole Nickname into Law, but Bill Dies in House," *Naples Daily News,* May 1, 1999.

47. Charlie Barnes, "Animals Are Mascots— Seminole Indians Are Symbols," *Florida State Times On-Line* September 1, 2001 [cited May 2003, available from http://www.fsu.edu/~fstime/FS-Times/Volume7/sep01web/2sep01.html].

48. Justin Rucki, "Senate Acts on Mascot Issue."

49. Readers' responses to "Senate Acts on Mascot Issue," FSUNews.com.

50. Clifford Geertz, "Religion as a Cultural System," *The Interpretation of Cultures,* edited by Clifford Geertz (New York: Basic Books, 1973).

51. Joseph L. Price, "Conclusion," *From Season to Season: Sports as American Religion,* edited by Joseph L. Price (Macon, GA: Macon University Press, 2001), 229.

9

New Orleans Becomes a Big-League City: The NFL-AFL Merger and the Creation of the New Orleans Saints

Michael S. Martin

On September 17, 1967, almost 81,000 fans packed into Tulane University's football stadium to watch the New Orleans Saints square off against the Los Angeles Rams. The Saints' first game of their inaugural season began auspiciously enough. The opening kick-off sailed into the outstretched arms of John Gilliam, who tucked the ball into his elbow, dodged would-be tacklers, and raced 94 yards to the Rams' end zone. From such glorious opening-minute heroics, the Saints promptly collapsed. Indeed, the final 59 minutes of that first game foreshadowed the team's future — both for the 1967 season and for much of the succeeding 35 years — with much greater precision than Gilliam's return. The Saints stumbled, bumbled, and fumbled their way to a 14–10 loss.[1]

The game played that day marked a culmination of events that brought a National Football League (NFL) team to the Crescent City. Professional football awarded New Orleans its franchise after political maneuvers in the United States Congress granted an anti-trust exemption allowing a merger for the NFL and its rival, the American Football League (AFL). Two Louisiana politicians, Senator Russell Long and Congressman Hale Boggs, were instrumental in the exemption's passage, and the granting of a New Orleans franchise was largely an act of gratitude for their actions. But the new franchise also reflected a long-developing trend: Following World War

II, professional sports leagues, led by Major League Baseball, spread out of Northeastern and Midwestern Rustbelt cities and into Western and Southern areas, where population and economic changes created demand for high-profile entertainment. By receiving a franchise, many New Orleanians believed that their city reached the ranks of "big-league" cities.

Early Efforts Toward a Professional Football Franchise for New Orleans

Led by local businessman Dave Dixon, New Orleans entrepreneurial and political leaders had sought the "big-league" badge via professional football since the late 1950s. Although Charles Erdmann, aide to Mayor DeLesseps "Chep" Morrison, had written in 1957 to the creators of one NFL rival, "We in the city were unable to come up with sponsors to get [a] franchise going,"[2] by 1959, Dixon and Houston businessman Bud Adams were corresponding about the possibility of New Orleans becoming a charter member of the American Football League.[3] In August 1959, Dixon wrote to Mayor Morrison seeking support in putting together a group of Crescent City professional football promoters. "Professional football would bring millions of dollars into New Orleans," Dixon wrote. "Not only would our city prosper economically but added prestige would be worth additional millions."[4] Mayor Morrison, sounding more like a football coach than his usual urbane self, replied that he supported Dixon "1000%."[5]

New Orleans did not receive an AFL team, probably because the city lacked plans for a new stadium, but the city did host NFL exhibition games over the first few years of the 1960s. By early 1961, Mayor Morrison had been impressed enough by the success of Bud Adams's Houston Oilers that he wrote, "After Houston's success in their initial venture, we are 'raring to go' here in New Orleans."[6] In 1962, rumors swirled that either the Dallas Texans or the Oakland Raiders might move to New Orleans. "Neither situation came to pass—tragically for New Orleans," Dixon later wrote.[7]

By 1964, Dixon and other football boosters in New Orleans had created New Orleans Professional Football, Inc., with the slogan "Bringing Professional Football to the South's Greatest City."[8] The next year, Dixon wrote to Mayor Victor Schiro, "We believe that our efforts to obtain major league sports for this great major league city of ours are about to bear fruit."[9] Early in 1965, New Orleans Professional Football, Inc., had entered into negotiations with "affluent and nationally prominent" individuals in Anaheim, Atlanta, Houston, Jacksonville, Los Angeles, Miami, New York, Oakland, Phoenix, and San Francisco to create a United States Football League. This was the fruit Dixon foresaw, but the league never materialized.[10]

Instead, by late 1965, the biggest of the big football leagues, the NFL, had entered into negotiations with New Orleans. Dixon and Governor John McKeithen met with NFL Commissioner Pete Rozelle to discuss the matter on December 2.[11]

During the summer and fall of 1966, NFL owners debated which city should receive an expansion franchise. The decision had been narrowed to three possibilities: Seattle, Cincinnati, and New Orleans. On May 18, Governor McKeithen, Mayor Schiro, and the members of the Louisiana Congressional delegation met with NFL owners in Washington, DC.[12] At first, New Orleans had no clear advantage, other than meeting one of the league's prerequisites: The city already had a large stadium on Tulane's campus that could be used until a new home was built. Other than that, the race for the expansion team looked to be a dead heat. That would be the case until Senator Russell Long worked a behind-the-scenes deal with NFL Commissioner Pete Rozelle.[13]

The NFL-AFL Merger

The NFL had encountered a growing problem during the 1960s: competition in the form of the fledgling American Football League. NFL owners traditionally tried to keep franchises scarce in order to control the supply-demand relationship and to foster competition between potential expansion sites. Additionally, due to the NFL's shared revenue system, expanding the league would, initially at least, decrease profits for team owners; bringing new franchises in would lessen the share received by each team owner until the newer teams produced profits. In other words, the profit pie at first would remain the same size, while more and smaller slices would be cut out of it. Rival leagues undermined such "monopoly profit considerations" by forcing the NFL to expand more rapidly and into different areas than might have been expected, usually through mergers with the rivals.[14]

Wealthy individuals such as Houston's Bud Adams and Dallas's Lamar Hunt had formed the AFL in 1960. The common denominator among the new leagues owners was that all originally had wanted NFL teams but could not get them. During the late 1950s, even many NFL owners had wanted to expand the league into new cities — Houston, Dallas, Miami, Minneapolis, and Buffalo were among the top candidates — but one or two owners exercised their veto power to stop this from happening. In reaction, the potential owners formed their own league. At first, the AFL of the 1960s sought to recreate the impact of earlier rival leagues — simply survive and the NFL would eventually merge with the league. These previous competitors, including the American Football League I (1926), AFL II (1936–1937), AFL

III (1940–1941), and the All-America Football Conference (1946–1949), had forced the dominant NFL to expand into new markets such as Cleveland, Baltimore, and San Francisco by absorbing successful teams.[15]

New technology, however, provided a key difference between the 1960s-era AFL and earlier rivals. Cross-country air travel allowed for a nationwide league, and television revenues offered the ability to actually compete, at least economically, with the NFL. Additionally, Congress passed the Sports Broadcasting Act of 1961, which allowed professional sports organizations to collectively negotiate national broadcast rights—a boon to NFL owners, certainly, but also good for the AFL. In 1964, the AFL and NBC signed a $42 million, five-year deal. It brought about $850,000 annually for each AFL team.[16]

Armed with a weapon the earlier rival leagues never had—a guaranteed source of revenue—the AFL competed with the NFL on a much more even playing field. The influx of television revenue did not guarantee the new league's survival, however. AFL owners realized that in order to put fans in stadiums, they had to put the best athletes on the field. This need for top-notch talents created a bidding war between the AFL and NFL for marquee college players. Joe Namath became the first player to benefit from the new circumstances. The former University of Alabama star quarterback signed a long-term, $400,000 deal with the AFL's New York Jets, a move that offered immediate benefits for the franchise, including increased season ticket sales. Over the next few years, the NFL and AFL offered increasingly higher wages to the top newcomers to the professional fold. The money issue peaked in 1966 when the salary wars shifted from rookies to veterans. Although certainly beneficial for the star players, the increasingly upward movement of the salary structure threatened the profits and control of both NFL and AFL owners.[17]

A merger presented the best option for owners from both leagues. However, bringing together the AFL and NFL would require an exemption from antitrust laws. Although Major League Baseball had been granted an exemption, no other professional sports leagues had one. In fact, the courts had explicitly ruled in the 1957 case *Radovich* v. *National Football League* that the NFL did not possess immunity from antitrust laws. The only way around such laws was to get a Congressional exemption.[18]

To prod Congress into action, the two leagues announced a proposed merger on June 8, 1966. The league would be known simply as the National Football League, with National and American conferences. Details of the fusion included a playoff system, an interleague championship game, and, most important for the owners, a common draft. Although these aspects of the combination would be instituted almost immediately, the complete merger into a unified league would not come until 1970. In the meantime, the new unified league's hopes rested on Congressional approval; without it, the courts undoubtedly would rule the merger illegal.[19]

In early October, the merger came before New York Representative Emanuel Celler's House Judiciary Committee. Celler looked disdainfully upon the new league, and he delayed any action on the antitrust exemption. He hoped to hold out until Congress adjourned on October 22. Some sportswriters declared that Celler, still fuming over the relocation of baseball's Dodgers from his native Brooklyn, simply disliked sports owners. More likely, Celler, who in his own words had crafted the antitrust legislation as "the product of 10 years of blood, sweat and tears with [Senator] Estes Kefauver," had a deep-rooted suspicion of any antitrust exemption, especially one that had been brought to him with little debate beforehand: "They're asking me to rush through a bill that the Senate didn't even have hearings on or a debate. I don't know what it would do, and I intend to find out." By October 14, the *New Orleans Times-Picayune* noted, "There appears little chance the House will get to act on the bill." Four days later, on October 18, Celler said that the exemption would allow "a group of employers virtually unlimited power over a group of employees. At the same time, no safeguard is given to protect the employees against abuse.... It is a shameful thing to do to any group of employees."[20]

At this point, Russell Long entered the scene. As an enthusiastic sports fan and, more important, a United States Senator, Long had been keeping up with the attempted merger. On June 30, he noted, "Plans for expansion are widely reported to include the city of New Orleans," and he commended "the owners and league officials for developing a constructive plan which will serve our country well...." When the antitrust legislation became bogged down in Celler's committee, Long contacted NFL Commissioner Pete Rozelle and arranged a meeting. Over dinner at a Washington, DC restaurant, and then later at Long's Watergate apartment, the two men struck a deal. Long proposed creating a tax bill, with the antitrust measures tucked into it, that would not be routed through Celler's Judiciary Committee. While in the Senate, Long would control the bill from his chair of the Finance Committee; once it reached the House, a supporter of the merger would control it in the Ways and Means Committee. Upon passage of the antitrust legislation, New Orleans would be awarded the NFL franchise.[21]

Long asked for and received from the Johnson administration a request to clarify admission and entertainment taxation. He used the request as a cover under which to craft the antitrust bill. He did not, however, include the antitrust language in the original bill. Instead, Commissioner Rozelle asked Senator Everett Dirksen, Republican of Illinois, to submit the antitrust amendment after the taxation bill came out of Long's committee. Dirksen agreed to do so because adding the amendment would benefit several franchises then encountering financial difficulties by allowing them to "receive income from charity games with special tax treatment."[22] The bill and amendment passed with little opposition. It then traveled to the House, where Democratic Whip Hale Boggs of New Orleans guided it through the Ways and Means Committee. Celler protested that the football leagues were "poor labor negotiators ... asking Congress to rescue them from their own ineptitude and folly"[23] and said on the House floor that an "end run was made around the public, who now have no way of knowing the whys and wherefores and results that may flow from this football merger."[24] The resulting Football Merger Act of 1966 exempted the National Football League from antitrust action and protected it from prosecution in the federal courts.[25]

Long's skill at manipulating the Congressional machinery to get the antitrust exemption passed should not be construed as sneaky, underhanded, or unethical. Neither he nor Boggs tried to cover up their involvement in the matter. Long himself stated on the floor of the Senate, "It is my hope that in the event the leagues are merged, New Orleans might be able to obtain a franchise." And Boggs wrote one constituent, "This is, of course, a subject in which I have long been interested, and I'm sure I don't have to tell you how pleased I am that a professional team for New Orleans may at last become a reality." The deal reaped almost immediate political dividends for Boggs. Within a week of the announcement that New Orleans had been awarded the franchise, the congressman won reelection with 69 percent of the vote.[26]

On October 25, Pete Rozelle and members of the NFL's joint committee on expansion arrived in New Orleans to meet with three prospective owners: Louis Roussel, Jack Sanders, and John Mecom, Jr. (who was eventually awarded ownership). The committee also met with representatives of Tulane University. Although Cincinnati and Seattle were ostensibly in the running and no official announcement had been made, New Orleans seemed a sure shot to most Louisiana observers. "All of this ... is just like a lot of window dressing as far as we're concerned," wrote *Times-Picayune* sports columnist Bob Roesler. "The decision has been made and our town is in like old Flynn." Governor McKeithen took a more cautious, but no less certain, approach: "Of course, I have no assurance that this is so, but I just think we have it [the expansion franchise]. If there were any doubts, they disappeared after what Senator Long and Congressman Boggs did in Washington last week."[27] Mayor Schiro wrote to Commissioner Rozelle, "It is a pleasure for me to join Pro Football fans throughout the Nation in expressing satisfaction at the House action which grants antitrust immunity to the National and American Football Leagues.... Naturally, we in

New Orleans are proud of the fine job done by Hale Boggs and Russell Long, and we are hopeful that the sixteenth franchise will find its home in this City."[28]

On Tuesday, November 1— All Saints' Day, appropriately enough — Pete Rozelle announced that NFL owners had unanimously chosen New Orleans for an expansion franchise. No owner for the franchise was announced, and the commissioner stressed the importance of building a new stadium for the team. Rozelle set up a temporary headquarters at the Royal Orleans hotel, where he oversaw more interviews of prospective team owners.[29]

Professional Sports, the Sunbelt, and Big-League Cities

Deeper causes were at work in the awarding of the new franchise than the politically expedient bargain Long and Rozelle struck. The NFL, by granting New Orleans a team, reflected a post–World War II trend among all professional sports leagues. At a time when sports became more and more significant in the lives of everyday Americans, the traditional regional stronghold of professional sports, the so-called Rustbelt of the industrial Northeast and Midwest, was being challenged and in some cases supplanted by the population-booming Sunbelt of the South and West as a potential source of fans— and of profits. Professional baseball had led the way in seeking out new markets when the Giants and Dodgers moved to California in 1958. The NFL, whose team owners tended to view their franchises as rare commodities that increased in value only due to scarcity, reluctantly followed baseball's lead, although they had allowed the Rams to move from Cleveland to Los Angeles and had absorbed the San Francisco 49ers from the All-America Football Conference in 1950.[30]

This reluctance on the part of the NFL owners opened the door for the success of the AFL in the early 1960s. The older league — or at least factions within it — refused to recognize the post–World War II population and business resettlement and failed to take advantage of expansion opportunities, sometimes due to the veto of only one team owner. In fact, the impetus to create the new rival league came from just such reluctance. In the late 1950s, business and civic leaders in Dallas, Houston, and Minneapolis-St. Paul clamored for expansion franchises. Tiring of delays, the groups, along with representatives from other Western and Southern cities, agreed to form the American Football League. The threat of aggressive AFL expansion, coupled with the salary wars, pressured the NFL into a new round of expansion in the mid–1960s. The New Orleans franchise would be the second new team in this movement, coming a year after the creation of the Atlanta Falcons.[31]

On the opposite side of the coin were the citizens and leaders of the cities themselves. For urban areas of the South and West, such as Miami, Atlanta, Houston, Denver, San Diego, Seattle, professional sports franchises further reflected their arrival on the scene as centers of population and business growth. Professional sports also brought media recognition; a football team or baseball team became a badge of honor, a status symbol, for cities. Professional sports, in other words, made a city "big league."[32]

In the eyes of most observers, the arrival of professional sports in New Orleans marked a new stage in the city's history: The Crescent City had finally become "big league." Attempts at defining just what exactly "big league" meant proved illusory at best and nonexistent at worst. What were the conditions for being a big-league city? What was the impact of having that descriptive term added to a city's public persona?

For cities as a whole, a professional sports franchise brought a number of positives that one might term "big league." Of course, proponents always pointed to the potential financial benefits of adding a sports team to a city's entertainment scene, but these financial benefits, which often went unrealized, do not completely explain the appeal of professional sports. Bringing an NFL team to New Orleans allowed the city to measure itself against other U.S. cities; without a team, measurement — good or bad — would be impossible. Just as important, a sports team created free publicity for a city, as Bob Roesler noted in the *Times-Picayune*: "The sports pages, and the front pages[,] of the nation's press, have New Orleans qualified as a major league city." Finally, receiving a sports franchise boosted the morale of the city as a whole. "A city without the stimulation and excitement of good sports," Roesler noted, "is a city without a spirit, a city that ultimately would grow gray and lifeless."[33]

New Orleans Mayor Victor Schiro remarked during a 1966 speech that the city's residents had always been football fans. New Orleanians had supported Tulane's teams until, in his words, "Tulane de-emphasized football." Since then, Crescent City citizens had begun trekking "every Saturday to Baton Rouge, filling the 68,000-seat Tiger Stadium, selling out virtually every home game.... They love [football] so much they don't mind driving miles and miles on crowded highways to and from the game to pull their team through." And with the advent of televised professional games, the city had become "National Football League conscious." Schiro concluded that if New Orleanians "had the opportunity to see top football, professional football, right at home, they would keep any stadium packed."[34]

For sports fans and residents of New Orleans, and other expansion cities, a professional franchise had more immediate and personal effects. For some city-dwellers, a professional team was a basic necessity of life. Not only did the new team place its city on a level with other cities, but it also brought the residents themselves up to the level of the residents of other "big-league" cities. Sports became a defining characteristic in a time when distinctiveness, even in such a distinctive city as New Orleans, gradually faded, thanks in large part to a media of mass culture that homogenized national and regional tastes and to suburbanization that fractured local communities. As Kenneth Jackson notes, "Citizen identification with the city is now less than it was a century or more ago," when 19th-century cities and their citizens "possessed a significant sense of local pride and spirit as a result of their struggles with other cities for canals, railroads, factories, and state institutions."[35] By the mid–20th century, this competition for infrastructure and institutional improvements had largely been replaced by a competition for sports franchises, and local pride and spirit had begun to be based on such "big-league" considerations. Although it might have been increasingly difficult to define exactly what a New Orleanian was by the mid–20th century — the influx of non-natives and American culture changed that definition — being a fan of the new football team certainly qualified a person as one. Additionally, for those city residents not terribly interested in sports, the new team did not endanger other forms of non-sports entertainment — theaters continued to show movies and plays, exhibits continued to arrive at museums and galleries, musicians continued to play concert halls and clubs. But for those who did care, even if only on occasion, a sports franchise became, in the words of authors James Quirk and Rodney Fort, a "common identification symbol, something that brings the citizens of the city together." This sense of togetherness characterized a "big-league" city.[36]

New Orleans, however, differed in one key way from most of the other U.S. cities clamoring for "big-league" status: its past. Compared to the other expansion cities of the South, and even the West, New Orleans had been a city of some consequence, in terms of population and economics, for quite a while longer. Therefore, the city did not really fit into the category of a "new growth" area. Just as important, though, New Orleans had a distinguished history as a center of professional sports.

Writing in 1968, a year after the Saints' first season, Crozat Duplantier addressed this issue. As early as 1837, he noted, New Orleans established itself as a center of sport — at first, horse racing. Following the Civil War and into the early 20th century, the city's sports emphasis shifted to professional boxing. As enthusiasm for boxing declined in New Orleans, the city's image as a "big-league" sports center waned, leading to "years of frustration when New Orleans watched its spectator sports decline while other cities moved ahead into the big league picture." Duplantier added, "Its citizens developed a complex that their city was a 'two-bit town.'" Not until the creation of the New Orleans Open, a Professional Golf Association tour stop, in 1957, did major professional sports once again make inroads into the Crescent City. The success of the golf tournament prompted calls for other professional sports possibilities, particularly professional football, which culminated in the awarding of the NFL franchise in 1966 and hopes for a major league baseball team, as well. "New Orleans," Duplantier concluded, "on the eve of its 250th birthday, was big league again."[37]

The Superdome

After the granting of an NFL expansion franchise, New Orleans needed to add one final piece to its "big-league" puzzle: a new stadium. Only eight days after the franchise announcement, Louisianans voted on Amendment 10, which allowed for the construction of a 60,000-seat, covered stadium in Orleans or Jefferson Parish, to be financed by a 4½ percent hotel tax in the two parishes. In addition to serving as a home to the new professional football team, the stadium would, according to proponents, attract other major sporting events, including high school football, baseball, basketball, tennis, polo, soccer, harness racing, professional and amateur boxing, track and field events, gymnastics—even the Spanish Riding School of Vienna and bullfighting.[38]

Although receiving the NFL franchise had been recognition of New Orleans as a "big-league" city, many observers viewed Amendment 10 as the chance to secure, once and for all, the city's right to that description. Months before the vote, businessman Dave Dixon had written to Governor McKeithen that in order to win support for a new stadium, citizens of the city and the state "don't need to like football, or baseball, or any other sport.... [They] need only to like money, because it will mean money in the pockets of every man, woman, and child." He added that, in order to win votes for the stadium, it might be useful to compare New Orleans to rival cities: "In New Orleans this may be more than normally effective, because there is a deep resentment here that Houston, Atlanta, Dallas, and Miami have moved past us during recent years."[39] To Mayor Schiro, Dixon noted, "Long after people will ever care over who appoints the registrar of voters, they will remember you and your role in passing our Superdome legislation. This stadium will be built during your administration, and it will be a monument such as few American mayors have ever possessed."[40]

Sports columnist Bob Roesler wrote, "Every city in the nation, cities that have written us off ten years ago, envious cities, are watching us. With the vote coming on the heels of the franchise announcement, we will have a double barrel load of great national publicity when the dome amendment is passed." Conversely, failure to pass the amendment would have only been detrimental, as *Times-Picayune* writer Ed Staton noted: "If Amendment No. 10 falls on its face, then New Orleans and Louisiana have fallen on their faces, locally and nationally. We'll look like a 10-horse town with a one-horse perspective."[41]

Louisiana politicians also emphasized the importance of a domed stadium in securing New Orleans' big-league status. Senator Allen Ellender said that the football team and stadium would "put our largest city and our state in the big leagues where they belong." Russell Long noted, "If we want to compete with the kind of leadership that exists in Houston, Dallas, Atlanta, and Miami, we must be prepared to go first class. That is what Amendment No. 10 proposes." Governor McKeithen added, "The domed stadium can do nothing but help the state."[42]

Louisiana voters approved Amendment 10 on November 8, 1966, but Governor McKeithen's prediction of it doing nothing but helping the state proved false. Indeed, it is ironical that so many observers hailed the expansion franchise and the stadium as proof of New Orleans' status as "big league," for both the team and the stadium turned out to be utter embarrassments. The New Orleans Saints became a virtual laughingstock, perhaps the worst franchise in professional sports. They certainly did provide New Orleanians with a common identifying symbol, as had been predicted, but the "Aints," as they were dubbed in the late 1970s and early 1980s, came to symbolize eternal losers. It seemed as if the "city that care forgot" had a team that care forgot, as well.[43]

The controversy surrounding the Superdome, as the home of the Saints came to be called, overshadowed even the frightfully poor play of the team itself. The last jewel in New Orleans' "big-league" crown, the Superdome did not open until 1975. Its construction displaced hundreds of families and dozens of businesses. At its completion, what was originally planned as a $35 million, 55,000-seat stadium, had been bloated to 97,000 seats at a cost of $163 million. Cost overruns weren't the only issue. "Except for the New Orleans Saints and the original New Orleans Jazz, who came and went, the major league professional teams that were going to flock to the city never materialized," noted *New Orleans Magazine* in an August 2000 article. "When the Dome opened, New Orleans had one major-league professional team, the Saints; a quarter century later that is still all it has."[44] Eventually, the city did profit from the domed stadium. It attracted papal visits, concerts, exhibits, Mardi Gras balls, and political and other conventions. The Superdome hosted Super Bowls and Sugar Bowls, the Bayou Classic and high school football tournaments. New office buildings and hotels line Poydras Street, which borders one side of the dome.

Conclusions

In 1966, however, New Orleanians could not have known what the future held. Instead, they focused on the present. Their city, which had once ranked among the biggest of the big leagues, had returned to its status as a professional sports market. Thanks to the efforts of Senator Russell Long and Representative Hale Boggs, the National and American Football Leagues had been granted an antitrust exemption, and New Orleans had been granted an expansion franchise. Capping the return, Louisiana voters had approved Amendment 10, which provided for the creation of a new stadium in New Orleans. The embarrassments would come soon enough — when the Saints took the field and when the Superdome costs piled up — and the successes would take longer but would come as well. For this brief period, however, New Orleans took its place in the spotlight as a "big-league" city once again.

Notes

1. *New Orleans Times-Picayune*, September 18, 1967.

2. Charles W. Erdmann to Millard T. Lang, June 10, 1957, Morrison, De Lesseps S., Collection, 1946–1961, City Archives, New Orleans Public Library (hereinafter Morrison Collection), Subject File, Carton S57–36, "United States Football League — 1957."

3. Dave Dixon to K. S. "Bud" Adams, Jr., August 10, 1959, Morrison Collection, Subject File, Carton S59–1, "American Football League — 1959."

4. Dixon to Morrison, August 10, 1959, Morrison Collection, Subject File, Carton S59–1, "American Football League — 1959."

5. Morrison to Dixon, August 14, 1959, Morrison Collection, Subject File, Carton S59–1, "American Football League — 1959."

6. Morrison to D. C. Smith, January 25, 1961, Morrison Collection, Subject File, Carton S61–10, "Football-Professional — 1961."

7. Dixon to Joseph V. Di Rosa, October 26, 1964, Di Rosa, Joseph V., Collection, 1962–1966, 1970–1978, City Archives, New Orleans Public Library.

8. Dixon to Mayor Victor H. Schiro, August 3, 1964, Schiro, Victor Hugo, Collection, 1957–1970, City Archives, New Orleans Public Library (hereinafter Schiro Collection), Subject File, Carton S64–12, "Football Club, Inc.— 1964."

9. Dixon to Schiro, Schiro Collection, Subject File, Carton S65–10, "Football Club, Inc.— 1965."

10. Dixon to Schiro, Schiro Collection, Subject File, Carton S65–10, "Football Club, Inc.— 1965."

11. Dixon to Schiro, Schiro Collection, Subject File, Carton S65–20, "N.O. FB Club Assn.— 1965."

12. NFL Trip to Washington, memo, May 13, 1966, Schiro Collection, Subject File, S66–6, "Football Club, Inc.— 1966."

13. *Times-Picayune*, October 25, 1966.

14. James Quirk and Rodney D. Fort, *Pay Dirt: The Business of Professional Team Sports* (Princeton: Princeton University Press, 1992), 145, 359.

15. Quirk and Fort, 334–347, 359; Steven A. Riess, *City Games: The Evolution of American Urban Society and the Rise of Sports* (Urbana: University of Illinois Press, 1989), 238

16. Randy Roberts and James S. Olson, *Winning Is the Only Thing: Sports in America Since 1945* (Baltimore: The Johns Hopkins University Press, 1989), 139; Benjamin G. Rader, *American Sports: From the Age of Folk Games to the Age of Spectators* (Englewood Cliffs, N.J.: Prentice-Hall, Inc., 1983), 256, 257

17. Jerry Gorman and Kirk Calhoun, with Skip Rozin, *The Name of the Game: The Business of Sports* (New York: John Wiley & Sons, Inc., 1994), 170; Roberts and Olson, 138; Quirk and Fort, 349.

18. Quirk and Fort, 340.

19. *U.S. News & World Report*, June 20, 1966, 10; *Times-Picayune*, October 7, 1966; *Time*, June 17, 1966, 68.

20. *Times-Picayune*, October 9, 1996, October 14, 1966, October 19, 1966; *Los Angeles Times*, January 25, 1981.

21. *Congressional Record* — *Senate* (hereinafter *CR*), June 30, 1966, 14809, 14810; *Los Angeles Times*, January 25, 1981; Robert Mann, *Legacy to Power: Senator Russell Long of Louisiana* (New York: Paragon House, 1992), 273.

22. *New York Times*, October 15, 1966.

23. *New York Times*, October 21, 1966.

24. *Congressional Record* — *House*, October 20, 1966, 28231.

25. *CR*, October 14, 1966, 26886; *Los Angeles Times*, 25 January 1981; Rader, 258.

26. *CR*, October 14, 1966, 26887; Hale Boggs to Dr. Walter J. Vinsant, October 19, 1966, Hale Boggs Papers, Legislation Series, Box 12, 1966–1967, "1966 Legislation, Ways and Means, October 1966"; *Los Angeles Times* , January 25, 1981.

27. *Times-Picayune*, October 25, 1966.

28. Schiro to Rozelle, October 21, 1966, Schiro Collection, Subject Files, Carton S66–8, "Football League — 1966."

29. *Times-Picayune.*, November 2, 1966, November 4, 1966.

30. Gorman and Calhoun, 216.

31. Roberts and Olson, 140–141; Quirk and Fort, 350–351,359; Gorman and Calhoun, 221.

32. Roberts and Olson, 141; Gorman and Calhoun, 45.

33. Gorman and Calhoun, 44; Roberts and Olson, 49; *Times-Picayune*, November 6, 1966.

34. The Victor Hugo Schiro and Margaret (Sunny) Schiro Collection, Manuscripts Collection 1001, Box 6, "VHS Speeches, 1966, Football team and stadium," n.d., Manuscripts Department, Howard-Tilton Memorial Library, Tulane University, New Orleans, Louisiana.

35. Kenneth Jackson, *Crabgrass Frontier: The Suburbanization of the United States* (Oxford: Oxford University Press, 1985), 272.

36. Gorman and Calhoun, 215, 221; Roberts and Olson, 216; Leonard Koppett, *Sports Illusion, Sports Reality: A Reporter's View of Sports, Journalism, and Society* (Urbana: University of Illinois Press, 1994), 62; Quirk and Fort, 176.

37. Crozat J. Duplantier, "A Sportsman's Town," in *The Past as Prelude: New Orleans, 1718–1968*, edited by Hodding Carter (New Orleans: Tulane University Press, 1968), 185–186, 189, 208, 209.

38. *Times-Picayune*, November 6, 1966.

39. Dixon to McKeithen, January 28, 1966, Schiro Collection, Subject Files, Carton S66–8, "Football Club, Inc.— 1966."

40. Dixon to Schiro, July 6, 1966, Schiro Collection, Subject Files, Carton S66–8, "Football Club, Inc.— 1966."

41. *Times-Picayune.*, November 4, 1966

42. *Ibid.*, October 30, 1966, November 3, 1966, November 4, 1966, November 10, 1966.

43. *Ibid.*, November 10, 1966.

44. Riess, *City Games*, 242; *New Orleans Magazine* 34 (August 2000), 13.

V. CAR RACING

10

Weekend Warriors: The Survival and Revival of American Dirt-Track Racing

Daniel Simone and Kendra Myers

The rising popularity of NASCAR, the National Association of Stock Car Auto Racing, is the major impetus for recent academic interpretations of auto racing in the United States. Scholarly work that concentrates on this top tier of racing often overlooks dirt-track racing, a vibrant part of the past and present of American auto racing. With the exception of a few articles and minor studies, academia has left the historic and contemporary significance of the popular culture pastime of dirt-track racing largely untouched.[1]

Most American auto racing takes place on oval tracks. Before World War II, auto racing was popular on fairground horse tracks, and on dirt, paved, board, and brick speedways throughout rural and urban America. Stock car racing, a tradition long associated with the South, gained popularity in the 1950s and has since grown into America's largest spectator sport. Other racing series such as the Indy Racing League (IRL), World of Outlaws, and even the European-based Formula One series are also popular in the United States. Motorsports is a bigger business in America now than at any other time in its history, and understanding this big business requires understanding its roots: dirt-track racing.[2]

Dirt-track auto racing flourishes in large markets as well as in small towns, where it is often woven into the fabric of the community. Geographic location might present a stumbling block to the promotion of top-level national and international races in rural areas, but local passion for motorsports is strong, and smaller cities enjoy well-attended racing events.[3] Dirt-track racing series such as the World of Outlaws and the Xtreme Dirt Series compete every summer in regional hubs such as Fargo, North Dakota, Oklahoma City, Oklahoma, and Dodge City, Kansas, as well as in the tinier enclaves of Batesville, Arkansas, Union Hill, Louisiana, and Cottage Grove, Oregon. Miniscule Knoxville, Iowa, hosts the Knoxville Nationals, the biggest dirt-track racing event of the year, and is also home to the National Sprint Car Hall of Fame.[4] Dirt-track racing is an institution in the state of Iowa much as Indy car racing is indispensable in Indianapolis or stock car racing is a fixture in Charlotte, North Carolina.[5]

Dirt-tracks are the cradles of American auto racing and the stages for the sport's popularity among the masses. American dirt-track racing traces part of its heritage to early–20th-century agricultural fairs. These state, county, and local fairs were prominent entertainment and social events where horse racing was popular. With the advent of the automobile came the first car races, which promoters staged at half-mile horse tracks to display the "exotic" new invention to a curious public. Auto races were often the top moneymaking attractions at fairs, and they generated an early grass-roots interest in motorsports.[6]

Some traditions from these early contests persist today. As horse races ran counterclockwise, so too do most contemporary auto races.[7] Modern American dirt-tracks vary in size. Many of these facilities are a half-mile in length, in keeping with the traditions of the International Motor Contest Association (IMCA) sanctioned races that predominantly took place on converted horse tracks from 1915 until 1977.[8] Some dirt-tracks are as short as a quarter of a mile, or as long as one mile. Some tracks are perfectly flat, while others are tilted, or "banked," in the turns. Racing surfaces vary as well. Facilities designate themselves as "dirt" tracks, "clay" tracks, "gumbo" tracks, or a combination of types of dirt. Drivers use this information to prepare for races, as different racing surfaces demand different car configurations and even different driving techniques.

Most dirt-tracks in the mid–South region are dirt or gumbo, which is a deep black mud dredged from the bottom of a river (in the case of Memphis Motorsports Park, the Mississippi River) and hauled to the track. Clay tracks are more common farther east, especially in the Southeast, where the soil is not the fertile, loamy gumbo of other regions, but hard, red clay.[9] Many tracks in the Northeast are gumbo, so named because of how it appears and how it behaves: It has a tacky, gooey consistency. It is an ideal racing surface because it holds moisture well and sticks together when it is squeezed in a person's hand or tamped down under a pack of cars. Whether the surface is dirt, clay, or gumbo, drivers spend an inordinate amount of time assessing the "mood" of the track before and during a night of racing. They crumble the dirt between their fingers and stick screwdrivers into the track surface to guess how it will behave through the night. Understanding the dirt is crucial as drivers decide how to prepare their cars and how to attack the race. Trying to know the dirt is all the more frustrating because it changes from week to week, day to day, and hour to hour, as it is battered by the weather and by hundreds of cars turning hundreds of laps on its surface. This unpredictability and inconsistency is at once exasperating and a large part of dirt-track racing's appeal to drivers and fans.

Many dirt-track purists disdain asphalt. A favorite fan and driver saying (and T-shirt and bumper sticker slogan) is, "Dirt's for racing. Asphalt's for getting there." The racing on dirt is closer. The drivers have to be better and the equipment has to be set up, or "dialed in," better to manage a racing surface that changes every four laps. Asphalt changes according to the weather and the rubber left on it by other cars, but nothing changes as much, or as fast, as dirt.[10]

Americans' increasing passion for motorsports and the growth of NASCAR into a multi-billion-dollar enterprise has created numerous opportunities for constructing new tracks, attracting corporate sponsorship dollars and drawing advertising and media coverage. The influx of large sums of money into racing has made competition more difficult for underfunded drivers and teams. NASCAR's exposure has also affected racing at the local level. Some hometown tracks have converted from dirt to paved surfaces in response to NASCAR's success and the demands of the market, but despite the popularity of stock car racing on paved super-speedways, many local fans still prefer racing on dirt. As a result, some paved tracks have suffered losses of revenue or racecars, changed their format back to dirt, or closed down entirely.[11]

At many local dirt-tracks scattered across the nation, the pressures of sponsorship, marketing, promotion, product endorsement, public relations, media and funding do not dominate the sport, and thousands of drivers race purely for fun. As they have since the early 1920s, the "weekend warriors" build and tinker with their race cars during the week and then compete in them on the weekends. Most of the drivers who participate in these small racing events do not aspire to advance to "the big leagues" of NASCAR, the Indy Racing League or the World of Outlaws. Many of them are not even competitive at their own, local level, yet they race weekend after weekend anyway, from April to October, spending all of their extra time and money to chase their passion for speed and competition on the dirt.

Competing in the upper echelons of auto racing has become a full-time job for drivers, mechanics, and businessmen. Money has become a major factor even in grassroots racing, where in some cases, the equipment, not the driver, wins the event; that is, he with the strongest engine that money can buy, wins.[12] This evolution from hobby to business began in the 1970s. Today, even at small dirt-tracks, some drivers roll into the pits with expensive and state-of-the-art haulers and equipment. The days of the small-time racer are not over though, because for every hundred-thousand-dollar rig stuffed with an array of shocks, tires, and headers, there is a deck hauler hitched to a pickup truck, bearing a beat-up car with its number duct-taped on its side. Sometimes, a wily veteran with superior knowledge of and experience on his home track can prevail in competition against better-funded, younger, drivers.[13] At small dirt-tracks in Tennessee, Pennsylvania, North Dakota, Mississippi, and Minnesota, local racing has survived and even thrived.

The effects of big money flowing into racing have trickled down to the grass-roots levels of American racing in many spheres beyond mechanical concerns. Even at the smallest local tracks, funding and sponsorship are becoming a necessity for competitors who harbor any hope of being successful. Drivers are putting more money into the sport than ever before. Race teams can spend tens of thousands of dollars to construct and maintain their cars, relying on donated funds or equipment from sponsors.[14] Unless they can obtain adequate sponsorship, most drivers will lose money trying to fund their hobby, and many of them are in deep debt.[15] Drivers and fans defend this sacrifice by comparing the hobby of racing to the hobbies of golf or hunting, which can also be very expensive, time-consuming and frustrating, albeit generally less dangerous.[16]

Track owners are also pouring more money into the sport. They invest in keeping their track surface consistent and good for racing, which attracts better drivers and larger audiences. They invest in their facilities such as restrooms and concession areas, appealing to more families and thus attracting more racers and sponsors.[17] In an effort to cover expenses, purses, and maintenance, some track owners have raised admission costs, especially at paved speedways. Tickets might become too expensive for many potential spectators.[18] Dirt-track facilities are committed to their fans because without the fans, there would be no racing: Direct fan support of drivers, tracks, and their sponsors keeps race teams, and therefore racing, afloat.[19] Staging weekly auto races at any level is terribly expensive for participants and for host tracks, and the economic relationship between racers, fans, sponsors and tracks is a delicate balance. Track owners hope to offer larger purses for winning to attract more drivers and fans, so to keep ticket prices manageable, they solicit sponsorships from local businesses, which range from insurance companies and lawnmower repair services to auto parts stores, restaurants and radio stations. Tracks also sell advertisements in their programs. With added income from sponsorships, they can afford to award more prize money without gouging the fans or requiring that drivers pay higher entry fees to race. Without these sponsorships, which can be as small as a few hundred dollars and as large as several thousand, dirt-track racing would stagnate. "There is only so much we can charge for a ticket," says Jason Rittenberry, general manager of Memphis Motorsports Park, "so we have to have sponsorships" if they want to grow.[20]

Despite a devotion to dirt among many racers and fans, many dirt-tracks across the United States have voluntarily switched, or been forced to convert, to asphalt racing surfaces. A paved speedway results in increased tire wear, thus making the sport even more expensive for the weekend warriors. Sometimes these tracks, which are easier to maintain than dirt-tracks and which also more closely mirror NASCAR tracks, are successful. In the 1950s, '60s, and '70s, weekend warriors could afford to build, keep up, and race one car for dirt and another for asphalt. Drivers rarely have that luxury today, and so they must choose sides, either based on their personal preference or their proximity to one type of track or the other. Some drivers and fans flock equally to dirt and to pavement. Often, though, dirt wins out with the purists.[21]

Economics is only one potential obstacle to the success and growth of American dirt-track racing. Growth and development can threaten racing facilities. Many American racetracks were originally constructed on the outskirts of towns, but in an increasing number of cases, suburban sprawl eventually engulfs those tracks, and environmentalists or developers usually prevail in disputes involving land use. In selected parts of the United States, soil, agriculture, and horses have been a way of life, and dirt-track racing traditions are firmly entrenched there. Dirt-track racing will likely endure in rural markets such as Sioux Falls, South Dakota and Lincoln, Nebraska, because of a relative lack of limiting ordinances and a dearth of environmental and social criticism of racing in these areas. Tracks in other parts of the country might feel more pressure.

Nationwide, small racetracks are often eliminated in areas that are experiencing suburbanization and highway development. The impact of development on auto racing is evident in the case of the once extremely popular Flemington Speedway in formerly rural Flemington, New Jersey. The track converted to asphalt in 1991 in an effort to control dust. The small town was in the process of heavy development, and by 2000, even though the track had reduced dust and adhered to strict noise ordinances, the rapid growth of a suburb conveniently located halfway between Philadelphia and New York City surrounded it. Single-lane State Road 31, where the track is located, has now become a four-lane highway. The track is scheduled for demolition, and a new shopping center will likely replace this facility, which has hosted auto races since 1915.[22] As a lifelong Flemington Speedway fan once stated, "The construction of homes nearby is never a good omen for a speedway."[23] New Jersey's East Windsor Speedway, for example, is surrounded by new $300,000 "mini-mansions." Racing has ceased at the facility, and its fate is undecided. In Tunica, Mississippi, town noise ordinances prevent racing at the year-old Delta Bowl Speedway from extending past midnight. If a large number of cars are competing or if the track requires maintenance during the race night, the track often has to shorten the races or cancel them entirely.

Some tracks can coexist with population growth. The Red River Valley Speedway in Fargo, North Dakota, nearly closed due to problems with noise and population growth in the 1980s. Development loomed close to the once isolated and rural West Fargo Fairgrounds, and noise from the track provoked a public outcry. There was considerable effort in the community to close the track down. The fair board saved the track by purchasing large chunks of land around the fairgrounds, thus confining the noise nuisance to a small number of residents close to the track.[24]

The widespread success of NASCAR has had conflicting effects on the local American racing scene. Many fans have decided that NASCAR races are their main interest, and they faithfully watch the races on television if they cannot travel to attend the events in person, thus abandoning live, local racing. At the same time, the popularity of NASCAR and the World of Outlaws has helped grass-roots racing in some areas to thrive. In areas with limited access to major racing venues, fans go to their local tracks every week to watch their sport and "get their fix." They also know that the big racing stars of tomorrow have to start somewhere, so they watch their local lads carefully, on the lookout for the next Jeff Gordon or Steve Kinser.[25] All over the country, children as young as five years old race in tiny quarter-midget racers and go-karts. This "Little League" version of auto racing includes both the youngsters and their families. It is not uncommon to see "Speedy Junior's" mom volunteering at the concession stand at these events while Dad acts as Junior's crew chief. In the words of sprint car driver Paul Sides, who has been at the races since he was a child, "The family that races together, stays together."[26]

In many parts of the country, local-level racing has been an integral part of the community for so long, it is as accepted as church or high school football. Here, dirt-track racing is an assumed part of life that is handed down from generation to generation, and people are racers or fans because they grew up with racing. Fans bring their babies and young children to the track, stuffing cotton in their little ears and giving them their first tastes of exhaust, dirt, and speed. The world of racing is tightly knit and well organized, and its long-standing traditions often hold communities together.

People know each other's private lives as well as they can deconstruct their techniques on the racetrack. Friday- and Saturday-night shows are as much social events as they are sporting events, and small communities rely on these congregations. Whether their interest is sparked by a nationally televised race or by living next door to a racer, faithful audiences head to their closest track, dirt or asphalt, and watch semiprofessional local competitors duke it out every weekend.[27]

These weekend warriors are local racing stars who have chosen not to cast their lot in the "big leagues." The dirt-track races are not unlike semipro baseball or pickup basketball games, even though the financial burden in racing is much higher, as drivers "play" their favorite sport together. Very few drivers make a living driving at this level. Most of them have day jobs, and many of them own their own businesses, so they can set their own hours and even write off some of their racing expenses as advertising for their companies.[28] It is possible to make a living running on dirt in one of the traveling series such as the American Sprint Car Series (ASCS) or the Mid-Atlantic Racing Series (MARS), and, of course, the World of Outlaws, but a nomadic lifestyle and demanding schedules require great personal sacrifices. Many grass-roots dirt drivers feel that such pressures "take the fun" out of racing.[29] There might be one or two guys who could have, should have, or would have made it to the fame and fortune of the "big time," but they choose to remain at their local tracks, racing for local glory.[30]

Although the state of American dirt-track racing is generally strong, competition for fan and sponsor support and dollars is also strong, and some racetracks suffer as a result. Tracks might feel the heat of competition with other local facilities as concurrent events split audiences and racers. Other racing events are not the only competition for these local tracks. For example, the Red River Valley Speedway is adversely affected when the independent minor league baseball team the Fargo-Moorhead Redhawks plays in town. Attendance at Memphis Motorsports Park often declines when high school football season starts and during the NBA's Memphis Grizzlies home games. Turnout at the racetrack also suffers when a big concert rolls into the FedEx Forum. While Memphis Motorsports Park commands the third-highest attendance of any sporting venue in Memphis and Shelby County, it still has to compete with the many other entertainment options that the city offers.[31]

Grass-roots racing in some locales has experienced a decline in interest and attendance due to the popularity of larger racing series. Most dirt-tracks operate far from large cities and major racing venues, but a few prosper in peaceful coexistence with larger tracks nearby, such as Charlotte, Fort Worth, and Las Vegas. In some cases, tracks have either been forced to shut down or they barely stay afloat with tiny purses and small crowds. Night racing at some local tracks has declined because fans prefer to watch NASCAR evening races on FOX or NBC from the comfort of their own homes.[32]

Increased interest in auto racing on a national scale can be a boon to local tracks. Fargo, North Dakota, is an example of a community that has benefited from the increased national popularity of racing. It is one of only a few markets that have three consecutive days of World of Outlaws races, and this event has become the city's biggest national sports attraction. Fargo's Red River Valley Speedway has its main program on Friday nights, thereby preventing the nationally televised NASCAR Nextel Cup or Indy Racing League Saturday evening events from having an adverse effect on local attendance. The World of Outlaws has boosted local attendance at the Red River Valley Speedway, but more important, the community now attracts racers and fans from all over the country.[33]

Most tracks do not worry about competition from racing events on television. Fans and drivers who prefer dirt do so because it is local, because the entire family can enjoy the event together, and because they can watch the people they live and work with compete. Race fans might also prefer local events because the races are shorter, more varied, and the racing show lasts only a couple of hours, whereas a NASCAR race can stretch up to five or more.[34] Finally, they prefer dirt-track racing because it is dirty, authentic, and more exciting than watching the sterile, corporate machines of NASCAR (or "NAS-bore," or "NAP-car") parade around yet another mile-and-a-half, D-shaped oval track built by rich men so they can get richer. There is a general disdain for the big-money NASCAR stars among drivers and fans at this level, where the perception is that the billion-dollar NASCAR guys are cushy, spoiled, and have forgotten their roots. And they race on asphalt![35] Dirt-track fans reserve their respect for NASCAR drivers who have connections to dirt, such as Tony Stewart, Dave Blaney, and Ken Schrader. These three drivers began their careers running on dirt, and they take every opportunity to return to their roots on NASCAR's off-weekends. Schrader occasionally travels with the Mid-Atlantic Racing Series (MARS), racing late-model cars, while Stewart and Blaney compete in sprint cars at selected dirt-tracks. These drivers remember where they came from, and even though they are rich and famous, they still get dirty when they can.[36]

Dirt-track racing is popular in countries such as Canada and Australia, but it remains a distinctly American pastime. Once considered a "minor league" sport composed of drivers who do not have the talent or money to race in top asphalt divisions, dirt-track racing is entering the mainstream in racing circles. A handful of World of Outlaws races have been broadcast nationally on cable channels, and much of the 2004 season will be aired on the Outdoor Life Network. NASCAR star Tony Stewart owns a team in the

World of Outlaws, which has brought more national interest to the series. Other dirt-track sanctioning bodies, such as the Southern California Racing Association (SCRA), Xtreme Dirtcar Series, and DIRT Motorsports Inc., are growing into big businesses.[37]

Perhaps to a larger degree than other popular American sports, auto racing has been in a continuous state of transition, and it is risky to declare that NASCAR's current boom will sustain itself. Stock car racing might have already reached its peak. The World of Outlaws and other successful regional sanctioning bodies have preserved dirt-track racing in America, which has allowed small racetracks to remain distinct features of American rural communities. Despite the national explosion of NASCAR and ongoing trends in American motorsports over the years, places like Fargo, North Dakota, and Memphis, Tennessee, have remained linked to the roots of racing. They remain dirt-track racing communities as they have for generations— places in which dirt-track automobile racing has not only survived but also continues to thrive as a key part of the local culture. The weekend warriors and their families continue to work on their cars and race for pure enjoyment and passion.[38]

Notes

1. There are many recent sources that address the popularity boom of NASCAR. The first scholarly work dedicated to the subject is Mark D. Howell, *From Moonshine to Madison Avenue: A Cultural History of the NASCAR Winston Cup Series* (Bowling Green, OH: Bowling Green University Press, 1997). Another recent full-length study is Robert J. Hagstrom, *The NASCAR Way: The Business that Drives the Sport* (New York: Wiley, 1998). See also Peter Golenbock, *American Zoom: Stock Car Racing—From Dirt-tracks to Daytona* (New York: Macmillan, 1993); Jim Wright, *Fixin' to Git: One Fan's Love Affair with NASCAR's Winston Cup* (Durham: Duke University Press, 2002).

2. Tom Jensen, "Tobacco Road Paved with Gold," *Street and Smith's Business Journal*, May 18–24, 1998, 19–20; Lee Walczak and Stephanie A. Forest, "Speed Sells," *Business Week*, August 11, 1997, 86–90; Roy S. Johnson, "Speed Sells," *Fortune*, April 12, 1999, 58–70. A useful recent resource on the general history of Formula One racing is Giuseppe Guzzardi and Enzo Rizzo, *The Century of Motor Racing: The Drivers and Their Machines*. Translated by Neil Davenport (New York: Barnes and Noble, 1998).

3. Daniel Simone produced a Master's thesis on dirt-track racing in North Dakota and Minnesota. Kendra Myers's Master's thesis in Southern Studies documents contemporary dirt-track racing in Tennessee and north Mississippi.

4. Jeff Olson, "Outlaws on the Upswing," *Racer,* October 1999, 98; Jeff Olson, "Rumor Not Humorous," *Racer,* November 1999, 98; Jeff Olson, "The Outlaws Question," *Racer,* August 2000, 94; Chuck Dressing, "WOO vs. IRL," *Racer,* October 1999, 38; Jeff Olson, "Never Enough," *Racer,* October 2000, 64–68; Doug Auld, "Ted and David," *Open Wheel,* June 2000, 40–45.

5. The Indianapolis 500 has been replaced by the Daytona 500 as America's most popular annual auto race. For information on the Indianapolis 500, see Rich Taylor, *Indy: Seventy-Five Years of Racing's Greatest Spectacle* (New York: St. Martin's Press, 1991); J. M. Fenster, "Indy," *American Heritage* 43 (May–June 1992): 66–81; Ed Hinton, "Whatever Happened to Indy?" *Sports Illustrated,* June 2, 1997, 26–33. For discussions of stock car racing's popularity in the Piedmont, see Richard Pillsbury, "Carolina Thunder: A Geography of Southern Stock Car Racing," in *Fast Food, Stock Cars, and Rock 'n' Roll: Place and Space in American Pop Culture,* edited by George O. Carney (Lanham, MD: Rowman and Littlefield, 1995), 229–238; Richard Pillsbury, "A Mythology at the Brink: Stock Car Racing in the American South," in *Fast Food, Stock Cars, and Rock 'n' Roll: Place and Space in American Pop Culture,* edited by George O. Carney, 239–248; Tom Kirkland and David

Thompson, *Darlington International Raceway: 1950–1967* (Osceola, WI: MBI, 1999); Pete Daniel, *Lost Revolutions: The South in the 1950s* (Chapel Hill: University of North Carolina Press, 2000), 91–120; Dan Pierce, "The Most Southern Sport on Earth: NASCAR and the Unions," *Southern Cultures* (Summer 2001): 8–33.

6. The history of motorsports in the Upper Midwest and Great Plains is more fully recounted in Daniel J. Simone, "Drivers, Dust, and Dirt: The History of Auto Racing in Fargo, North Dakota (1903–1969)," MA Thesis, North Dakota State University, 2002. Derek Nelson, *The American State Fair* (Osceola, WI: MBI, 1999), 70–72, 78–79; Allan E. Brown, ed., *The History of America's Speedways: Past and Present* (Comstock Park, MI: Slideways, 1994), 11–12; J. L. Beardsley, "Rise of the Dirt-tracks," *Speed Age*, April 1951, 10–13.

7. Formula One racing is a notable exception. Most F-1 races are run clockwise.

8. Many sanctioning bodies are pronounced as an acronym. However, in the case of the IMCA, the individual letters are stated. For additional information on the formation and history of the IMCA, see Simone, "Drivers, Dust, and Dirt;" Lee O'Brien, *Dirt-track Legends: A History of Sprint Car Racing at the Iowa State Fairgrounds Vol. 1, 1907–1949* (Lake Mills, IA: Graphic Publishing Company Inc., 1984); Joe Scalzo, *Stand on the Gas! Sprint Car Racing in America* (Englewood Cliffs, NJ: Prentice Hall, 1974), 106–113.

9. A study of contemporary dirt-track racing in the mid–South is Kendra Myers, "Drive: A Season in the Life of a Dirt-track Racer, or, Confessions of a Dirty Girl," MA Thesis, University of Mississippi, 2004.

10. Mauk, "Sprinting to the Top," *Racer*, February 2001, 70–72; Paul Dean, "The Sprint Car Connection," *Road and Track*, December 1998, 186.

11. Rob Sneedon, "21 Predictions for the 21st Century: The Long View from America's Short Track Operators," *Speedway Illustrated*, July 2000, 81–86; Jeff Olson, "Rural Legend Revival," *Racer,* April 2000, 82. Clay Hill Raceway in Atwood, Tennessee, is an example of a track that began its life on dirt, converted to an asphalt surface, returned to dirt, and ultimately closed.

12. Jason Rittenberry, interview by Myers, Memphis, TN, November 6, 2003.

13. Mauk, "Sprinting to the Top," 70–72; Debby Sonis Jackson, "The Fun Comes in Winning: Dirt-track Racing," *Goldenseal*, Fall 1995, 51; "Dirt-tracks Pave Way for Racing Life," *USA Today*, March 13, 1989, sec. D, 1–2; Earl Krause, interview by Simone, Succasunna, NJ, March 31, 2004.

14. Paul Sides, interview by Myers, Millington, TN April 25, 2003.

15. Mark Hardee, interview by Myers, Millington, TN, May 2, 2003.

16. Thompson, interview by Myers.

17. Rittenberry, interview by Myers.

18. Sneedon, "21 Predictions for the 21st Century," 81–86; Krause, interview by Simone.

19. Allen Swinford, interview by Myers, Millington, TN, April 25, 2003.

20. Rittenberry, interview by Myers.

21. Rick Thompson, interview by Myers, Southaven, MS, February 4, 2003; Tom Cummings, interview by Simone, Fargo, ND, December 5, 2001; Sneedon, "21 Predictions for the 21st Century," 81–86; Krause, interview by Simone.

22. Gordon Eliot White, *Lost Racetracks: Treasures of Automobile Racing* (Hudson, WI: Iconographix, 2002), 65; Scott Cooley, interview by Simone, Flemington, NJ, July 1, 2001; Sneedon, "21 Predictions for the 21st Century."

23. Cooley, interview by Simone.

24. Bruce Byers, interview by Simone, West Fargo, ND, April 3, 2000

25. Jeff Gordon, a superstar in NASCAR, started his racing career when he was five years old and came up through the ranks of racing in open-wheel competitions in Indiana. Steve Kinser, "the King of the [World of] Outlaws," has been a dirt-track driver for his entire career. He won his 500th race in 2004.

26. Krause, interview by Simone; Paul Sides, interview by Myers, Millington, TN, April 25, 2003.

27. For additional information and detail regarding the culture of the dirt-track, see Myers, "Drive: A Season in the Life of a Dirt-track Racer."

28. Rittenberry, interview by Myers.

29. Sides, interview by Myers.

30. The World of Outlaws runs a blistering schedule, racing nearly every weekend from the beginning of March to the beginning of November. They race all over the country, bouncing between Nevada, Wisconsin, Texas, Iowa, Pennsylvania, Indiana, Alabama, and Washington. In 2005, approximately 18 drivers will run the full schedule, and as many as 30 more will run a limited schedule. For more details regarding the World of Outlaws, see the World of Outlaws Web page, http://

www.worldofoutlawsracing.com/; Wayne Rhodes, interview by Myers, April 2, 2004; Jeff Olson, "Outlaws Under the Gun," *Racer,* August 2003, 14; Rocky Entriken, "Jumpstart: IMCA," *Racer,* December 2003, 98.

31. Rittenberry, interview by Myers.

32. Olson, "The Outlaws Question," 94; Olson, "Outlaws on the Upswing," 98; Olson, "Rural Legend Revival," 82; Bob Myers, "Prime-Time Saturday Night," *Circle Track,* December 1999, 10.

33. Byers, interview by Simone; Cummings, interview by Simone.

34. Thompson, interview by Myers.

35. *Ibid.*

36. Ben Blake, "Dirty Minds," *Racer,* January 2004, 66–69.

37. Dressing, "WOO vs. IRL," 38; Auld, "Ted and David," 40–45; Ron Hedger, "Special Report: Dirty Pool," *Speedway Illustrated,* June 2004, 81–87.

38. Ben Blake, "Will NASCAR's New Found Fan Base Prove to Be Fickle in the End?," *Racer,* October 2000, 30.

11

Racing's Roots in the Virginia Landscape

Brian Katen

In the late 1940s, rural Virginia and North Carolina saw the rise of a regional sport — stock car racing — that would come to epitomize for many people a mid- to late–20th-century image of the rural South. The evolution of this sport was accompanied by the development of numerous local racetracks that collectively compose a significant physical and social Virginia landscape neglected by most contemporary scholarship. To date, more than 100 Virginia racing sites have been identified. Most of these venues were developed in the 25 years following World War II. These new speedways, carved from farmers' fields and natural amphitheaters, and their featured event, now known as "Saturday Night Racing," became significant gathering places in the social and recreational landscapes of small towns throughout Virginia. A study of the Virginia speedways can provide new insights and understandings of the richness of the vernacular Virginia landscape and offer an important window into the early development of stock car racing in the American South.

Automobile racing in Virginia did not begin with the development of the post–World War II speedways. The earliest automobile racing landscape in Virginia was intended to be the northern part of the 80-mile stretch of beach from Cape Henry, just above Virginia Beach, south to Oregon Inlet in North Carolina. In March of 1904, 21 New York "automobilists," including "[American Automobile Association] officials, operators, racing men, reporters, and photographers ... left New York ... for a trip that was expected to supply a convenient course where the elimination trials and other speed contests could be held."[1] The trip was hosted by the Virginia Beach Automobile Club, specifically formed for "the promotion of an annual tournament on the coast at Virginia Beach."[2] The New York contingent had hoped that Virginia Beach would provide it with a closer venue than the group's originally selected site at Ormond–Daytona Beach in Florida. However, the Virginia sands proved to be unfit for racing competition, and racing remained at Daytona, today one of America's premier racing sites.

Although the Virginia Beach course proved unsuitable, automobile racing quickly began to gain a foothold in the South and mid–Atlantic region. Cumberland Park in Nashville hosted races in 1904,[3] as did Benning's Race Track in Washington, DC.[4] Electric Park in Baltimore hosted a race in 1905,[5] and Piedmont Park in Atlanta saw a match race between Barney Oldfield and Paul Albert in 1906.[6] In Virginia the earliest documented automobile race occurred on the horse track at Mariner's Park in Norfolk on September 16, 1904, and by 1907 automobiles were racing on the one-mile oval at the Virginia State Fairgrounds in Richmond.[7] The Virginia fairground tracks, typically one-mile or half-mile dirt ovals for horse racing, with wide, sweeping curves and a grandstand for spectators, were easily adapted for the new sport of automobile racing. Fairgrounds at Lynchburg, Bluefield, Norfolk, Suffolk, Roanoke, Emporia, Tasley on the Eastern Shore, and the Virginia State Fairgrounds in Richmond all hosted open-wheel, Indianapolis-style automobile races prior to World War II. Most of these races were sponsored by the American Automobile Association (AAA).[8] It was natural that the fairgrounds, focuses of community and regional celebration and competition, and with existing tracks, would become the sites of the state's early automobile races. Prior to World War II, automobile racing at the fairgrounds was a special, occasional event associated with the fall fair or special holidays such as Labor Day or the Fourth of July.

By 1941, a new type of automobile racing, stock car racing, was beginning to draw the attention of promoters throughout the country.[9] What was likely the first sanctioned "stock car" race in Virginia was held at the State Fairgrounds in Richmond on July 4, 1941. The race was advertised as a race between "passenger cars"[10] only with the "headlamps, hub caps, and bumpers removed."[11] The race was a success, with approximately 4,000 spectators in attendance.[12] But the advent of the Second World War quickly brought a close to racing at the Virginia fairgrounds, and it would be another five years before racing would resume.

After the war, open-wheel racing made a comeback at the State Fairgrounds in Richmond. Three AAA-sanctioned races were held there in 1946 and again in 1947. Additional AAA-sanctioned races were held at the fairground at Keller on the Eastern Shore in 1947, and at fairgrounds in Winchester, Staunton, Martinsville, and Lynchburg in 1948.[13] Open-wheel races with Indianapolis-style cars continued to be a featured event at Virginia's fairground tracks well into the 1950s. But during the decade following World War II, stock car racing was gaining in popularity and soon supplanted open-wheel racing at fairgrounds and speedways throughout Virginia.

By the early 1950s, the fairgrounds at Lynchburg, Petersburg, Starkey, Galax, Tazwell, Fredericksburg, Danville, Norfolk, Princess Anne, Fincastle, and Wise all were hosting stock car racing.[14] The popularity of this new type of racing soon resulted in the construction of a new generation of Virginia racetracks designed specifically for racing automobiles. More local in character and intimate in scale than the earlier fairground tracks, these new speedways proliferated. The first documented stock car race in Virginia on a track built for that purpose occurred in May 1947 near Marion. That track, Southwest Virginia Speedway, was carved out of a farm field alongside the South Holston River. Though it was open for only one racing season, its construction heralded both the growing regional popularity of stock car racing and the sport's deep roots in the Virginia landscape. In the two decades that followed, new speedways would be built across the state. The most significant concentration of the new speedways was located in the southwestern part of the state.[15]

Beginning in the late 1940s, the consistent and recognizable landscape of the early Virginia fairgrounds was augmented by a rich fabric of automobile speedway sites and designs. Many of the original fairground tracks in Virginia were flat tracks suited to horse races. But fairground tracks that featured harness racing had elevated or banked turns. The banked turns at the Tazwell fairground were steep enough to allow the construction of a tunnel under the first turn to provide access to the infield. Following the precedents of the fairground tracks, two general types of automobile speedways developed: flat tracks and those with elevated or banked turns. In general, four typical site types were selected for speedways. First, many flat tracks were located, like the earlier fairground tracks, on large, flat, open sites. In many cases, these sites were adjacent to streams that supplied the water necessary for track maintenance. Second, a significant number of the new speedways were sited in natural amphitheaters or narrow valleys. These speedways took advantage of existing topography to provide spectators with natural hillside vantage points for viewing the race. Eventually, at many speedways, these hillsides would be augmented with temporary and, later, permanent seating. A steeper, lower part of these natural slopes served an important safety function, separating spectators from the action on the track. A third group of speedways, less permanent in nature, was sited on rolling upland agricultural fields. On most of these sites, only the banked turns required significant ground manipulation. Occasionally, however, significant effort was undertaken to create a speedway site. For example, Route 58 Speedway, located outside of Danville, was carved out of an existing ridge to create a three-sided amphitheater. Suitable clay to surface the track was then brought in from a nearby location. A fourth group of new speedways was located in existing outdoor stadiums and indoor arenas. Victory Stadium in Roanoke; Richmond City Stadium; the Norfolk and Salem Civic Centers; and Norfolk's Scope Arena all became racing venues. Victory Stadium hosted races into the 1990s, and today the Scope in Norfolk is the site of indoor races sponsored by Arena Racing USA.

The new automobile speedways varied in size and configuration. Many of the first new speedways continued the half-mile dirt-track tradition of many earlier fairgrounds. But, as new speedways were built on a variety of sites, shorter speedways evolved. Four-tenths, one-third, and quarter-mile speedways all became common. The length of the speedway was determined in part by the character and topography of the chosen site. Length directly influenced the quality of racing at many sites. A shorter speedway required fewer cars for exciting racing. As a result, some half-mile speedways were shortened to improve the racing when the number of racers dwindled. In the 1950s, some speedways were shortened to more nearly conform to the length of the speedways on the developing NASCAR (National Association for Stock Car Auto Racing) circuit. The newly shortened speedways hoped to make themselves more attractive venues to NASCAR drivers, who could now race there without having to change the race setup on their cars.

The configuration of the new speedways varied considerably. Most tracks held true to the traditional oval configuration but with variations of width, straightaway length, curve radii, and degree of banking. D-shaped tri-ovals and more circular configurations were also employed.[16] Figure-eight courses were eventually laid out over some speedway ovals to boost flagging attendance. Other factors also affected the evolution of the Virginia speedways. Dirt tracks suffered from the clouds of dust that enveloped them as the race progressed. A new, "no dust" paved surface became an attractive marketing feature for many speedways. As a result, a new generation of paved speedways began to emerge in the 1950s. In some cases the new, paved ovals were built inside longer dirt tracks. Other paved ovals were built adjacent to existing dirt tracks. Finally, in some cases the existing dirt track was simply paved over and often shortened in the process. As the speedways were reconfigured, the overlays and traces of the earlier venues transformed them into sites of memory, the visible repositories of racing history.

The local speedways were designed and laid out in the field by property owners, promoters, and in some cases by the racers themselves. Influenced by their experiences and observations at other, nearby speed-

ways, these men create their tracks without the assistance of trained designers. They had seen the crowds that racing could command and saw in the
speedways real financial opportunity. Bluestone Speedway near Bluefield
was reportedly constructed in 1948, a year after its promoters attended races
at the Southwest Virginia Speedway outside of Marion.[17] Similarly, New
River Speedway in Ivanhoe was built in the early 1950s soon after the owners of the property had attended a race at the nearby Piney Speedway.[18]
Piney Speedway, located near Fort Chiswell, had been laid out by local drivers after other nearby tracks had closed, limiting their opportunities for
racing.[19] Many of these early efforts were true design experiments, and the
speedway surfaces, layouts, banking, and facilities were adjusted in response
to the actual conditions of the racing. The soil at the chosen site made all
the difference. Complaints of poor track conditions, particularly rocky
ground and excessive dust, were common. Speedway promoters did whatever they could to alleviate these conditions, and their newspaper advertisements boasted of improved conditions and "no dust." Those speedways
that had superior clay surfaces are still talked about with awe by the early
drivers.[20]

As racing grew in popularity and track promoters refined their sites,
a distinct design vocabulary began to develop at the speedways. The track
was at the center of the speedway composition, but around it evolved a
hierarchy of landscape spaces that gave spatial form to the racing hierarchy
that developed at each track. At most speedways, a pit area was created
inside the track. Here cars were readied for the competition. They emerged
from the pits for each race and returned to the pits for repairs and service
as the race progressed and again upon its completion. The most popular
racing division and its cars and drivers would be assigned those pit locations most visible from the spectator areas. The action in the pits could at
times rival the competition on the track itself. At some smaller tracks or at
tracks with low seating where spectator sight lines would be interrupted,
the pits were located outside the track. A few speedways had two pit areas.
Inside the track was a pit for the speedway's premier race division, while
the remaining race cars pitted outside the track.

Each speedway had viewing areas that overlooked the action on the
track. At the early speedways, this might simply be an unimproved hillside
that provided an elevated vantage point. Often this was a steep slope for
spectators only. At other speedways, with more gentle slopes or terraced hillsides, the spectators could park on the hillsides that overlooked the track
and watch the race from their car. This was the case at Radford Speedway,
which in 1959 was advertised as "the only drive-in track in the South."[21]
Over time, most speedways constructed more permanent seating, either
wooden or concrete bleachers. Casual seating areas at the speedways con-

tinued to allow spectators to bring their own chairs or blankets from which to watch the race. Some still provide areas where spectators can watch a race from their vehicle. At the New River Valley Speedway, some of these vehicles are permanent features. Today, window vans and Volkswagen buses serve as vernacular luxury boxes for season ticket holders at the speedway.

Many of the early dirt tracks had no safety walls or barriers to keep the cars from leaving the track. As noted earlier, at many of these speedways, the natural slopes themselves served to separate the spectators from the dangers of the action on the track. The bottom of the slope acted as a type of crude Jersey barrier. The steep cut of these slopes often never revegetated, and the eroded bottom part of the slope is a signature landscape feature of many former speedway sites. To prevent drivers from cutting the corners to gain an advantage, barriers such as cut-off telephone poles or half-buried tires were installed on the inside edge of the track. As safety became more of a concern, various barriers to separate the action on the track from the pit and spectator areas began to appear at the speedways. These barriers included guard rails and wire safety fences to protect spectators from flying debris. By today's standards, many of these "safety" devices simply look dangerous, but they, along with the grade separation between the track and the viewing areas, were the first steps toward creating the safety elements that characterize today's modern speedways.

Many speedways also added wooden board fences along the backstretch and through the turns. These fences would often extend behind the spectator seating areas. They ensured that only the paying customers would be able to see the action on the track. Such screening was often a necessity. At the inaugural race at Southwest Virginia Speedway, the non-paying spectators watching the race from nearby hillsides likely outnumbered the paying customers.[22] At many abandoned speedway sites, the posts from these fences are tangible reminders of the site's racing history and important clues to the layout and spatial structure of the site.

The sense of mystery created by fences that screened the action from public view is an important clue in understanding the spectator experience at the speedways. That experience began with the approach to the track. Fairground sites were often at least partially visible from the nearby roads, but speedways located in valleys and more rural settings were often hidden from view and approached along long, narrow entry dives. Along the approach, anticipation would build until the speedway, alive with the energy and excitement of racing, finally came into view. Some speedways were approached from below. Spectators would drive along the valley to the speedway site and then climb up to their preferred vantage point. At other speedways, spectators approached from above, arriving at the top of the slope overlooking the track and then moving down to their seat. In both cases there was a developing sense of anticipation until the hidden landscape of the speedway was finally revealed.

Water was a significant landscape feature at most of the early dirt tracks. At these speedways, water was required to prepare the track surface for competition. A water truck would be filled from the nearby stream or pond and would then wet down the track surface in preparation for the evening's races. At a few speedways, the pond was located in the speedway infield.[23] At least one speedway had an irrigation system that was used to wet down the track before each night's racing card.[24] Occasionally, the nearby pond would become a particularly spectacular race hazard.

There was little architectural embellishment to the speedway landscapes. However, the early speedways did develop a vocabulary of typical speedway structures. The most prominent structure at the first speedways was the flag or starter's stand. This was often nothing more than an elevated wooden platform from which the race officials could view the track and give flag commands to the participants. More permanent towers constructed of cinder block were erected at some later speedways. They housed speedway offices and rest rooms and provided protected seating for important guests. Some towers also included concession stands, but at most of the early speedways, the concession stands were simple wooden structures. Early on, most stock car races were held in the afternoon on Saturday and Sunday. Over time, many speedways added lights for night racing. Weeknight races were soon added to the schedules at many speedways. Today, remnant light poles are evocative reminders of past action at many of the abandoned speedway sites.

Documenting the sites, spatial organization, and structures of the speedways can provide only a partial understanding of the landscape of the Virginia speedways. A unique social landscape soon developed at the speedways. From its inception, stock car racing was, and remains today, a family activity. Fathers and sons, brothers, uncles, cousins, and wives and husbands participated in the sport as drivers, crew members, and in various support positions. The race was a day-long event, with drivers and crews arriving early to prepare for the testing and qualifying trials that preceded the afternoon or evening races. The speedways became places of family competition and celebration. Rooted in their communities through strong family ties, the speedways served an additional role as community social and recreational gathering places. Families and friends sat together in the same seating area each week, and the competition in the stands could rival that on the race track. Many participants note that the social landscape of the early speedways flourished in that time just before television became a central feature in American homes. In some communities the speedway became the site for numerous local events, including the circus, wrestling

matches, thrill shows, rodeos, motorcycle races, and drag races. Many speedways served as informal community centers in which gatherings for special events and for holidays such as the Fourth of July and Christmas
occurred. Many speedways still serve in this capacity today.[25]

Competitive by nature, drivers were eager to test their cars and skills
on other speedways and against the best drivers they could compete
against.[26] In response, speedways often coordinated their racing schedules
to allow drivers to race on several nights of the week at different speedways.
It was not at all uncommon for drivers to race on Friday and Saturday nights
and then again on Sunday afternoon, all at speedways within easy driving
distance of home. These informal racing circuits quickly extended the social
landscape of the speedways throughout the state. Hilltop Speedway at Zion
Crossroads, Cavalier Speedway in Charlottesville, and Douglas Speedway
in Ruckersville composed an early mid-state circuit in the 1950s.

Additional circuits evolved throughout the state. Prominent among
the early circuits was the circuit that included Fredericksburg Speedway at
the Fredericksburg Fairgrounds, Old Dominion Speedway in Manassas, and
Marlboro Motor Raceway in Marlboro, Maryland. Another early circuit in
the Shenandoah Valley included East Side Speedway in Waynesboro, Mas-
sanutten Speedway in Keezletown, and Valley Speedway in Staunton. Later,
Eastside Speedway would be part of a circuit that also included Natural
Bridge Speedway and the Craigsville Motor Speedway.[27] In Richmond in
the 1950s, drivers raced at Royall Speedway, New Richmond Speedway, the
Fairgrounds, and Cockade Speedway in Petersburg. In Tidewater, Dude
Ranch Speedway, Virginia Beach Speedway, and Princes Anne Speedway
constituted an early circuit that would later include Dog Track Speedway
in Moyock, North Carolina. In the New River Valley, several circuits developed, most notably a late–1960s circuit of Pulaski County Speedway,
Hillsville Speedway, and Pilot Speedway in Floyd County. Similar informal, regional circuits existed at various times throughout the state. A step
up in scale and competition was the more formally organized and promoted
Dixie Racing Circuit, which in 1952 sponsored races at Lynchburg, Danville,
and Roanoke, Virginia and at Henderson and Camp Butner, North Carolina.[28] Drivers from both states traveled the Dixie Circuit on a regular
basis. Bill France, Sr., the founder and head of NASCAR, worked during
this same period to establish that circuit as a regular feature of racing in
Virginia.[29] France promoted many early races in Martinsville, Roanoke,
Lynchburg, Danville, and Richmond in addition to Winston-Salem and
other nearby North Carolina cities.

As the sport grew, some speedways began to offer larger purses and better competition through the sponsorship of sanctioning bodies such as the
Dixie Racing Circuit and NASCAR. The result was the development of a

multi-level racing circuit frequented by the state's better drivers. These drivers often raced at local speedways on weeknights and then, seeking better competition and larger prize money, traveled farther distances to more competitive speedways with races on Saturday nights and Sunday afternoons. Some drivers raced as often as five times each week, racing at local speedways on Wednesday, Thursday, and Friday nights in preparation for each weekend's higher-level competition.[30] These drivers became local and regional celebrities with devoted followings. Their names were often included in the speedway advertisements, and some speedways paid appearance money to ensure the crowd would not be disappointed. Guaranteed appearance money induced the better drivers to appear regularly at tracks throughout the state. In the 1950s, for example, attracted by the guarantee of a $50 appearance fee, drivers from the New River Valley would regularly appear at races in the coal-field areas of far southwest Virginia.[31]

Many of the old Virginia speedways have long been abandoned and returned to crop fields, pasture, or forest. Others have been converted to parkland. Only a few speedways located in growing urban areas have been demolished and their sites built upon. The Virginia speedways, once active social spaces charged by racing competition and the racing circuits they delineated, constitute a significant cultural landscape that spanned the entire state and extended into North Carolina and other nearby states. The energy of the gatherings at the speedways is evident in panoramas of the lost speedway landscapes.

Today more than 20 Virginia racing venues remain in operation. Deeply rooted in their communities, they, like their predecessors, are landscapes of community pride, social intercourse, ritual, and entertainment. They are the heirs of the state's rich racing heritage and constitute, with their nearly forgotten predecessors, a Virginia landscape of historical importance and economic potential.

Notes

1. "Virginia Beach Inspection Trip," *The Automobile* (March 19, 1904): 315. See Randal L. Hall's "Before Nascar: The Corporate and Civic Promotion of Automobile Racing in the American South, 1903–1927" in *The Journal of Southern History*, vol. LXVIII, no. 3, August 2002. I'm indebted to Hall's discussion of this early interest in Virginia Beach as a racing venue.

2. "Virginia East Coast Association Formed," *The Automobile* (February 20, 1904): 240.

3. "Racing in Nashville," *The Automobile* (September 10, 1904): 302.

4. "Poor Sport in Washington," *The Automobile* (September 10, 1904): 298.

5. Baltimore Races July 4, *The Automobile* (July 13, 1905).

6. "Oldfield's Southern Circuit," *The Automobile* (March 29, 1906): 560.

7. Allan E. Brown, *The History of America's Speedways* (Comstock Park, Michigan: America's Speedways, 1994), 14.

8. Brown, 518–526.

9. The *Richmond Times Dispatch* noted on June 29, 1941, "Stock car racing … is sweeping the country like a prairie fire…." Stock car racing was not a new phenomenon. America's first stock

car race might have been held as early as 1907. It gained only a limited following in the years leading up to World War II. After the war, stock car racing was reintroduced by promoters and saw
growing popularity in the Midwest before finding its strongest support in the Southern states. See
Brown, 75–78.

10. *Richmond Times Dispatch*, July 1, 1941.

11. *Richmond Times Dispatch*, June 29, 1941.

12. *Richmond Times Dispatch*, July, 5, 1941.

13. Brown, 519–520 and the "AAA Contest Records, reel #23, Sanction Books, 1909–1950," Gordon White Archives.

14. Brown, 518–526. Period newspaper ads and articles often note the fact that a speedway was
located at the fairgrounds.

15. The importance of that region to the history of racing in Virginia was acknowledged when
the Virginia Legislature designated the counties of Halifax, Patrick, and Pittsylvania and the cities
of Martinsville, Danville, and South Boston as "Virginia's Racing Region." In reality, the region is
much larger.

16. Craigsville Motor Speedway was a true tri-oval. Period air photos of the Fincastle Fairgrounds reveal that its track might have been the state's first tri-oval. Alan Brown notes the New
Brunswick Speedway was a circular track. See Brown, 518.

17. Interviews with Lawrence Richardson, July 2002. Richardson attended the very first race at
Southwest Virginia Speedway in 1947.

18. Interview with Jim Jackson, son of the speedway owner and promoter, March 2002.

19. Interview with Carl Davis, March 2003.

20. A good clay surface would compact until it was hard, slick, and fast. A poor surface could
spell the end of a speedway. Piney Speedway near Fort Chiswell and Ararat Speedway just inside
Virginia north of Mt. Airy, North Carolina, were notorious for their poor racing surfaces. Neither
lasted more than a few years.

21. *Roanoke Times*, July 11, 1959, p. 11.

22. Interviews with Lawrence Richardson, July 2002.

23. Interview with Harlan Reynolds, Lynchburg, Virginia, December 2001. Harlan and others
have noted that 501 Speedway north of Volens had a pond in its infield.

24. Interview with Peanut Turman, Dugspur, Virginia, November 2001. The speedway was Log
Cabin Speedway in Henry County.

25. A good example is the New River Valley Speedway in Dublin, Virginia, which served as a
primary collection site for relief supplies for victims of flooding in nearby West Virginia in the
summer of 2001. The speedway also serves as a collection point for an annual Christmas toy drive
for needy children. The drivers compete as fiercely to collect the most toys as they do on the track.

26. Competition between drivers in different regions of the state was part of racing from the
beginning. In 1924 drivers in Norfolk challenged the drivers from Richmond to race at Norfolk's
Dixie Speedway. See the *Richmond Times Dispatch* article from May 1924 (date illegible) in the
Gordon White Archives.

27. Interview with Richard Fox and Arbil Welcher, Craigsville, Virginia, December 2001.

28. Advertisement, *The Lynchburg Virginia News*, April 18, 1952, collection of Harlan Reynolds.

29. The growth of the Virginia speedways parallels the growing popularity of stock car racing
throughout the South. The primary organizing body for stock car racing throughout the region
was NASCAR, founded in 1947 by Bill France.

30. Interview with Carlton Pugh, Danville, Virginia, November 2001.

31. Interview with Jim Jackson, Ivanhoe, Virginia, March 2002.

12

Kickin' Up Dirt and Puttin' Down Roots: Keith Simmons and NASCAR's Dodge Weekly Racing Series in Eastern Iowa

As Told to David "Turbo" Thompson

My whole life, I've been ate up by racin'.
— *Keith Simmons*

Keith Simmons is a renowned engine builder for NASCAR's Busch and Winston Cup series.[1] At Bill Davis Racing, he built motors for Jeff Gordon and Bobby Labonte. At Sabco Racing, he built the power plants for Kyle Petty, Joe Nemecheck, Kenny Irwin, Sterling Marlin, Wally Dallenbach, and Ted Musgrave. Simmons spent some time at Darrell Waltrip Motorsports, and he built motors for Dale Earnhardt while working at Childress Racing.

He resigned from big-time stock car racing in 2001 to begin a new career at age 46 as a dirt-track owner and stock car racing promoter in eastern Iowa. Simmons left North Carolina and moved to Iowa. He formed Simmons Promotions, Inc.,[2] which owns Farley Speedway in Farley, Iowa, a half-mile high-banked clay oval track. Simmons also holds the rights to hold stock car races at the Dubuque County Fairgrounds in Dubuque, Iowa, a three-eights-mile high-banked clay oval. And he promotes special events races at Scott County Fairgrounds in Davenport, Iowa. From 2001–2003, he promoted stock car races at West Liberty Speedway, a fairgrounds speedway in West Liberty, Iowa. These are all dirt tracks.

It takes awhile to get to know Keith Simmons.[3] He says he has always been shy and rarely makes eye contact. He usually looks down and to the left. But his words hit home. Simmons seems to have a rare ability to remember just about everything about stock car racing. He has a passion for preserving the history of the sport, and he remembers details about races, drivers and tracks that others might not have even noticed.

I have seen him walk through the pits during a race, then interview the winning driver by saying something like, "I'll tell you what. That was a heckuva move you put on the number 35 car in turn four on that last lap." Simmons had not seen the move, but he knew. He says he relies on what others tell him. I suspect he knows the sounds of the engines so well, he can hear one car pass another.

To know Keith Simmons, visit his race shop. It is a metal building near the pit gate at turn two of the Farley Speedway. The tools are put away. The floor is spotless. Two classic stock cars from the 1960s are in the process of being restored, a couple of new stock cars are being built, and a car hauler (a truck that carries a race car) is parked inside. But look closely at the walls.

I have interviewed a number of racers, from grass-roots racers in home garages or rotting barns to pro shops for ARCA and Winston Cup teams. There always has been a girlie poster on the wall. It was usually a calendar, a promotional product from a performance parts manufacturer that features long-legged, busty young beauties.

Not in Keith Simmons's shop. The only poster on his wall features a racing engine. No girl. No background. No words, except "Pontiac" on the valve cover. Pure, sexy power.

Simmons has three children and a nearly ex–wife. His 21-year-old daughter, Rachel, tried her hand at race promotion before moving back to North Carolina. Kyle, 19 years old, graduated from high school last year and now works at the track with his father. Kyle drove in several races during the 2003 season. Cliff, 15 years old, is a "damn good football player," his father says. Cliff lives in Davenport with his mother.

Simmons lives in the Palace Ballroom at the Farley Speedway. His big-screen television is near the bar. A black leather couch and recliner are positioned near the front door of the ballroom, a large metal building that is rented for special occasions, such as wedding receptions and company parties. He has a full restaurant-grade kitchen. His bed is in a corner near the kitchen. In the corner of the restroom is a shower stall and dressing area. A sign on the wall says "Private Shower."

This is not a first for Simmons. A machine shop he owned had a similar setup. "I'm always there," he says. "I'm never late for work."

Simmons is not all business, though. He has a surprising sense of humor. His version of the "ultimate racer's yard ornament" rests in the far end of the Palace Ballroom. It used to be an outdoor Christmas decoration. He calls it a reindeer, but it looks more like a "Chris-moose." It's about seven feet tall, six feet long and four feet wide. It has four Hoosier racing tires, a spoiler, and header pipes.

Cash flow is an issue for a stock car racing promoter. This is a sport that relies on good weather between April and September. When it rains, the track turns to mud and the week's racing program is cancelled. To minimize the financial impact of bad weather on his business, Simmons is a sales representative for 10 different companies that make high-performance automotive products. "I noticed these companies didn't have any sales reps going around to parts dealers to promote their product lines." Simmons says, "I figured, who better to represent high-performance products than a former Winston Cup engine builder?"

In 2004, Simmons was 50 years old. He continues to find his place in his new life as a track owner. An important part of that is mentoring. He does what he can to share his knowledge with those who are willing to listen and learn. He enjoys seeing young drivers develop their skills. He seems happiest, though, in the company of the living legends of Iowa dirt-track racing — the drivers he watched as a young man.

Drivers and mechanics gather around Simmons after the weekly racing program to drink a few beers and to hear his stories of life at the top as a Winston Cup engine builder. So gather 'round. Here is his story in his own words.

— David "Turbo" Thompson

I've been very, very fortunate to be associated with good people.
I've kinda let my talents shine through them.

— Keith Simmons

I'm originally from the Freeport, Illinois, area. I started out, like everybody, in the hobby stock support division. A car I built raced in the first event they ever had at the Farley Speedway back in 1969. I built my first car when I was 14 years old, but I didn't tell my dad about it until we started winning races.

I got into building engines basically because I couldn't get anybody to do it the way I wanted to do it. So I just did it myself. As I started doing my own racing engines, I needed more equipment. The only way I could really justify that was to start doing them for other people. So pretty soon I had a whole shop full of equipment. My dad and I were in the auto parts business, and I started a machine shop there.

The engine was always the most expensive thing. I never had any extra money, so the more I could do myself, the further my money went.

We got to where we were really consistent winners at the local level. We were the very first NASCAR Weekly Racing Series champions back in 1982. Tom Hurst was our driver at the time. We got a lot of exposure from that championship, and I got to meet a lot of people in NASCAR. I used that exposure to make some contacts with some teams down South.

Sometimes in life opportunity is there at the right time. I got into Winston Cup racing at the time the growth was really phenomenal. It got to be a really well-paying profession. The last year I was there I made right around $300,000. Ten years before that, the top guy in the sport wouldn't have made that.

Kickin' Up Dirt: Becoming a Race Promoter

There are a couple of reasons I decided to leave Winston Cup and buy the track at Farley. For one thing, the rule book in Winston Cup was getting way too thick for me. Eventually they're going to end up with a spec-type engine. So jobs as an engine builder for a race team will be tough to find. The jobs are just being eliminated.

I had the opportunity to start the Dodge program with Ray Evernham; I was seriously considering it. But I just didn't know if I could muster the energy to do what it takes to start over again.

The thing of it is, I was just too old. But I probably would have stayed in Winston Cup a few more years if the opportunity to buy the Farley Speedway hadn't come along at the same time.

Al Frieden owned Farley Speedway before I bought it. His health was starting to fail. I always told him, "Don't ever sell the place without letting me have first chance at it." He called me one day and said, "If you really are thinking about it, you'd better get up here and take a look at what's going on because I'm just not going to be able to do it much longer.

He was about 67 years old at the time. He passed away in the summer of 2000, shortly after I bought the track from him.

This wasn't the first track in Farley. You can still see a berm from one of the turns of the original track in a corn field just north of the current speedway. That first track was very successful from about 1948 until about '51.

The current Farley Speedway has been through several different owners. It was originally carved out by Irv Valentine and his family. There are quite a few of his descendents still left in the area. His oldest son, Butch, owns a car that races in our Pro Stock division. His grandson drives that car.

The Valentines really worked hard. They had about everything go against them, though. The weather, in particular. They were supposed to open in June of '69, and they didn't get going until September. They had a lot of setbacks, and they had one whole year that they had nothing but outgoing expenses and nothing coming in. I believe 1973 was their last year.

Then it sat for a few years.

Chuck Martell got it going again, and he had things turned around pretty well. He ran it for a year and a half. I believe that would have been 1979 and part of 1980. Then Chuck had a falling out with a few competitors and decided it was way too much work for the hassle. So he threw in the towel.

Then it sat vacant for another year.

The Bechen family reopened the track in '82. They ran that season, and I think they made it through all of '83, too.

Then it sat idle 'til '89, when Al Frieden bought it and resurrected it. Farley Speedway has been in continuous operation since then.

Improving the Property

The first year I got here, 2001, the biggest bad rap the place had was that it was a single-groove race track. It was tough to pass. So the races weren't as competitive as they should have been. Some of that was due to the tires they used to run. Some of it was due to the way they prepped the track. Some of it was due to the dirt that was on it.

We reconfigured the track in 2001. We've hauled in a different dirt surface. We've changed the way we prep the track. We've changed the equipment we prep it with. We've done everything in our power to turn that around. It seems to be paying off.

There are only five privately owned speedways in Iowa: Farley, Burlington, Stewart, Boone, and, I think it's Hawkeye Raceway in Blue Grass. All the other dirt tracks in Iowa are at fairgrounds and operated by county fair boards.

I can see why it ends up that way. Fairgrounds don't pay any property or sales tax. I've doubled my property tax in the past few years with all the improvements I've made here. And fairgrounds are tax-exempt. So they get to keep that 7 percent of concessions sales that a private owner gives up to the state as sales tax.

We've put in playgrounds, sky boxes, and better lighting. We installed Musco [brand] lighting, the same as some of the Winston Cup tracks have. It's TV-quality lighting.

We've put everything into one corporation, Simmons Promotions Incorporated, or SPI. The Palace Ballroom has been a real bright spot. When we have rain and during the winter when we can't race, we've got something going on in the ballroom that brings a little bit of revenue in. We rent the ballroom for wedding receptions and other parties. And we hold engine builder seminars there, too.

Nascar Weekly Racing Series

I've kind of come full circle. My car won the first NASCAR Weekly Racing Series national championship in 1982. That was the inaugural season for the NASCAR Weekly Racing Series. Now I'm a track owner with a NASCAR Dodge Weekly Racing Series sanction.

There's not much comparison between NASCAR's Weekly Racing Series and the next best thing in terms of point funds, quality of membership, instructional meetings, insurance, banquets, and promoters gatherings. There's nobody even in NASCAR's league.

Two years ago, the NASCAR Weekly Racing Series had almost 100 tracks. Now that number is down to 80. NASCAR is looking for the premier facilities in the country; they aren't interested in every racetrack that's out there. They're trying to bring more national corporate involvement into the Weekly Racing Series. Until about two years ago, the Weekly Racing Series of NASCAR was kind of separate from the NASCAR family as a whole. Now every company they bring in as a national sponsor is included in the NASCAR Weekly Racing Series. NASCAR is using all of its assets to promote this deal. It's really going to help promoters.

NASCAR does a lot for local tracks. It's great for local drivers to be able to tap into NASCAR's national point fund. For example, we paid Gary Webb $165,000 to be national champion. Jeff Aikey got about $40,000. In 2003, Ronnie Barker won a regional championship. Aikey won two track championships. It can be a big boost for a local weekly racer.

There may be an intangible value for drivers, too. If a driver is deciding whether to race at Darlington [Wisconsin], which doesn't have a NASCAR sanction, or Farley, then maybe he'll decide to run at Farley because of the connection to NASCAR.

On the promoters' side of it, there are advantages to being associated with NASCAR. There are dangers associated with this sport. If some catastrophic event were to happen, NASCAR's legal team would step in to help us out.

At Farley and Dubuque, we have a Craftsman night at the races. We have a U.S. Army night where they're out there soliciting people to sign up. On 3M night, they do a customer-appreciation thing. A lot of those promotions wouldn't be available to me if I didn't have the NASCAR sanction.

On the other side of the coin, sometimes NASCAR is our biggest competitor. If it's held on a night we race here, a televised Cup race takes 500 people out of our crowd.

Some people wonder why I run two tracks so close to each other. Farley and Dubuque are only about 20 miles away from each other. I think if you do it right, you build more of a following by doing it that way. We share a lot of the same fans, but not totally. Probably a third of our crowd attends both. If I were to give up promoting at Dubuque, somebody else would come in and do it. I think we're better off controlling our own destiny.

The Big Challenge: Attracting Spectators

This business really depends on good weather and getting a good crowd to every race. We can't do anything about the weather, but we do everything we can to attract attention to the speedways at Farley and Dubuque.

Now that NASCAR is directing its national sponsors to the Weekly Racing Series, we get the benefit of some of their national advertising.

Media coverage is another way to get some attention. It's really tough to get exposure for local auto racing in local newspapers. We're very, very fortunate that the *Dubuque Telegraph-Herald* is interested in racing. We get a front-page article every Saturday morning about our Friday-night races at Farley, and they do a front-page story every Monday morning on our Sunday-night races at Dubuque. That's tremendous. That really helps us, and we don't have to pay for that.

My predecessor didn't do much in the way of fan promotions. He was more on the competitors' side of things, which you can't ignore. But the fan side of the business pays the bills.

Not everyone's a race fan. But we can try to get everyone to come out once and see if they take an interest in racing. But it's like this: If somebody came and gave me a ticket to an art show, I wouldn't go even though it's free. We find the same thing when we give away race tickets. We've given away several hundred tickets at a time. Our actual response on a free ticket is only 27 percent. That's one of our biggest challenges — to make people race fans. We find that 60 percent of the people, if we get them there one time, will come back. But it's a battle to get them to the track the first time.

I know there are some people who say all there is to stock car racing is a bunch of cars going around in a circle. Well, to me, that's like someone who says, "Why play golf? You just chase the ball around." It's your perception of the sport. My argument is that if you go to a movie it's more expensive than going to a race. Probably someone has already told you the outcome of the movie, or you can figure it out way before it's over. But if you go to the race, it's never over 'til it's over. Something different happens with every race. And there's a family atmosphere at the track.

Stock car racing is exciting once you know what's going on. The best way to learn is to talk to the people who race. That's the really good thing about our sport at the local level. The competitors are so accessible. When the race is over, fans can walk across the straightaway, go into the pits and talk to drivers and mechanics. Most racers are really down-to-earth people. They're doing something they love, and they'll take time to talk to you if you're interested in what they do. They really like it when people take time to talk with them about their passion.

A lot of people that attend get started because a guy down the block has a car, or it's their nephew or whatever. And that's what gets them to come to the track in the first place.

In 2003, I had a consulting firm come in to do a market analysis. We found that 72 percent of our fans are homeowners. We're attractive to a more affluent resident of eastern Iowa than I thought we were. That surprised me. I really thought that we were on the low end of economics in terms of our fan base. Maybe that's our downfall. We don't have as many tried-and-true, blue-collar apartment renters coming out to see us.

This wasn't our first survey, though. The first year we did our survey, our average fan was 47 years old. I said, "Whoa! This is bad. That means we have a lot of 70-year-olds that aren't going to be with us here in a couple of years."

To attract a younger crowd and to make entry-level racing more afford-able, we introduced a four-cylinder class, the "Farley Flyers." Our weekly car count went up, which told us more competitors and their crews were coming out. And the average age of our fan lowered to 36. So I was pretty happy with that.

I still think a lot of the real young people are out of tune with what we do here. I really struggle on how to correct that. The young people of years ago were gearheads. You don't see much of that any more.

In terms of gender, the NASCAR demographic for a Winston Cup race is about 60 percent men and 40 percent women. But I think the reason for that is a lot of them travel to races as couples because you're there for a few of days and you make a long trip to get there.

At Farley, we get about 30 percent women. I don't have any actual black-and-white documentation on what that was 10 years ago, but I think it's probably a bigger share of women now than what it was.

Special Promotions

We've had at least one Winston Cup driver appear every year I've been here. I call in some old favors to get them to come.

Those are highly successful events if the weather cooperates. It's amazing the number of people that turn out to see the Winston Cup or Nextel Cup drivers. I have a hard time with that. I think there are more race fans now than there ever have been. But they're TV fans. It's real hard for us to draw them off the couch to come out and watch our events.

In 2003 when we had Ray Evernham, Kenny Schrader, and Bill Elliott — and they all raced; it was a heck of a night — it was the biggest crowd we've ever had, including the Yankee [Dirt Track Classic].[4] We put on a good show.

I thought, "Boy, this is great!" People are coming up to me smiling and saying, "This is cool! I haven't been here in 20 years; you've got the place fixed up so nice." And other people are saying, "We never knew this was here; this is great!"

I thought this is really doing just what I want it to do — get people excited about coming back to the speedway week after week.

We held that event on a Thursday night. We had eight days until the following Friday night when we raced again. That Friday, the weather was nice. People had another paycheck cycle go through their pockets, so they should have had money to spend. And we had less than an average crowd that week for our regular show. Evidently, we didn't entertain those people enough to make them want to come back.

We're looking for ways to make our events more entertaining and more fan-friendly. I've been going to hockey games and things like that to see what they do.

We are giving some ticket discounts to try to lure families in. We have raised the age for kids to get in free hoping that that'll make it easier for the whole family to come to the races.

I'm in this to make money. There's no doubt about it. But it's a long way to the bottom line. As I go along in this, I can see that I have to come up with some new idea in order to forge ahead. It's just like when I was on the competitive side of the business in Winston Cup. You've got to branch out and work in the gray areas of the rule book to get ahead.

Every expense that we have continues to go up. For example, after September 11, 2001, all of our insurance rates went up about 30 percent. But it's hard to relay that into the ticket price. So our challenge, and our only other option, is to sell more tickets.

We are so influenced by weather. We can do everything possible to get a big turnout. But if the weather's no good, it was all for nothing.

Legends Night

When I was a little kid, I remember all the champions and all the races my dad took me to. The first season I remember was 1959. I remember all those cars and all those drivers. I think we lose something if we lose that history. My idea is to have a tri-state [eastern Iowa, southwest Wisconsin, northwest Illinois] racing museum out there at Farley.

We have had a lot of really talented race people from this area. This place is rich in racing tradition and history from right after World War II. Racing in Freeport [Illinois] dates back to the early '30s. Every year, we're losing a few of the guys who raced around here right after the war. I try to keep up with gathering their memorabilia, if they want to get rid of it, and keeping it safe so it'll be around.

It's important. You can't go forward unless you know where you've been.

We have a Legends Night every year at Farley Speedway. Those guys who were my heroes, the guys I started with, come to the track to be honored. That's one reason I hold the Legends Night — because without them, I wouldn't have had the career I've had. Another reason I do it is a lot of those guys are getting into their early to mid–70s now. They really enjoy the camaraderie. They don't get to see each other much anymore.

You have a bond with your fellow competitors. You might hate the son of a bitch on race night. But you're all in it together. You all share the same frustrations. You all, at one time or another, shared the same glory. You all had bad things happen to you and you stuck it out and kept going through the years. I suppose you find that kind of bond in other sports. But racers really are a family of competitors.

I also hold the Legends event because so many of the new fans think racing in the tri-state area started just a couple of years ago. Racing around here really took off after World War II. There were a million old pre-war coupes around, and that's how it started. Without those guys putting forth the effort to get it going, we wouldn't have what we have today.

Legends Night is our chance to give something back to them.

Puttin' Down Roots: Growing the Sport

Fatherhood

I was not the best soccer dad or any of that because every weekend there was a race someplace. I missed out on a lot of that.

My oldest boy, Kyle, works for me at the race track; he just graduated from high school in 2003. He's trying to figure out what he wants to do with his life. He bought a race car last year, and I helped him with it.

That caused some controversy at the track. I think he won 11 features in a row. Some people thought he was getting preferential treatment, although I did disqualify him from a win out at Dubuque for being five pounds light. He said, "But Dad, can't you do something about that?!" I said, "You've gotta be the most legal car here, man. There's nothing I can do for ya. You're out." He understands. He catches a lot of flack from everyone because he's the promoter's kid. The truth is he really outworks those guys.

I don't know what Kyle will do with his life. I'd like for him to get a college education to go along with the practical experience. Maybe get a little bit of engineering. He has aspirations of doing the Nextel Cup thing as a mechanic of some kind. I could open some doors for him, but I'm not going to let him go until he's ready. If he really wants to do it, I'll help him every way I can.

If I were a good football player, I'd be neglecting my duty as a dad not to help my son play football if that's what he wants to do. My expertise is in racing, so I do teach him a lot. But he does all the work. This is finally my chance to be soccer dad.

The kids never really said anything, but I'm sure my time on the road with race teams [about 50 weeks a year] had some effect over the years.

I'm sure if they had their druthers, they would've wished I was there a little bit more. I gave up a lot to race. Maybe it's not too late to get a little back.

Mentoring

I help anybody that wants help. I'll let anybody use the shop as long as they're really trying hard. I don't charge anything for my help. A lot of kids that are just starting out don't have any extra money. They've got everything tied up in the car already.

You never know when another Jeff Gordon will come along. The way these guys hone their skills is to race local tracks like Farley and Dubuque.

These days, the learning curve for Nextel Cup drivers seems to get shorter and shorter. The equipment at NASCAR's top level is so much better than it ever has been. That seems to make it easier for these young kids to come in and drive. It used to be you had to work your way up into a good car. It appears now that damn near all of them are good. It's really having the reflexes and the brash youngness that just gives you a little bit more balls to go fast. Now it seems like these kids can get into a car and be competitive right away.

But you have to have it all at that level. It's not enough just to have driving talent. You have to be able to talk to people and get along well in the environment that they throw you into. It's really intense. It's as intense off the track as it is on the track. How you handle yourself and how you communicate with your crew. How you intermingle with your sponsors and team owner. That is just as important as how well you can drive. These kids are hitting the big time with all that.

Drivers don't have much time to prove themselves these days. They've got to be on their way to North Carolina by 18.

I don't try to push what I know onto anybody. A lot of guys are pretty set in their own ways. They've been successful, and they have their own way of doing things. I respect them for that. On the other hand, some guys want to get some information. Maybe they don't have it all figured out. If they ask, I'll give my advice. But in the end, they have to decide what to do.

Everybody races for a different reason. Some people get to a certain intensity level, then, as they get older and they get a family and what not, that deteriorates. There are very few guys who stay in this for 25 or 30 years. Most racers are as far as they're going to go in 5 or 6 years, and then they either maintain that for a couple of years or they're out. If you look at the history of racing, it has always been that way.

Priorities in life change.

The Future for Keith Simmons at Farley Speedway

I really like doing this. It can be frustrating too, though. The more I'm around it, the more I don't understand it.

When I started this three years ago, I had a million ideas, and I thought they would all work. I've gone through so many of those ideas, and very few of them have worked. The people business is really funny. There are so many things competing for the entertainment dollar in eastern Iowa — bars, bands, casinos. On top of all that, we compete for people's time spent with the Internet and 100 TV channels. When you look back at pictures of crowds that are in this area at the races in the '50s, it's just unbelievable. We couldn't get anywhere near those crowds today, and our show is so much better and so much better organized. But back then they had three TV stations if they had TV at all. Nobody had air conditioning. So on a cool night, the best place to be was outside. People got tired of watching three TV stations. There was no casino, and there was no civic center. So when you put all that into the mix, it just cuts our segment of the pie much smaller.

But I like to watch people starting out in racing. And I like to see the veterans who were here when I started. It's just a good mix of people. I like being around race people.

I'm real content with what I'm doing, but I've dug myself a pretty big debt here. I've about knifed my living expenses back to nothing, and I can stand the test here for quite a while. Unless something unforeseen happens health-wise, I'll be here quite awhile. When it's all said and done and they put me in the ground, I guess they'll write on my tombstone, "Racer."

I really feel this part of the country is where I belong. My roots are here. It all goes back to the early days.

Joe Finn from Stockton, Illinois, was the guy who was winning all the races when I was a kid. He was my hero. I never talked to Joe Finn back then. Dad used to take me down to the pits after the races were over. I was pretty shy; I never had much to say. But I was watching everything and taking it all in.

I found one of Joe Finn's old race cars, a '39 Chevy. It last raced in 1963. I've restored it.

Then I actually found the car that belonged to Finn's tooth-and-nail competitor. I'm restoring it, too. It's about half done. It's a '38 Dodge with a 392 Hemi in it. It was driven by Todd Cole from Monroe, Wisconsin.

When I get them both done, my buddy and I will take them out on the track one night, turn the lights on and settle the score — find out which one's really faster.

Notes

1. In 2004, Nextel became the primary sponsor for NASCAR's premier stock car racing series. Now the Winston Cup series is known as the Nextel Cup series. NASCAR is the National Association for Stock Car Auto Racing (http://www.nascar.com).

2. The official Web site of Simmons Promotions Inc. may be found at http://www.simmonspromotionsinc.com.

3. This chapter is the result of three years of getting to know Keith Simmons. The information presented here was gathered during three interviews: November 6, 2002; November 12, 2003; and March 21, 2004. I gathered additional material by observing races, and by participating (twice) as a competitor at the speedways in Farley and Dubuque.

4. The Yankee Dirt Track Classic is an annual four-day special event held in mid–September, after the regular racing season. Promoter Al Frieden began "the Yankee" in 1978.

13

The NASCAR Fan as Emotional Stakeholder: Changing the Sport, Changing the Fan Culture

Barbara S. Hugenberg and
Lawrence W. Hugenberg

By all recent accounts in marketing and sports publications, the fastest-growing spectator sport in the United States is NASCAR.[1] Racing fans flock to tracks across the country to participate in the NASCAR experience — camping, tailgating, qualifying time trials, frequently the Busch Series Race, pre-race rituals, the race, and post-race celebrations — weekend after weekend from February through November. NASCAR fans have evolved from the early days as a Southern phenomenon drawing good ol' boys to tracks all over the Southeast. David Ronfeldt, author of *Social Science at 190 MPH on NASCAR's Biggest Speedways* argued NASCAR fans are no longer only Southern rednecks; NASCAR fans are now urbanites, well-educated, middle-class professionals.[2] A staff writer for *Retail Merchandiser* suggested;

> NASCAR fans today reflect a cross section of America: rural, suburban, and urban dwellers, professionals and blue-collar workers, male and female, young and old. What do they have in common? They all love the thunderous sound of fast cars driven side-by-side by regular guys from regular families.[3]

We have said elsewhere, "NASCAR fans are different from fans of other professional sports in several ways — loyalty to sponsors, lack of specific geographic boundaries, and loyalty to the individual driver."[4] Although the geographic center for NASCAR fandom is gravitating north and west away from the Southeast, today's NASCAR fans are no less passionate and devoted than the fans following the pioneers of NASCAR from the beaches at Daytona to the dirt tracks in North Carolina. NASCAR forced changes in fandom by organizational decisions designed to alter the sport and the historic competition while trying to maintain many of the traditions noted in pre-race and victory lane ceremonies.

Although there have been many decisions made by NASCAR over the years that have affected the fan culture (e.g., developing common race-car templates, restrictor-plate racing, racing to the yellow flag, the "Lucky Dog" rule,[5] using the red flag during a race,[6] changing championship cup sponsors, focusing on diversity recruitment, recruiting Magic Johnson to assist in this all-important issue, negotiating television broadcast contracts and broadcasting expectations), two high-profile decisions made for the 2004 and 2005 Nextel Cup seasons have brought controversial changes to the sport. First, NASCAR made the decision, beginning with the 2004 season, to change the championship points race from a 36-race competition to a 26-race "qualifying season" and then a 10-race sprint to the championship for the top 10 drivers (or all drivers within 400 championship points of the leader after the first 26 races)—otherwise known as the "Race for the Championship." Second, NASCAR decided, beginning with the 2005 racing season, to move two races from historic and fan-popular Southern tracks (Darlington Raceway in Darlington, South Carolina, and North Carolina Speedway in Rockingham) to different tracks (Texas Motor Speedway in Fort Worth and Phoenix International Raceway in Avondale, Arizona). This decision reduces the number of NASCAR races at Darlington and means that Rockingham will no longer host a NASCAR race.

NASCAR fans, because of their emotional attachment to the NASCAR nation, are forced into the position of accepting the cultural changes and their impact or giving up their relationship with NASCAR and their favorite driver(s). As noted by David Poole, who covers NASCAR racing for the *Charlotte Observer*, NASCAR

> is in the same place that professional baseball was in Brooklyn (New York) in the 1950s—there is a [deep] connection with the fans.... The Brooklyn Dodgers were more than just Brooklyn's baseball team, they were part of the fabric of the community. That's what racing is to many fans. They are very parochial, intense and protective of their sport.[7]

Because fans are so emotionally attached to the weekly NASCAR experience, they view themselves as important stakeholders in the NASCAR organization. Regardless of whether NASCAR shares this perception with its fans, it is the socially created reality shared by the fans.

The NASCAR Fan as Organizational Stakeholder

Abbass Alkhafaji's description of organizational stakeholders in sports organizations includes the community of fans. Stakeholders, he wrote, are "those groups with a direct interest in the survival of the corporation; without their support the corporation might cease to exist."[8] Stanley Deetz included in his description of stakeholders all members in a host community who will be influenced by the organization.[9] Fans are groups upon which sports franchises depend for their existence, but there is something at stake for the fans, also. Fans are important to their drivers and their drivers' teams, and teams are important to their fans. The emotional attachment between the fan and driver cannot be underestimated. Nick Trujillo, in his landmark baseball and ballpark culture study, discovered that fans and athletes "unite in ritual and tradition" and "share a common sense of reality."[10] This dynamic view of fans as stakeholders, he claimed, "explains why fans attend games even when their team is losing and why 'hard core' fans remain in the ballpark for hours during rain delays."[11] NASCAR fans, no less "hard core" than baseball, football, or soccer fans, endure long races of four to five hours, occasionally with interminable rain delays, long post-crash clean-ups at the larger tracks, and searing summer heat. They are more than spectacle watchers, they are cultural collaborators—participating members of a fan culture shaped and reshaped with each new race and each new season. Therefore, conceptualizing fans as stakeholders is appropriate because of the symbiotic relationship between NASCAR administrators, owners, drivers, and fans.

Because fans represent an affective and not financial connection to the NASCAR organization and its drivers, they may be thought of as emotional stakeholders. Fans are emotional stakeholders according to their "affective sensibilities" and "affective alliances."[12] Fans let NASCAR "organize their emotional and narrative lives and identities" as they manage the sport — the spectacle of NASCAR.[13]

Much of fan behavior has been portrayed as irrational, dysfunctional, and/or pathological.[14] Few studies have attempted to represent the "authentic voices of the fans."[15] "Fans are typically marginalized," Kari Whittenberger-Keith says and labeled "crazies" by the media.[16] Henry Jenkins, in discussing sports fans, observed,

> To speak as a fan is to accept what has been labeled a subordinated position within the cultural hierarchy, to accept an identity constantly belittled or criticized by institutional authorities. Yet it is also to speak from a position of collective identity, to forge an alliance with a community of others in defense of tastes which, as a result, cannot be read as totally aberrant or idiosyncratic.[17]

NASCAR fans portray their emotional connections, and the commonly held notion that fans' emotional behaviors are irrational or faulty. Fans are important organizational stakeholders whose views and values are vital to NASCAR and its financial success.

Corporate responsibility is key to the success of an organization in the contemporary marketplace.[18] An institution is permitted to exist only if it meets its constituents', or in NASCAR's case fans', expectations and does what society demands. Is NASCAR listening to the voices of its fan constituency groups? Does NASCAR take the fans seriously as important organizational stakeholders? In a true organizational democracy the interests of all groups affected by the organization should be carefully and ethically considered.[19] Listening to the voices of the various constituency groups is important to a broader understanding of the meanings constructed in organizing. NASCAR fans are emotional stakeholders whose socially experienced values, beliefs, behaviors, and practices shape their identities as members of the larger NASCAR community — regardless of their driver loyalty.

For example, for decades fans of NASCAR were able to understand the scoring system used to determine NASCAR's annual champion driver.[20] They might not have always agreed that the person deemed champion was indeed the best driver in any given year, but they came to understand the weekly racing strategies used by drivers and their race teams to position themselves to contend for the title. For example, sometimes making a late-race pit stop for fuel prevents a driver from contending for first place but keeps the car from running out of gas, just as changing tires late in the race costs valuable time but improves the handling of the car. In this way the driver collects more championship points by finishing 12th or 15th than by running out of gas and finishing 34th or 35th. In 2004, NASCAR the organization turned this familiar NASCAR tradition over by changing the rules to determine the drivers' championship. In the weeks and months prior to the 2004 season, NASCAR fans demonstrated their displeasure with the new system. NASCAR owners responded by pointing out that no driver in history had won the championship points race after being 400 points behind with 10 races left in the season. They argued that the last 10 races would be more exciting. Even the drivers expressed their displeasure with the new format. In fact, Ryan Newman, a talented young driver, was openly critical of the 10-race chase. However, in a twist of irony, he found himself over 400 points behind after the first 26 races yet in the top 10 in the standings. As a result, he was seeded in the "Race for the Cup."[21] One driver and his fans who might not be too happy with the new "Race for the Cup" is Jeff Gordon, who, under the old scoring system, would have captured his fifth NASCAR championship in 2004 instead of finishing third. To be fair, it might take several seasons using the new format to render an informed judgment about its impact on NASCAR, its teams and drivers, and the fans.[22]

Changing the Championship Point System

For several decades, the Winston Cup Championship point system used the entire NASCAR racing season to determine its champion. As noted previously, points were awarded based on the driver's particular finish in each race (first place receiving the most points, second the second most, and so on) with additional points awarded if the driver led a lap during the race or led the most laps during the race. Over the 36-race season, the driver with the most points was recognized as the Winston Cup Champion. Being the Winston Cup Champion was the goal for all the drivers because of the prestige of the award and the monetary prize associated with being the champion. Frequently, however, the driver who won the most races during the year did not win the Winston Cup. The point system rewards consistently high finishes throughout the racing season (top fives and top tens), and few DNFs ("did not finish") or poor finishes (30th or lower). For example, the 2002 Winston Cup Champion, Tony Stewart, won three races, two fewer than Matt Kenseth, who finished eight in the final standings. However, Stewart had fifteen races where he finished in the top five — more than any other driver that year. Stewart did not clinch the championship until the results of the last race of the 2002 season at Homestead, Florida. In 2003, the last Winston Cup Champion, Matt Kenseth, won only one race all season — far fewer than Ryan Newman. Yet Kenseth clinched the championship well before the last race of the season and, in fact, finished last during that final race of the 2003 season at Homestead. All of the drama regarding the championship was over weeks before the final race — a concern for NASCAR, its sponsors, and the networks. This concern was a direct result of television ratings, money, and sponsor exposure. Whenever a champion is crowned based on the results of 36 different events, there are going to be fans and, unfortunately, media commentators who do not like the system that determined that champion. Their reasons for complaining are as varied as a crowd of NASCAR fans. However, the tradition of NASCAR was to reward consistent performance instead of drivers with too many peaks (wins and top-five finishes) and valleys (DNFs or finishing out of the top 20 places in races). Fans, drivers and sponsors were, for the most part, comfortable with this system of determining the points champion at the end of the season.

Before the 2004 season, NASCAR announced a change in the point system "race" for the Cup Championship. This announcement coincided with NASCAR's finding a new corporate sponsor, Nextel. The former cup sponsor, Winston, and NASCAR mutually agreed to end their long-standing relationship. Because NASCAR continues to market the sport to young, technologically sophisticated potential fans, Nextel was a perfect fit. Although the points would be awarded to the drivers in the same way, the points for the first 26 races of the season would determine which drivers would be eligible to compete for the 2004 Nextel Cup Championship. The top 10 drivers at the end of these 26 races—and all drivers within 400 points of the leader—would be eligible to compete for the 2004 championship. NASCAR selected the 400-point exception rule based on their research that no driver had ever come from 400 points behind the leader with 10 races to go to win the annual championship.

Fans, willing to express their opinions regarding the change in the scoring system, were overwhelmingly against it. One wrote in *Scene Magazine*, "You have fans and media clamoring for a revision in points, because things didn't work out the way they thought they should. New fans and new media don't seem to have a lot of respect for the sport and where it came from. The instant gratification generation strikes again. The lack of respect isn't all on the track."[23] The theme of discontent continued when a fan wrote the next month, "NASCAR can color me goodbye at the end of 26 races this season. As a longtime fan, my interest has been waning in recent years with all the Mickey Mouse stuff NASCAR has been pulling—mostly in favor of the almighty dollar."[24] Another fan, also unhappy with the new scoring system, wrote,

> I have been a fan for 30 years, attending numerous cup events, watch nearly all the televised races that I did not attend, and spent thousands of dollars on souvenirs. The present point system had properly crowned the season champion in all of the NASCAR divisions.... To show my disapproval to the proposed plan, I have renewed my last race ticket and will not view the final 10 races. If the proposal comes to fruition, this will be my last year as a fan of NASCAR.[25]

In the same issue, another fan lamented, "NASCAR has finally taken the excitement out of the sport with this playoff thing for 2004. I have been a NASCAR fan since 1968 and attended six races a year minimum, and sometimes eight to ten, but that will all change in 2005. (I have already paid for the 2004 season.) Goodbye, NASCAR, I will not be returning."[26] A more adamant fan stated, "You told us straight to our faces that we were less important than channel-flipping National Football League and Major League Baseball fans. You swapped history and tradition for an artificially created farce for the championship."[27]

Fans, who recognized their lack of importance within the NASCAR organization, expressed their opinions to *Scene Magazine*. Although they understand that their dollars support NASCAR in many ways, many fans concluded they were not an important consideration when it came to NASCAR's deliberations on changing the championship scoring system. One wrote, "NASCAR has always boasted that it is a fan-driven sport, yet they refuse to listen to the fans about the new system. Well, fans, maybe it's time to think of boycotting NASCAR and/or its sponsors to show them that we feel the new system stinks."[28] In the same issue, another fan let his feelings be known and reiterated the call for a boycott:

> Though I am not alone in my contempt for NASCAR's new scoring system, it is obvious that fan opinion means nothing to Nextel, NASCAR Chairman Brian France and President Mike Helton. What does matter is money. So, if you want to get their attention, put your money where your mouth is and treat Nextel and other official sponsors of NASCAR as if they were covered in anthrax.[29]

Although the overwhelming sentiment among NASCAR fans was that the change to the new scoring system was a mistake, there were those who thought the change was a good idea. One fan wrote, "I can deal with all the changes that NASCAR has made this year...."[30] Another wrote:

> I just find it hard to hear people say they won't watch races, whether it is the last 10 or the whole season if they are honest-to-goodness fans. I have been watching races since the days of Cale Yarborough, Richard Petty, Bobby and Donnie Alison and will continue to watch races with Ryan Newman, Jamie MacMurray and the new drivers. I don't always agree with some of the attitudes of these youngsters, but I love the sport. Give it a chance.[31]

Finally, another follower wrote in the same issue, "All I have been hearing and reading is that nobody likes the new point system. No matter what officials try to do to update or improve NASCAR, they can't please everybody."[32] With the overwhelming evidence illustrating that fans believed the new points system is not an improvement *and* that their opinions on the issue do not interest NASCAR, it is no wonder that when examining the evidence, one might conclude that NASCAR management is forcing this cultural change on the rest of the organization (owners, crews and drivers), including the fans.

NASCAR Changes Tracks

The second decision made by NASCAR beginning with the 2005 season was to move two races from popular, historic venues. One of two races held at Darlington Raceway will be moved to Fort Worth, Texas, and the remaining race will take place on an entirely different weekend (Mother's Day weekend). The only NASCAR race held at the North Carolina Speedway in Rockingham will be moved to Arondale, Arizona. Both Darlington and Rockingham have been traditional NASCAR tracks for more than five decades, and the move signifies an obvious distancing by NASCAR of some of its Southern roots and stereotypes (a rural, white male sport). Art Weinstein noted,

> NASCAR, born and bred in the Carolinas and in Daytona Beach, Fla., continues to push westward like a modern-day Lewis and Clark expedition. In the last decade or so, NASCAR has added races in Chicago, Kansas City, Indianapolis, Las Vegas, Texas and California. In the past year, two of those tracks, Texas and California, along with Phoenix have been granted second races.[33]

Even before the final decision was announced by NASCAR on May 14, 2004, one fan wrote *Scene Magazine*, "I am tired of flipping through the letters to find nothing but Southern boys whining about North Carolina Speedway losing a date. You guys don't even sell out the races you have in the South…. You keep saying that this is a national sport, so let's make it a little more national. We like racing out here, too."[34] The two new racing locations are in Texas and Arizona — newer superspeedways located near a growing geographic base of fans. The decision to change racing venues does have some context. Mark Ashenfelter concluded;

> Sure North Carolina Speedway will be missed. And there are those who will have only one chance per season to tame Darlington Raceway. Those views, however, took a back seat to the harsh economic realities of the sport when NASCAR released its 2005 schedule on May 14 [2004].[35]

Depending on whose interpretation of events one believes, the decision to move two races from the traditional Southeast NASCAR "homeland" to different locations was the result of different things. First, it is clear that these decisions resolved a long-standing lawsuit against NASCAR and Bill France, Jr., president of NASCAR, regarding their monopoly on determining race locations and dates. According to an analysis by the staff at *Scene Magazine*, Bill France, Jr., and his family received approximately $96 million by selling Martinsville Speedway in Martinsville, Virginia, to Speedway Motorsports, Inc. (SMI).[36] The additional race for Phoenix International Speedway merely means that International Speedway Corporation (ISC) moved races from one of its tracks, North Carolina Speedway, to another. Second, SMI received a second race at its Texas Motor Speedway. Third, both Darlington Raceway and North Carolina Speedway failed to sell out their races, while both Phoenix International Raceway and Texas Motor Speedway sell out their NASCAR races. Kenny Bruce wrote, "Both Rockingham and Darlington have been the subject of rumors in previous years. Despite exciting racing, lagging ticket sales have left both facilities fighting to keep their races."[37] A fourth reason for the decision to change race venues is that television broadcasts gain larger markets (Dallas–Fort Worth and Phoenix [the 15th largest media market] instead of Rockingham, North Carolina, and Darlington, South Carolina). By racing in these larger markets a second time each season, NASCAR, its sponsors, and the networks hoped for increased ratings for the other races by growing the fan base. Similarly, one might suggest that the decision makers at NASCAR believe that their fan bases in the Carolinas will not abandon NASCAR as a result of the change. Since most of the official explanations for these changes focus on the financial gains by all parties, one fan wrote to *Scene Magazine*, "It's a sad time in auto racing when millionaires decide to fill their stands and their pockets, while many of us tune out and go to the mall."[38] Steve Waid, a regular contributor to the magazine, agreed with this fan's perspective:

[G]ood business comes with a price. It has alienated many longtime NASCAR supporters who feel the sanctioning body has shunned their allegiance for the dollars. NASCAR has tried, and continues to try, to convince them that it is not shunning them but rather it is bringing to them a whole new and bigger world of racing that is, after all, something it must do and will continue to do. It will be hard to convince the grassroots fans of this. For them, tradition has become a myth, and their choices are to accept it or move on. Some will accept it. Others will move on.[39]

NASCAR fans like competitive racing regardless of the track. North Carolina Speedway in Rockingham has historically provided tremendous racing competition. Jeff Owens wrote, "But who outside the state of Texas can honestly say they would rather see a race at Texas than at gritty, old Rockingham? Certainly not the competitors. And certainly not the fans. This year's thrilling finish aside, the races at Texas—and most other 1.5-mile tracks—pale in comparison to shows at The Rock."[40] His comment refers to the fact that the competitors on longer tracks are better able to distance themselves from each other than on the shorter, more traditional tracks such as Rockingham.

The decisions made resulting in relocating two races to new tracks provide additional justification to many NASCAR fans who already feel marginalized by the organization. One fan wrote in *Scene Magazine*,

NASCAR makes such a big deal about being fan friendly and how important the fans are, and yet they go right ahead and give second races to two tracks at the expense of two of the tracks that helped make NASCAR what it is today. If NASCAR really cared about longtime fans, they would never take races away from Rockingham and Darlington.[41]

Another wrote in the same issue, "NASCAR has done it again, taking away from tracks that made the sport what it is today. All because they didn't want to open their financial records to the public."[42] As part of the lawsuit resolved by these decisions, plaintiffs sought to have privately owned NASCAR reveal it finances. This was something NASCAR was not willing to do and, as a result, it made the organization more willing to settle the lawsuit before it went to court. It did not want to risk losing on this financial disclosure component of the original lawsuit. In the same issue of *Scene Magazinge*, still another lamented, "Do the fans who buy tickets to these events mean anything? Do the fans who watch the races on TV mean anything? Do the fans who support these sponsors mean anything?"[43] Finally, one fan concluded, "Taking away the last race date at The Rock is paramount to tearing down Doubleday Field because it doesn't draw as many fans as Yankee Stadium."[44]

Fans believe NASCAR betrayed the sport in taking races away from two of the tracks that helped define NASCAR for decades. Not only do the fans in North Carolina and South Carolina support NASCAR at the tracks, they are also among the largest NASCAR television broadcast audiences.[45] Because of the high emotional stakes NASCAR fans create for themselves, they bemoan the fact that they are not considered important when these decisions are made that affect their sport. As evidenced by the two examples discussed here, NASCAR fans are loud and passionate about their sport. They have strong, emotional feelings about how NASCAR should promote itself and its competition.

Conclusion

NASCAR is making organizational decisions in an attempt to alter its older image as a Southern, redneck, white male sport. NASCAR wants to move itself into the information age by using available technologies to promote the sport, communicate with its fans, and develop communications media to solicit and secure new fans. A subtle example of this transformation was pointed out by a fan in *Scene Magazine*: "The soundtrack of the sport slowly changed from country to western to high-energy rock 'n' roll.... It's kind of interesting that as the music changed to the more aggressive rock, so did the personality shown by some of the drivers and the 'fans.'"[46] The change of corporate sponsors from Winston to Nextel is another indicator that NASCAR is taking the sport into a new era. One fan warns, "You cannot move forward without respecting your past. Sure, you can take a date from Rockingham and even mess with tradition and swap dates to give California the Labor Day weekend, but remember NASCAR started in the Southeast, and that's where its home is. Remember your past!"[47]

NASCAR is changing — maybe because it has to, maybe because it wants to — but it is changing. Change is inevitable for such an organization as it continues to try to grow in popularity by increasing track attendance, Nielsen ratings, and sponsorship dollars. The organizational decisions made within NASCAR affect its fans, from the most passionate to the disengaged. One wrote, "There are too many changes at one time for fans to absorb. We're exhausted trying to keep up with them all.... And, the worst thing of all that NASCAR has done is to never pay attention to what the fans want."[48] It would behoove NASCAR to listen better to its fans as emotional stakeholders in what is going on with the tracks, the competition, and the Cup. NASCAR fans carry different cultural determinants and possess multiple cultural perspectives. However, it seems NASCAR is dragging its fans along — some willingly and others begrudgingly — as emotional stakeholders into one vision for the sport. Why does it do this to its millions of fans? The answer rests in the current success of the sport on and off the tracks: *Because it can!* However, if its successes mean the sport retains fewer fans or its television ratings drop, the relationship between NASCAR and its fans will also change. Tom Sorensen perhaps sums up why NASCAR pulls its emotional stakeholders along in any direction it sees fit:

> If baseball and basketball pushed their fans as hard as NASCAR pushes its, asking them to spend a half day in their cars to get to and from a game that is called because of dampness, fans would revolt. To race fans the concept of revolt is so alien there is no word for it. I have a dog, and I sometimes pretend I'm going to throw the ball into the yard. But I don't let the ball go. Still, the dog will run as if I did, and it will do it every time. NASCAR fans are like that. No matter how often their sport teases them, they believe that the next time, they won't.... Racing is the most technologically advanced sport in the land, but race fans still live in 1955. They don't demand. They accept.[49]

A change announced by NASCAR for the 2005 Nextel Cup season shortens race weekends for race teams by eliminating "Happy Hour," moving track testing to Fridays, and conducting race qualifying on Saturdays. Track owners of Atlanta Motor Speedway, Bristol Motor Speedway, Las Vegas Motor Speedway, Lowe's Motor Speedway, and Martinsville Speedway announced their resistance to NASCAR's decision and will keep the traditional, fan-friendly weekend schedule.[50] Given these dramatic organizational decisions, fans should not be surprised if NASCAR takes one or both races from Martinsville and the remaining race at Darlington and moves them to new and larger markets in the Pacific Northwest and the New York City area. The organization might also level the racing field by handicapping "field-fillers"[51] — giving them a head start so they can compete with the higher-profile teams that have more sponsor money. And don't be surprised if NASCAR's traditional "made-in-America" moniker is supplanted when teams racing Toyotas enter the Nextel Cup Series. (Toyotas were raced for the first time in the Craftsman Truck series in 2004.) Fans might also suffer NASCAR's revenue-sharing plan, so all teams can afford the necessary equipment and testing facilities, and a ban on coolers at the tracks.

Notes

1. Scott Huler, *A Little Bit Sideways: One Week Inside a NASCAR Winston Cup Race Team* (Osceola, WI: MBI Publishing, 1999); Lewis Lord, "The Fastest-Growing Sport Loses Its Hero." *U.S. News & World Report* 130 (2001): 52.

2. David Ronfeldt, "Social Science at 190 MPH on NASCAR's Biggest Speedways," *First Monday* 5 (2000): 1–29.

3. "Fan-tastic Fans: NASCAR Fans Are Younger and More Affluent than the U.S. Population and Spread Coast-to-Coast," *Retailer Merchandiser* 42 (June 2002): 14.

4. Barbara S. Hugenberg and Lawrence W. Hugenberg, "If It Ain't Rubbin,' It Ain't Racin': NASCAR, American Values and Fandom," *The Journal of Popular Culture* (at press).

5. The "Lucky Dog Rule" was introduced by NASCAR near the end of the 2003 season to prevent drivers from racing to the start-finish line when a caution or yellow flag is used due to a wreck on the track, an oil spill, or the spotting of debris on the track. Historically, drivers created dangerous conditions when they would try to race the leader back to the start-finish line to get a lap back. The "Lucky Dog Rule" stops racing back to the start-finish line first by freezing the field at that instant and second by automatically allowing the first driver one lap down to get his lap back and start at the end of the racing line of all drivers on the lead lap when the caution ends.

6. NASCAR uses the red flag when race conditions are too dangerous to continue racing. Typically, a red flag is used when it rains or when the safety of the clean-up crews is in danger because there is too much debris or oil on the track. All cars are stopped on the track until racing conditions become safe again. Drivers and crews are not permitted to work on their cars during a red flag. When the race is restarted, there is a single line of cars starting in the same position in the race as when the red flag was issued. Sometimes during red flag periods caused by debris on the track or an oil spill, cars are stopped right on the track. Other times, as when the red flag is caused by weather, cars are parked in pit row.

7. In Richard Ernsberger, Jr., *God, Pepsi, and Groovin' on the High Side: Tales from the NASCAR Circuit.* (New York: M. Evans and Company, 2003), 8–9.

8. Abbass Alkhafaji, *A Stakeholder Approach to Corporate Governance: Managing in a Dynamic Environment.* (New York: Quorum, 1989), 103.

9. Stanley Deetz, *Transforming Communication, Transforming Business: Building Responsive and Responsible Workplaces.* (Cresskill, NJ: Hampton Press, 1995). See also: Joanne Martin, *Cultures in Organizations: Three Perspectives* (New York, Oxford Press, 1992) for an excellent discussion of the importance of organizational cultures to all stakeholders in the organization.

10. Nick Trujillo, "Interpreting (the work and the talk of) Baseball: Perspectives on Ballpark Culture," *Western Journal of Communication* 56 (1992): 363. For another interesting study on baseball fans see, Nick Trujillo, "Hegemonic Masculinity on the Mound: Media Representations of Nolan Ryan and American Sports Culture," *Critical Studies in Mass Communication* 8 (1991): 290–308.

11. Trujillo, 364.

12. Lawrence Grossberg, "Is There a Fan in the House?: The Affective Sensibility of Fandom," in *The Adoring Audience: Fan Culture and Popular Media,* edited by Lisa A. Lewis (New York: Routledge, 1992), 59.

13. Grossberg, 59.

14. See for example: Henry Jenkins, "Television Fans, Poachers, Nomads," in *The Subcultures Reader,* edited by Ken Gelder and Sarah Thornton (London: Routledge, 1997), 506–522; Leonard Koppett, *Sports Illusion, Sports Reality.* (Boston: Houghton Mifflin, 1981); and Robert Lipsyte, *SportsWorld: An American Dreamland.* (New York: The New York Times Book Company, 1975).

15. Cheryl Harris and Allison Alexander, ed., *Theorizing Fandom: Fans, Subculture and Identity* (Cresskill, NJ: Hampton Press, 1998), 5. For a study of sport fan culture and fans' relationships to their team, see Barbara S. Hugenberg, *Communicatively Constructed Stakeholder Identity: A Critical Ethnography of Cleveland Browns Fan Culture.* Unpublished doctoral dissertation (Bowling Green, OH: Bowling Green State University, 2002).

16. Kari Whittenberger-Keith, "Understanding Fandom Rhetorically: The Case of 'Beauty and the Beast,'" in *Postmodern Political Communication: The Fringe Challenges the Center,* edited by Andrew King (Westport, CN: Praeger, 1992), 131–152.

17. Jenkins, 507.

18. Rogene A. Buchholz, *Business Environment and Public Policy: Implications for Management and Strategy Formulation* (Englewood Cliffs, NJ: Prentice-Hall, 1986).

19. Deetz, 1995.

20. Driver points are awarded in the following manner: first place—175 points; second place—170 points; third place—165 points; fourth place—160 points; fifth place—155 points; sixth place—150 points; seventh place—146 points; eighth place—142 points; ninth place—138 points; 10th place—134 points; 11th place—130 points; 12th place—127 points; 13th place—124 points; 14th place—121 points; 15th place—118 points; 16th place—115 points; 17th place—112 points; 18th place—109 points; 19th place—106 points; 20th place—103 points; and subsequent reductions in points to 43rd place—34 points. Five bonus points are awarded to all drivers who lead at least one lap during the race, and five additional points are awarded to the driver who leads the most laps during the race. This summary of NASCAR championship points was taken from Mark Martin, *NASCAR for Dummies: Your Complete Guide to NASCAR* (New York: Hungry Minds, Inc., 2000): 177–178.

21. For the final 10 races in 2004, the top 10 drivers were seeded based on the points they earned in the first 26 races. To begin the final 10 races, drivers were positioned 5 points apart. So 2nd place was 5 points behind 1st, 3rd place was 5 points behind 2nd, 4th was 5 points behind 3rd, etc. So 10th place was only 45 points behind 1st place at the beginning of the "Race for the Cup"—the final 10 races.

22. The "Race for the Chase" for the 2004 season could not have concluded more dramatically for NASCAR. It ended on the last lap of the last Cup race of the season in Homestead, Florida. Kurt Busch finished 5th in this race to secure the championship by the most narrow margin in history: 8 points over Jimmie Johnson, who finished 2nd at Homestead. Third place in the "Chase" went to Jeff Gordon, a total of 16 points behind and who finished 3rd in the final race. To illustrate just how close this championship finish was, if Jimmie Johnson had won the race and picked up the 5 championship points for leading a lap in the race and the 5 championship points for winning the race, Johnson would have been the 2004 Nextel Cup Series Champion—by 2 points.

23. From Our Readers. *Scene Magazine* 27 (December 11, 2003): 116–117.

24. From Our Readers. *Scene Magazine* 27 (January 15, 2004): 10.

25. From Our Readers. *Scene Magazine* 27 (January 22, 2004): 11.

26. From Our Readers. *Scene Magazine* 27 (January 22, 2004): 11.

27. From Our Readers. *Scene Magazine* 27 (February 19, 2004): 11.

28. From Our Readers. *Scene Magazine* 27 (February 12, 2004): 94.

29. From Our Readers. *Scene Magazine* 27 (February 12, 2004): 94.

30. From Our Readers. *Scene Magazine* 27 (March 4, 2004): 76.

31. From Our Readers. *Scene Magazine* 27 (February 5, 2004): 10.

32. From Our Readers. *Scene Magazine* 27 (February 5, 2004): 10.

33. Art Weinstein, "Sorting Out a Day of Change in NASCAR," *Scene Magazine* 28 (May 20, 2004): 88.

34. From Our Readers. *Scene Magazine* 27 (February 26, 2004): 76.

35. Mark Ashenfelter. "Good for Business," *Scene Magazine* 28 (May 20, 2004): 24.

36. Scene on the Circuit. *Scene Magazine* 28 (May 20, 2004): 16.

37. Kenny Bruce. "Rockingham, Darlington Officials Couldn't Postpone the Inevitable," *Scene Magazine* 28 (May 20, 2004): 22.

38. From Our Readers. *Scene Magazine* 28 (May 20, 2004): 87.

39. Steve Waid, "Tradition Always Loses in Fight with the Bottom Line," *Scene Magazine* 28 (May 20, 2004): 8.

40. Jeff Owens, "The Rock Is Gone, But Not Forgotten," *Scene Magazine* 28 (May 20, 2004): 88.

41. From Our Readers. *Scene Magazine* 28 (May 27, 2004): 10.

42. From Our Readers. *Scene Magazine* 28 (May 27, 2004): 11.

43. From Our Readers. *Scene Magazine* 28 (May 27, 2004): 10.

44. From Our Readers. *Scene Magazine* 28 (May 27, 2004): 106.

45. Bob Moore, "Southern Cities Remain NASCAR TV Strongholds," *Scene Magazine* 28 (November 25, 2004): 96. Nine of the top 10 markets for NASCAR television broadcasts are in the South. The markets are: 1. (tie) Greensboro-High Point-Winston-Salem, NC: Greenville-Spartanburg, SC, 3. Knoxville, TN, 4. Charlotte, NC, 5. (tie) Indianapolis, IN: Richmond, VA, 7. Orlando-Daytona Beach, FL, 8. Atlanta, GA, 9. (tie) Louisville, KY: Birmingham, AL.

46. From Our Readers. *Scene Magazine* 27 (January 29, 2004): 11.

47. From Our Readers. *Scene Magazine* 27 (March 25, 2004): 10.

48. From Our Readers. *Scene Magazine* 27 (April 1, 2004): 84.

49. Tom Sorensen, "NASCAR's Fans Continually Loyal, Almost to a Fault, Knight Ridder/ Tribune News Service. Accessed April 5, 2004; http://infotrac-college.thompsonlearning.com/itw/ infomark/940/869/73986491w3/4!ar_fmt

50. Mike Hembree, "Speedway Motorsports Tracks Resist Qualifying Changes" *Scene Magazine* 28 (November 25, 2004): 20.

51. "Field-fillers" are those race teams/drivers that constantly qualify higher than 30th in the field of 43 cars for every NASCAR race. They have little or no chance of winning the race but are needed to fill the field to the required 43 cars. There has been some discussion about reducing the race field from 43 to 40 or 39 cars to reduce the number of field-fillers needed each week. Many of these cars leave the race within the first few laps, are quickly lapped by the lead cars, or stay in the race and get in the way of faster cars.

VI. SPORTS NOT FOR MEN ONLY

14

Marketing Multiple Mythologies of Masculinity: Television Advertising and the National Hockey League

Kimberly Tony Korol

Players All: Hockey and Acting

When is a hockey player not a hockey player? When he is an actor promoting the National Hockey League (NHL).[1] Since the league first began expansion in 1967, it has used various devices to market multiple mythologies of masculinity. As time passed and more teams entered the NHL, the league executives became increasingly creative with their marketing strategies. By the dawn of the 21st century, the NHL was exercising several approaches to garner greater audiences. One of the more recent and innovative measures has been the use of players as actors in commercials to commodify various mythologies of masculinity. The NHL has employed television advertising to market four distinct masculinities in order to attract a larger and more diverse viewing audience.

Erving Goffman's *Frame Analysis* and Roland Barthes's *Mythologies* form the basis of the critical methodology to explore how television advertising has promoted multiple mythologies of masculinity for the NHL. Goffman writes that a primary framework renders "what would otherwise be a meaningless aspect of the scene into something that is meaningful."[2] The NHL rekeyed the frame of hockey to attract more viewers. Barthes's concept of mythology is paramount in that one can consider the multiple identities the NHL commodifies to be part of mythologies of masculinity, each with its own distinct and coded characteristics that the audience reads and assigns. Every player has a role and a character on the ice. Whether that character is congruent with his personality off the ice is of little matter, though physical appearance often will play a part in how an audience views the individual.

The media have played a significant part in the labeling of multiple masculinities within the sporting culture. ESPN, the major television carrier for the NHL, has helped the league divide its players into categories of varying masculinity. In a marketing campaign from the mid-1990s, ESPN described five basic types of players, both in hockey and in life: Grinder, Playmaker, Stopper, Scorer, and Superstar. By looking carefully at the multiple masculinities the ESPN campaign deployed and viewing them through the lens of gender theory on masculinity, one can condense and combine the classifications and construct a list of four primary mythologies of masculinity that exist within the NHL: the bully, the hero-protector, the sexual athlete, and the New Man. From 1967 to 2002, the NHL has at one time marketed each of these masculinities and often has promoted all four simultaneously as a means of attracting wider audiences.

The first masculinity NHL teams appeared to market was the bully. This mythology begins with the ESPN campaign definition of a Grinder: "The Grinder's willing to sacrifice the body. Stopping a speeding puck with your face isn't pretty but then again, neither is the name 'Grinder.' The Grinder always sticks up for his teammates. Why? Because they're teammates. And the other guys aren't."[3] This type resembles gender theorist David Savran's concept of the "angry white male" and gender commentator Jonathon Rutherford's theory of retributive man: "John Wayne with the gloves off."[4] Thus the bully is the tough guy who will fight, gloves off, to defend his teammates and his honor.

The second mythology of masculinity is the hero-protector. This category begins with the NHL's Stopper, "the one you count on to succeed after everyone else has failed."[5] Sports scholar Garry Whannel's definition of hero explicates this mythology. Whannel explains that the etymology of the term *hero* is complex but comes from such diverse sources as Greek mythology and Arthurian legend: "Heroic tales do provide a fund of metaphoric allusion—think of the resonances of the tales of Theseus killing the Minotaur, Ulysses and the sirens, Jonah and the whale, David and Goliath, Samson and the lion, Perseus and the head of Medusa. Representations of sport draw upon the connections to the traditional and the legendary that such allusions facilitate."[6] The hero-protector then is the masculinity that conquers evil, shields the less able, and safeguards all that is good and right.

The third mythology the NHL has marketed is quite different from the bully and hero-protector. Equating bullies and heroes with professional hockey is a relatively simple accomplishment even for the uninitiated. Certainly, to those unfamiliar with the nuances of the sport, these are the most readily understood identities. The third masculine mythology, the sexual athlete, is a bit more complex. This particular masculinity begins with the NHL's Scorer. "The Scorer's the one who doesn't study all semester, goes out the night before, and still manages to ace the final."[7] This image is similar to Barthes's description of the wrestler Mazaud, "(short and arrogant like a cock) that of grotesque conceit," Savran's concept of the "male searching for the Wild Man within," and sports theorist Donald Sabo's conceptualization of the sexual myth of masculinity.[8] Sabo writes, "The phrase 'sexual athlete' commonly refers to male heterosexual virtuosity in the bedroom. Images of potency, agility, technical expertise, and an ability to attract and satisfy women come to mind."[9] The sexual athlete is the team member for whom "scoring" is a natural product of his inner and instinctive primitive self.

The final myth of masculinity is the New Man. This is a combination of the NHL's Playmaker, who makes his teammates look good, and Superstar, who "should be watched and enjoyed. Because the Superstar doesn't come along that often."[10] The New Man also contains Savran's "sensitive male" and Whannel's New Man, whom Whannel defines as "men who had responded to and taken on board aspects of the critique of masculinity offered by feminism. Such men endeavoured to become more involved with domestic labour and childcare. They got in touch with their emotions and tried to combat their own sexism."[11] Unlike the bully and hero, and even less than the sexual athlete, it might seem difficult for the audience to assign this identity to a hockey player. How then does the sensitive man even play a sport that is as aggressive as hockey? Savran suggests an answer: "The new, countercultural masculinity represents a much more deeply contradictory identity than either its supporters or its detractors acknowledge. John Wayne may be an anachronism, but the relatively androgynous new (white) male by no means signals a repudiation of traditionally masculine goals."[12] The New Man, therefore, uses hockey as an outlet for the conventional male needs, while still playing the role of caring, sensitive man.

NHL Expansion and the New Marketing Strategies

From 1942 until 1967, there were only six teams participating at the top level of professional hockey in the United States and Canada; the Solid Six represented a single masculinity to their viewing audience.[13] Michael

A. Robidoux, a former junior hockey player and current assistant professor of kinesiology at the University of Lethbridge, helps to explain the overall dominating masculinity that existed within professional hockey at that time. Robidoux writes, "The result is a shared identity, one informed by a physically dominant, white, heterosexual male model that has been validated through annual rituals and everyday behaviour. It is this model that is privileged within the community as ultimately the only legitimate masculinity."[14] However, in 1967 the NHL doubled in size, a massive undertaking for the league. Expansion has continued, and by 2000 the NHL comprised 30 teams. The more recent waves of expansion were the brainchild of then–league president Gil Stein, who explained the need to expand hockey across the country and the importance of television to the continued survival of the sport: "The normal expansion indicates that you're adding teams. But what I'm talking about is expanding our market, where we are going in the U.S. Where do we need to go to build what we need in the U.S. to make our sport attractive to network television?"[15] In less than 35 years, the league quintupled in size, placing teams in cities such as Miami and Los Angeles, cities in which ice is not a naturally occurring phenomenon and which are thus seemingly illogical sites for the sport.

The first wave of expansion in 1967 had two primary effects on the NHL. First, it severely reduced the talent pool available to the league — the six new teams were "stocked with twenty players each drafted from the established teams"— thereby decreasing the quality of the games played.[16] Because the quality level of the sport in the individual games dropped dramatically, the sport in its entirety weakened and suffered. Second, the league and the individual teams now had to find a way to sell to audiences a watered-down product. Over the course of five waves of expansion, an aggressive marketing campaign became necessary for an NHL franchise to survive as an individual and for the league's continued existence as a whole. In the 1990s more than ever, as growing numbers of theatricalized events competed for the consumer dollar, the NHL began an assertive effort to bring its stars to the forefront, not just with their on-ice abilities, but also with characteristics that appeal to different segments of the population. General managers constructed teams composed of players that fill various roles, necessary both for on-ice success and off-ice appeal. The league and individual teams then marketed these players at the national and local levels.

Television commercials were instrumental in promoting the mythologies of masculinity exhibited by individual players. "The need of television for star personalities, and the conventions of television, particularly narrativisation, had a transformative impact on athletics."[17] To illustrate the importance of the television advertising and marketing of player masculinities within the NHL, one can examine the local marketing campaign for the Washington Capitals as well as the national advertising scheme for the NHL on ESPN and ESPN2. These advertising campaigns illuminate that the league is self-aware of the necessity of increasing the theatricality of its product through creation and recognition of multiple masculinities that appeal to a broad and diverse audience. By promoting the teams' and the league's stars in theatrical roles not specifically limited to on-ice activities, the advertising executives are creating masculinities and delivering a new concept of those mythological identities as Barthes proposes.

The Washington Capitals' advertising campaign began in 1999. Mark Tamar, director of game operations for the Capitals, explained that the inspiration for the campaign was a collaborative effort between Capitals' executives and Hill Holliday, a Boston advertising firm. They chose the players who acted in the commercials based on their personalities and abilities to fit the roles the advertisements required. "You had to decide if a player's personality was like the ad piece. If you have a tough guy role, you want one of our tough guys playing the role in the commercial."[18] These commercials were part of a larger marketing strategy featuring the Capitals' new motto: "Always Intense." Somewhat contradictory to the motto, each of the commercials contained strong elements of comedy, thus offering dual levels of appeal to the potential audience.

Equally aware of the need to market the NHL's stars was ESPN in its 2000–2001 campaign entitled "Every Player Has a Story." The brainchild of associate marketing manager Kevin Kirksey of ESPN's consumer marketing department and the Portland, Oregon, advertising agency of Widen and Kennedy, the campaign featured several of the league's biggest stars in individual vignettes, each taken from a different literary genre. "The objectives were to communicate that the NHL is a passionate sport," Kirksey says. "Like every other sport, there are stories behind the games: rivalries, faces. There's a reason to watch beyond the action on the ice."[19] Therefore, the concept behind the campaign evolved from a desire to illuminate more than the on-ice action for the fans. Through these commercials ESPN created multiple mythologies of masculinity. Each advertisement stars a different player in a literary genre, typing a story while the viewing audience hears a voice-over of the player.

Through these television commercials the NHL and its member teams and players have increasingly created mythologies of multiple masculinities. These four primary mythologies of masculinity — the bully, the hero-protector, the sexual athlete, and the New Man — reflect the league's desire to widen its audience base and rekey the frame of hockey in order to compete for the fans' entertainment dollar.

The Bully Masculinity

Sometimes the masculinity revealed is more physically represented than artistically portrayed. Teams are made of up different characters who each fill a role in one of the masculinities the franchises market. From 1997 until 2001, Chris Simon was the player the Washington Capitals cast in the role of tough guy.[20] In the Capitals' advertising campaign, subtlety is at a premium as the commercial starring Simon clearly portrays his off-ice personality as carrying on in complete harmony with the on-ice character. Goffman writes that as time passes, the framing of combatlike contests has changed: "Typically these changes have been seen as signs of the decline of toleration for cruelty and performer risk, at least in the recreational sphere … so cock fighting, bearbaiting, ratting, and other blood sports have been prohibited."[21] Yet fighting has remained an important part of hockey, in part because it requires a different type of character, a role hockey audiences strongly desire to see portrayed on the ice.

Writing about tennis matches in the early 1980s, Whannel explains the fan desire to view the bully and the issues it creates within sports. "[Bjorn] Borg was every bit as good a player, but [John] McEnroe and [Jimmy] Connors were more interesting and more exciting to watch. Coaches, managers and officials demanded dedication, concentration and application; whilst television producers and the public sought drama and excitement."[22] The bad-boy masculinity Whannel ascribes to Connors and McEnroe is very much like the tough-guy roles within hockey. This mythology of the bully masculinity is part and parcel of the product the NHL has marketed since the beginnings of modern expansion, and television delivers it to the fans who want it.

In the Washington Capitals' advertisement featuring Simon, he and Peter Bondra, one of the team's superstar scorers, are shopping in a grocery store. When an elderly woman's cart accidentally collides with Bondra's, they share a few polite apologies, and she attempts to offer some advice on how to be more careful. Simon, having witnessed the crash from the far end of the aisle, runs barreling up to the two and knocks the woman over with his shopping cart. The background sound is a heart beating, and this, along with the actions of the woman as she falls, moves the scene from one of unprecipitated violence to one of dark humor. As the scene changes to the on-ice play of Simon placing devastating hits on opponents, Capitals' play-by-play television announcer Joe Beninati's voice-over at the end of the advertisement succinctly describes the respective roles Bondra and Simon play for the team: "Chris Simon gives Bondra all the room he's gonna need."[23] This statement clearly illustrates the difference in Simon and Bondra's on-ice roles. Simon provides the backdrop against which Bondra takes center stage. Both his role and his character are clearly indicative of the bully masculinity.

This commercial featuring Simon and Bondra illustrates Simon's role on the ice as an integral part of successful play. Simon is reputed for standing up for his teammates, a role substantiated by the statistic that he led the Capitals in penalty minutes per game played for the majority of his career with the team. However, when injuries to Bondra and other players initially forced Simon into a different role, the Capitals' audience did not readily accept the transformation. Because the team was relying on Simon to score more often, he fought less. By booing loudly, the fans would often express their resentment at his reluctance to drop the gloves to fight just because he had become a goal scorer. It was only when for the 2001–2002 season the Capitals cast rookie Stephen Peat in the bully role, as Simon became more of a complete player, that the audience began to approve of Simon's new character.

The segment of the audience to whom the league caters when marketing the bully masculinity is appreciative of the efforts to maintain this violent aspect of the sport. A certain amount of showmanship exists in the preparation for a hockey fight, but it occurs only as complement to the spectacle about to take place, which is what the audience desires. Writing about French wrestling, Barthes explains the mythology: "What the public wants is the image of passion, not passion itself. There is no more a problem of truth in wrestling than in theatre. In both, what is expected is the intelligible representation of moral situations which are usually private. This emptying out of interiority to the benefit of its exterior signs, this exhaustion of the content by the form, is the very principle of triumphant classical art."[24] This feeds into the role of the bully masculinity as a purgation of violence with which the audience can identify. Not only does the player partake in the eradication of his need for violence, but the fans are also allowed to share in the release. By casting players to be bullies on the team and then illustrating that character in off-ice situations through advertisements, NHL teams seek to reinforce in the minds of the fans that this masculinity is flourishing in the league even as the other masculinities have slowly crept in and attempted to steal some of the bully's audience while acquiring new spectators.

The Hero-Protector Masculinity

The National Hockey League realized that some potential spectators would not be enticed by, interested in, or attracted to the bully masculinity. For some, undoubtedly, the bully mythology represented everything that was wrong with the sport. Other mythologies were necessary if the

NHL was to continue to successfully implement its expansion policy. To attract new fans, a second mythology of masculinity began to emerge: that of the hero-protector. This mythology remains in the new millennium an important part of the masculinities the NHL markets to attract new audiences.

Commercials on ESPN/ESPN2 clearly marketed players to the cable television audience as hero-protectors. One advertisement in the series features Colorado Avalanche player Chris Drury, who had just completed his second full season in the NHL when ESPN tapped him for the campaign. The writers keyed into Drury's age and newness on the scene as they created a science-fiction genre commercial for him. In a darkened room, lit only by firelight and a small lamp, Drury sits at a desk typing on a laptop computer. The music creates a tense atmosphere, and the camera angles that alternately pan around the room and close in on Drury's intense blue eyes set the perfect scene for his story. He writes, "As he looked past the three moons of Dominion towards his home planet, it hit him like a teleportation booster. The rebellion would start on the ice because hockey was where the robots were vulnerable. And as the game's young superstar, the fate of his people rested solely on his shoulders and tomorrow's game."[25] The commercial specifically references hockey, but places it in the science fiction genre and thus captures both the masculine mythology associated with the hero-protector masculinity (the hockey players) triumphing over evil invaders (the robots).

Choosing Drury as the "game's young superstar" was hardly inspired casting. Following a win of the Hobey Baker Award as best collegiate player of the year in 1997, Drury won the Calder Trophy as NHL Rookie of the Year in 1999. By plugging him into a literary genre associated with youth popular culture, the writers created a hero-protector mythology that perfectly blended Drury's on-ice talent with his looks and age. Again the duality of performance exists as Drury's on-ice persona melds with the character his off-ice self is creating at the computer for the fans who both watch him at the arena and the audience currently viewing the commercial.

As with all of the ESPN commercials, Drury is not only author but main character in the story as well. He is the young hero, handsome and intelligent, prepared to face the enemy robots head on in a physical clash of strength and will. This masculinity appeals to members of the audience who identify with the bully mythology, while also drawing in new fans who see the hero-protector not simply through the physicality manifested in the bully, but through the righteousness wielded by those identified as saviors. Drury is not taking on the robots just to prove he can, as the bully would, though the physical aspect is certainly attractive to fans of the bully masculinity. Rather, the young Colorado star embodies the modern hero who is doing it not for his own good or gratification, but for that of his people who desperately need his help to survive. Notice that he calls the hockey game a "rebellion," illustrating that the humans must rise up against the robots. In order to do so, someone must lead them into the battle fray, and Drury is that hero-protector who will sacrifice everything to save his race.

Another of the ESPN *Every Player Has a Story* commercials starred Detroit Red Wings forward Brendan Shanahan, who was 31 years old when ESPN filmed the commercials. At six feet, three inches tall and 215 pounds, with dark wavy hair, the handsome Shanahan looked every bit the role in which ESPN cast him: the successful detective. The only reference to the Red Wings in the commercial is the mouse pad for Shanahan's desktop computer, which sits next to a replica Maltese Falcon, perhaps itself a reference to Humphrey Bogart's detective roles. As haunting piano music sets the tone, the Detroit player types, "Inspector Shanahan knew he was close. Thirteen years in the game, battles in the corners, big-game goals, raising two Cups. He saw things so clearly now. He stuck to the clues and followed the tracks of the skate blades right to the scene. He pointed towards his suspect. For it was the goalie who did it all along."[26] The hero-protector mythology is clearly evident in the detective drama, as the male inspector succeeds in tracking down the perpetrator, and all of the signs— especially the Maltese Falcon — serve as clues for the audience to read as such.

Shanahan epitomizes the cop who always gets his man. It might not be easy work, but somebody has to do it. Shanahan references the difficulty facing him: "thirteen years in the game" and "battles in the corners." However, he also illustrates that if the hero-protector stays his course, using his brain as well as his brawn —follows the clues— he will ultimately succeed. This down-to-earth hero, who is willing to do whatever it takes to protect his turf, is fascinating to the same audience that finds the Capitals' defensive corps attractive. This hero-protector appeals to the man on the streets, the blue-collar worker who does his job simply because it is his job.

Another advertisement in the ESPN campaign featured the New Jersey Devils' Scott Stevens. The Devils had won the NHL championship that summer (2000), capturing the Stanley Cup for the second time in five years. Stevens is a hard-hitting defenseman and captain of the Devils. When New Jersey won its second Stanley Cup in 2000, Stevens had been in the league for 17 years, a well-known and respected veteran player. The commercial's writers focused both on Stevens's personality and reputation as a leader as well as on the Devils' Stanley Cup victory to create the Arthurian legend story for the New Jersey captain. Standing in a room lit only by candles, medieval flute music playing in the background, a suit of armor with the Devils' logo clearly visible over his right shoulder, Stevens shares his story: "The whole township of Jersey came to the feast for the capture of Lord Stanley's Chalice. They merrily drank their grog, ate their pheasant, and cheered their chivalrous knights. But their leader, good Sir Stevens, watched prudently for he knew defending the Cup from men with black hearts would be a hardship equal to that of its capture."[27] Midway through he picks up a chicken leg and unceremoniously thrusts it into his mouth as he finishes typing, continuing the dual persona of author and character that reflect his on-ice identity.

The chicken leg conjures the image familiar in popular culture of Henry VIII and the turkey leg. Along with the suit of armor and the language Stevens employs to tell the story, the commercial creates a mythology of character for Stevens by combining what viewers know of his on-ice talents with the off-ice tale he tells. By recalling the Arthurian legends, Stevens captures the hero-protector mythology of Camelot that portrays the ultimate in good triumphing over evil, reminiscent of the Knights of the Round Table. Through language recounting the need to defend the Cup, the Devils' player even creates regional and national identity associated with territorial defense.

By invoking the Arthurian legend, the Stevens commercial appeals to a wide audience appreciative of the hero-protector mythology. Not only does it attract those who would be drawn to the defender concept, it entices those who are interested in the Arthurian mythology. Whannel specifically referenced the Arthurian mythology when creating his description of the hero genealogy. By continuously harking back to the medieval legend through the script, the background music, the set design, and the props, the Stevens commercial helps to transport the viewer to a time and place with which 21st-century viewers automatically equate the hero-protector masculinity. Camelot was a place where men were heroes, and knights had the mission to protect the people of their realm.

Although the bully is often a draw more for men and not women, the hero-protector is attractive to both sexes. Females comprise almost half of all audience members at the arena.[28] Therefore, marketing a masculinity that appeals to the female audience is important to the NHL. The hero-protector appeals to a segment of the audience that responds to the bully mythology that showcases brute strength, while simultaneously captivating new spectators who are more charmed by the ideals the hero-protector mythology symbolizes. The NHL helps to perpetuate the mythology of the hero-protector masculinity as it epitomizes the principles of security and safety within our American culture. With marketing the hero/protector, the league attempts to attract both male and female members of the potential audience.

The Sexual Athlete Masculinity

The incredibly strong image of the hero-protector in Camelot portrayed in the Stevens commercial also holds a touch of romance, since the

Arthurian legend often conjures the images of Gwenevere and Sir Lancelot. The romantic mythology linked with the Arthurian legend, however, is buried in this particular advertisement, as Stevens makes no particular mention of it. The following examples will more clearly illustrate the masculinity the National Hockey League has marketed to reflect both romance and eroticism. This mythology of the sexual athlete, like that of the hero-protector, has appeal for both male and female audience members.

The marketing of the sexual athlete mythology can be either implicit or explicit. Sometimes images will be read one way by certain audience members and in another manner altogether by others. While the NHL might not have set out with the conscious idea of marketing sex appeal, the groundwork for showcasing it has clearly been laid. In his book *The Erotic in Sports*, Allen Guttmann discusses the fallout following the publication of basketball Hall of Fame member Wilt Chamberlain's assertion of his sexual prowess and promiscuity. "Wilt Chamberlain's notorious claim that he had slept with 20,000 different women produced a spate of journalism in which other athletes boasted that they too had had their pick of young women eager for vicarious involvement in baseball, basketball, football, and ice hockey."[29] The athletes' declarations of the number of women interested in them as objects of sexual desire inevitably led to an even greater marketing of the players as sexual athletes.

The Washington Capitals were unrestrained in marketing their individual players as part of the sexual athlete mythology. While goaltenders and tough guys have their place, playmakers and goal scorers are necessities in the NHL. Adam Oates was the assist leader for the Capitals from 1997 to 2001.[30] His purpose was to create scoring opportunities for other players, and he also provided solid defense. Although Oates's ability to pass is legendary, and his defensive capabilities were often rated at the top of the ranks for forwards, he often lacks personal scoring punch. More than once, as Oates has skated in alone on a goaltender and failed to score, audience members have moaned, "That's why he's the league's leading playmaker." The Capitals commercial featuring Oates played upon the inability to finish the conquest. This contradiction again showcases the playfulness with which the NHL markets its players.

This advertisement shows the five-foot, eleven-inch Oates walking into a laundromat. The Washington player is clad in a gray sweatshirt; his dark hair is slightly ruffled. As he begins to take his dirty clothes out of his duffel bag, he catches the eye of an attractive young woman standing by the dryers. She smiles at him, and he smiles at her. All appears to be going well until he starts to pull bloodstained clothing from the bag. Ignorant of the horror with which she is now looking at him, Oates nods his head at his would-be mark and winks.[31] The potential sexual athlete is completely unaware that his hockey life has intruded upon his personal life because, for his intended, the bloody clothes conjure an image of the bully masculinity, not the sexual athlete he is trying to evoke.

Oates is oblivious to the young woman's changed attitude toward his advances. His seduction will not succeed, but he is yet unaware of his failure. This mythology of the sexual athlete masculinity is appealing as it renders the player as seducer, but the woman as the ultimate decision-maker in the potential seduction. It is also attractive and amusing to knowing female hockey fans, who laugh at the young woman's misreading of the situation. It is important to note that she was indeed initially attracted by Oates's physical appearance. The male in this case is objectified, and Guttmann notes that the athletes are well aware of this objectification. "The athletes whom the Broadway entrepreneurs and the Hollywood moguls and the Madison Avenue hucksters showcase are not unaware of their physical attractiveness. 'Broadway Joe' Namath marketed his sex appeal almost as successfully as he sold his skills as a quarterback for the New York Jets."[32] The NHL franchises learned an important lesson from the National Football League teams and players that sex appeal was marketable on its own. However, while the Oates commercial illustrates that he is keenly aware of his sexual charm, it also shows that he is just as acutely unaware that the masculinity his bloody clothes project is not that of sexual athlete, but that of bully. The Capitals thus marketed with the sex appeal of the NFL's Namath, while leaving the consumer the final laugh.

Unlike the Oates commercial, in which the gore fans associate with the game ultimately foils the seduction, in another advertisement the Capitals used the hockey terminology to their distinct advantage. For more than 30 years hockey announcers have used a saying that has become part of the vernacular of the game: "He shoots; he scores!" With the "Always Intense" advertising campaign, the Capitals adapted a line as familiar to hockey fans as "Now is the winter of our discontent" is to Shakespeare fans, and the writers melded slang of popular culture with hockey vernacular to create another commercial illustrating the mythology of the sexual athlete.

This television advertisement features Washington's Sergei Gonchar, one of the franchise's leading defensemen, and it is overtly indicative of the sexual athlete masculinity. In the NHL there are generally considered to be two types of defensemen: stay-at-home and offensive-minded.[33] Gonchar falls squarely into the latter category as one of the league's top scoring defenseman for 1999 through 2002. For the 2001–2002 season, Gonchar led all NHL defensemen in goal scoring. His on-ice character is taken off the ice and combined with his youthful appearance (Gonchar was 25 at the time the commercial was filmed) as he and a date stumble into his house, completely entwined with each other. The background music "Hold Me" plays as the still-embracing couple climbs up the stairs and practically falls into Gonchar's bedroom. Shortly after he slams the door shut, a loud siren sounds and a red light flashes on his door, just as happens when the home team scores a goal at an NHL game. As the scene switches to Gonchar scoring a goal on the ice, Capitals play-by-play man Joe Beninati screams excitedly, "Gonchar shoots; he scores!"[34]

Although this commercial certainly has a comedic value in the double entendre, it definitely also contains vital sexual imagery. The players in the NHL are all men, and the concept of using the slang term of *scoring*, which means to succeed sexually, to correlate with on-ice behavior is understandable in the league — which allows women only as passive viewers, not active participants. It is simply another example of the NHL's ongoing creation of the sexual athlete mythology as a marketing tool to attract new audiences. The handsome young Gonchar is tempting to female audience members. His overt sexuality and successful conquest contrast with Oates's vain attempt to woo a member of the opposite sex. Gonchar epitomizes the sexual athlete about whom Sabo wrote. This player certainly conjures up imagery of "potency, agility, technical expertise, and an ability to attract and satisfy women."[35] This commercial clearly illustrates the heterosexual virtuosity in the bedroom that Sabo ascribes to the sexual athlete.

The Capitals were not alone in their use of the sexual athlete mythology to market hockey. The ESPN campaign also employed this particular mythology of masculinity to its distinct advantage. The advertising executives chose to market familiar characteristics of a player through an unusual genre. Mark Recchi of the Philadelphia Flyers has a reputation as a tough player who takes a great deal of abuse in front of the net in order to score goals. The five-foot, ten-inch, 185-pound, 32-year-old forward (at the time of commercial filming) has the rugged good looks of a Hollywood leading man. Kirksey and the ESPN advertising team did not pass up a golden opportunity as they cast Recchi as the lead character and writer of a dark melodrama rife with overt sexuality and which conjures up memories of the American classic *The Postman Always Rings Twice*, a part of popular culture in the United States as both a novel and as film noir.

Standing at a counter in a dark kitchen, light filtering in through dirty, partially open windows, Recchi is clad in pants and a white sleeveless T-shirt known colloquially as a "wife beater." His attire is designed to showcase his physical attributes and create a heightened sense of sexuality. As Whannel comments, "Men's bodies are now far more commonly objectified in representation, and there is a greater sexualisation of these bodies, most markedly in movies and in advertising."[36] The advertisement begins with the sweating player turning toward the camera and forcefully sticking a knife into a cutting board. The music resonates, growing to a crescendo as he types. As fire flares in a pan on the stove, Recchi writes, "She walked through the door with enough heat to melt the ice at First Union Center. She was trouble from the start. She wanted to know my credentials. I told her about being the alternate captain, about the seven all-star appearances. I told her I was one of the best two-way players around. And that's when she slapped me. I guess I had to explain that one."[37]

The scene clearly invokes the sexual athlete mythology of masculinity as it frames this particular member of the fierce Flyer team as a tough ladies' man. Recchi's good looks and deep, resonating voice create a sensuousness about him that boils over much as the pot on the stove flares. While the commercial ends with the image of the object of his desire slapping him, the unspoken narrative read by the audience is that he will be able to explain his abilities as a two-way player and garner the attentions of the vixen. He thus appeals to the masculine segment of the potential audience who relate to his ability to overcome adversity and still score. The commercial also engages the female fans, like the groupies who surround sport stars waiting to be asked out, who are enticed by his overwhelming and undeniable manliness.

ESPN also took a less overtly sexual path, focusing more on the romantic angle of the sexual athlete mythology. Only two of the commercials featured non–North American players. The first of the two starred former Florida Panthers scoring ace Pavel Bure of Russia.[38] In his second season with the Panthers, Bure led the NHL in goals to capture the Maurice "Rocket" Richard Trophy as the league's top goal scorer. In the advertisement, Bure is lounging on a comfortable and posh sofa, a beautiful, fluffy snow-white cat next to him. The player's off-ice personality is brought into the commercial with the revelation that he is writing a romance novel. The press had documented Bure's off-ice life well for a year before the filming of the commercial because of his on-again/off-again relationship with tennis player and model Anna Kournikova.

As the advertisement begins, rain is falling outside. More than a bit wistfully, underscored by violin music, Bure writes of his fictional love, "Before he stepped on the ice, he gave her one last glance. He wanted to remember her. He looked into her eyes. They were dark, like two pucks in a puddle. Her face was a goalie mask of beauty, as pretty as a no-look backhand pass leading to a one-timer to the top shelf."[39] The hockey references Bure uses to describe the beauty of his love are strengthened by the single tie to the Panthers organization, a jersey framed as if it were an expensive piece of artwork hanging on the wall to Bure's right. Otherwise the scene is rich and luxurious, a perfect setting for writing the typical dime store romance novels that are part of the American popular culture and that appeal to a definitive segment of the female population.

These ESPN commercials, along with the two different sexual-athlete advertisements the Capitals created, illustrate that even within the varying mythologies of masculinity, there is room for diversity. Though this masculinity I have termed sexual athlete always has sexual overtones, they might be displayed explicitly or implicitly, depending upon the actor the NHL is using and the sector of the potential devotees the league hopes to reach with the marketing. The conquests these characters attempt might be either tremendous successes (Gonchar) or dismal failures (Oates). These sexual-athlete masculinities have a wide range of appeal for both male and female fans, and the NHL has used this mythology of masculinity to its benefit primarily during the past decade.

The New Man Masculinity

Changes within the entire structure of the NHL governing body might have played a role in the new marketing strategies designed to entice different fans around the country. An upheaval at the very top of the NHL board of governors certainly played a part in the acquisition and marketing of the New Man mythology of masculinity. There were bullies aplenty and hero-protectors galore in the league. Sexual-athlete characters would appeal to a certain segment of the population, but there was still a masculinity unused by the NHL — the New Man, the sensitive, family-oriented male. This mythology would attract two new audiences. First, the New Man is incredibly attractive to female viewers, the caring, gentle type who could entice fans who would ordinarily be repulsed by the violence associated with the game of hockey. Second, the New Man is attractive as a father figure to younger audiences, a complete new generation of fans for the NHL.

The Washington Capitals television advertising markets goaltender Olaf Kolzig as a New Man. Two of the "Always Intense" commercials featured Kolzig. The first one illustrates the New Man mythology as the advertisement begins with Kolzig and his "wife" at a restaurant to celebrate their fifth anniversary. After they toast with their glasses, sharing an incredibly romantic moment, Kolzig places his wine glass on the table, grasps the bottle, drinks straight from it, spits out the wine, and then pours the rest of the bottle's contents over his face.

The scene then changes to Kolzig on the ice doing virtually the same thing with a water bottle during a game situation. As this game situation plays, announcer Joe Beninati does a voice-over: "Kolzig's been hot tonight."[40] This commercial, and all the others in the series, end with the Capitals' logo and marketing catch phrase "Always Intense." The inference is clear: You can take the player out of the hockey game, but you can not take the hockey game out of the player. As with the other commercials in the series, the advertising executives used a variety of techniques to perpetuate the multiple masculinities. Even as the commercial portrays Kolzig as the New Man, it reminds the audience that no matter what his mythology of masculinity might be, he is a hockey player first.

The second Kolzig commercial again portrays the at-home side of the goaltender. He appears in front of a house in a suburban neighborhood, clad in T-shirt, backwards baseball cap, sweatpants, and a plaid bathrobe, awaiting the daily paper from the delivery boy. As the boy approaches Kolzig, he winds up and begins furiously firing paper after paper at the Capitals' net-minder. Kolzig deftly blocks numerous papers before catching one and bestowing an appreciative smile upon the newspaper boy. Again the action of the scene then changes to Kolzig on the ice, and Beninati intones, "Oh, Kolzig with a dynamite save."[41] The New Man's appeal to the younger fan base is clear. Kolzig may be an NHL goaltender, but he still has time to play with the local paperboy.[42]

The ESPN campaign marketed St. Louis Blues defenseman and team captain Chris Pronger, a six-foot, six-inch, 220-pound, hard-hitting player, against his on-ice image by portraying him as a New Man in the commercial. Pronger, who has won both the Norris Trophy as the league's top defenseman and the Hart Trophy as the league's Most Valuable Player, has also appeared in four consecutive All-Star games. In the spot for ESPN/ESPN2, Pronger is lying on a bed, dressed in khaki shorts, a gray T-shirt, and white tube socks, typing a diary entry into his laptop. The only clues to his on-ice identity are a hockey stick in the background and a single pillow on the bed with the St. Louis Blues logo on it. Soft piano music fills the air, the lighting is subdued, and rain is falling outside the windows as he writes, "Dear diary, Today it's raining and I'm sad. If only people knew the true me, and not the so-called 'nasty defenseman.' They never see the master horticulturalist, the feng-shui artist, or the man who never turns away a stray dog. Because underneath the tough hockey player exterior, there's a sensitive boy trying to get out."[43] As Pronger writes, a large dog lays comfortably nearby on a chair. When he has finished typing, the campaign logo, "Every Player Has a Story," appears as it does in all the other commercials, in white letters at the top right of the screen.

By invoking the diary-writing genre, the writers have given Pronger an alternative identity and created a New Man mythology about him that underlines the words he types. Diary writing is associated with femininity, sensitivity, soulfulness. This, of course, is the complete antithesis for Pronger's on-ice persona. The advertisement creates in Pronger a New Man masculinity, whose qualities he can share only with his diary. Yet the commercial achieves a dual purpose by also illustrating that even on the ice, Pronger contains his off-ice character and ethics, the feng-shui artist and lover of stray animals. In this case the advertisement creates a mirror-image identity of the player: Everything about him on the ice is exactly opposite of his personality off the ice, inner versus outer character. The bully on the ice is really a New Man off the ice, and the question remains as to whether the two can actually be separated.

Pronger is a handsome young man, and the New Man mythology is appealing to female audiences. It is easy to look upon the character in the commercial and be attracted to the sensitive, wistful manner with which he writes. There is a feeling that Pronger is sharing a very special, private moment with the fan, and there is a need to join in the mythology he is creating. Even when he is back on the ice, being the "nasty defenseman," viewers will carry the image of the New Man with them. The spectator who is attracted to the New Man mythology will never be able to completely lose the impression of Pronger as ESPN shows him off the ice, even as he viciously confronts opposing forwards on the ice. Garry Whannel writes of the New Man that he "is arguably something more than a media label but certainly less than a major new social movement or a transformative social force, yet does signify forms of unsettling of some mainstream assumptions about gender relations."[44] For the NHL the New Man exists to aid in attracting females to the sport through the calculated use of the television media.

The NHL also markets a New Man who does not offer a contrasting personality on the ice. The second European-born player featured in the ESPN commercials is the Czech Republic's Jaromir Jagr, whom Kirksey and the advertising team specifically cast as a character first before creating the advertisement. "We picked Jaromir Jagr and then wrote a script to fit him," Kirksey says. At the time ESPN filmed the commercial, Jagr played for the Penguins and was clad in a Pittsburgh T-shirt.[45] Jagr won the scoring title for the NHL four consecutive years, from 1998 to 2001. The six-foot, two-inch, 232-pound forward with ruffled, slightly curly hair and a huge smile has an innocent quality about him that made him perfect for the children's story he told in his advertisement, again appealing to fans of the New Man.

To create the mythology of New Man, the scene is well lit, with bright colors all around. The music playing in the background is bouncy and vibrant as Jagr writes, "Jimmy's eyes opened wide with excitement. 'Look,' Jimmy said as he pointed at Jaromir's stick. 'The goblin was wrong. That's not the magic stick, and you scored six goals. The Wizard's curse has been lifted.' That meant that the magic had been inside Jaromir all the time."[46] Once again the writers combined both the on-ice talent (Jagr is capable of scoring multiple goals in a game) with off-ice looks to create a believable character for the viewing audience. The commercial reflects the Harry Potter craze that has become a major force in popular culture at the beginning of the new millennium.

The Jagr commercial entices the young audience, who, though perhaps unfamiliar with hockey, is certainly well acquainted with Harry Potter. By relating Jagr to the popular cultural icon, ESPN created a New Man masculinity for Jagr that will appeal both to children and their parents, especially mothers who are attracted to this particular mythology. Perhaps hockey is not such a violent and evil sport, mothers can muse after viewing the commercial. After all, Jagr seems like the prototypical New Man, unafraid to share his innermost fears through a children's story. Jagr rarely is involved in scuffles on the ice. He is certainly not known for his defensive capabilities. His innocent looks make it difficult to view him as a sexual athlete. The New Man mythology, however, is perfect for the superstar.

The NHL and its member teams continue to market the New Man mythology through individuals such as Kolzig, Pronger, and Jagr. The differences between these players illustrate, as with the sexual-athlete masculinity, that even within a particular mythology there is room for variations. Kolzig illustrates the family man, whereas Pronger demonstrates that differences exist between real person and player. Jagr, on the other hand, typifies the New Man both on and off the ice. These New Men all help to attract a wider audience for the NHL, targeting new fans largely consisting of younger audiences and women.

Conclusion

As the NHL marketed each of the four masculinities— bully, hero-protector, sexual athlete, and New Man — the league rekeyed the frame previously defined as hockey to include these mythologies. As Goffman wrote, "Thus, the systematic transformation that a particular keying introduces may alter only slightly the activity thus transformed, but it utterly changes what it is a participant would say was going on."[47] This rekeying precipitated a growing number of audience members who participated in the culture of hockey, and a growing worth for the league, even if the new additions to the frame identified the sport they were watching in a radically different manner from those who were spectators before the 1967 expansion. Therefore, the appropriation of the theatrical elements that helped the NHL to market these mythologies of masculinity was instrumental in the continued survival of the league as it expanded into areas where the previous frame was unknown and unaccepted. The NHL has also begun to market its stars by having them act not just in the roles they fill on the ice, but also in characters off of the ice.

In the two advertising campaigns, one local and one national, there were similarities that are important to identifying how they built character for the players. Both campaigns featured actual players as actors. For

Mark Tamar, the director of game operations for the Capitals, this does not appear to be incongruent. "They're not actors, but it's not a real far stretch from being a professional athlete to being an actor because they perform in front of thousands of people. They're professional and used to being on camera and good at taking direction. They understand timing and hitting their marks."[48] Both campaigns also featured a wide range of stars, from rising stars (Gonchar and Drury) to experienced players (Bondra and Stevens), as well as both offensive players (Jagr and Shanahan) and defensive players (Gonchar and Pronger). By deploying different players in appropriate situations, those casting the actors created believable characterizations of all the masculinities the NHL sought to market. Each of the mythologies—bully, hero-protector, sexual athlete, and New Man—provides an opportunity for different audiences to actively participate in hockey's culture.

Notes

1. I will use the terms National Hockey League, NHL, and the league interchangeably to all represent the same professional sports entity within the United States and Canada.

2. Erving Goffman, *Frame Analysis: An Essay on the Organization of Experience* (New York: Harper and Row, 1974; reprint, Boston: Northwestern University Press, 1986), 21 (reprint ed.).

3. "Hockey Is More Like Life than Life Itself," *Sports Illustrated*, February 13, 1995, 6.

4. See David Savran, *Taking It Like a Man: White Masculinity, Masochism, and Contemporary American Culture* (Princeton, NJ: Princeton University Press, 1998), 5; and Garry Whannel, *Media Sport Stars: Masculinities and Moralities* (London: Routledge, 2000), 69.

5. "Hockey," 11.

6. Whannel, 41.

7. "Hockey," 13.

8. See Roland Barthes, *Mythologies*, trans. Annette Lavers (New York: Hill and Wang, 1972), 18; and Savran, 5.

9. Michael A. Messner and Donald F. Sabo, *Sex, Violence & Power in Sports: Rethinking Masculinity* (Freedom, CA: The Crossing Press, 1994), 7.

10. "Hockey," 13.

11. Whannel, 75.

12. Savran, 125.

13. The Original Six or Solid Six are the teams that composed the National Hockey League from 1942 to 1967. Those teams are the Boston Bruins, Chicago Blackhawks, Detroit Red Wings, Montreal Canadiens, New York Rangers, and Toronto Maple Leafs. See Zander Hollander, ed., *Inside Sports Magazine: Hockey* (Detroit: Visible Ink Press, 1998), 61.

14. Michael A. Robidoux, *Men at Play: A Working Understanding of Professional Hockey* (Montreal: McGill-Queen's University Press, 2001), 127.

15. Gil Stein, *Power Plays: An Inside Look at the Big Business of the National Hockey League* (Secaucus, NJ: Carol Publishing Group, 1997), 92.

16. Hollander, 116.

17. Whannel, 130.

18. Mark Tamar, director of game operations for the Washington Capitals, interview with the author, by telephone to Washington, DC, from Deale, MD, April 4, 2002.

19. Kevin Kirksey, associate marketing manager for ESPN consumer marketing, interview by author, by telephone to New York from Deale, MD, November 8, 2001.

20. During the 2002–2003 season, the Capitals traded Simon to the Chicago Blackhawks. He was subsequently signed by the New York Rangers.

21. Goffman, 56–57.

22. Whannel, 132.

23. *Nice Shoes*, prod. and dir. Washington Capitals, 5 min., Hill Holiday, 1999, videocassette.

24. Barthes, 109–111.

25. *NHL Image All: Every Player Has a Story*, prod. and dir. ESPN, 4 min., Widen and Kennedy, 2000, videocassette.

26. *Ibid.*

27. *Ibid.*

28. Estimates by the league show that in 1998, 45 percent of game attendees at NHL contests were female. Bernard J. Mullin, Stephen Hardy, and William A. Sutton, *Sport Marketing*, 2nd ed. (Champaign, IL: Human Kinetics, 2000), 30. Although, unfortunately, there are no statistics illustrating the makeup of the audience in 1967, films of old games illustrate that the fans in attendance were primarily male and white.

29. Allen Guttmann, *The Erotic in Sports* (New York: Columbia University Press, 1996), 87.

30. Washington traded Oates to Philadelphia in March 2002. He was leading the Capitals in assists at the time of the trade. As of May 2003, Oates was playing with the Mighty Ducks of Anaheim.

31. *Nice Shoes.*

32. Guttmann, 87.

33. Stay-at-home defensemen are those whose primary purpose is to defend against the opponents' forwards. They rarely take shots on net and score with even less frequency. Offensive-minded defensemen, while they are also tasked with defending against opposing scorers, often actively participate on the offensive side of the ice and some score more frequently than many of their team's forwards.

34. *Nice Shoes.*

35. Messner and Sabo, 36.

36. Whannel, 19.

37. *NHL Image All.*

38. Like Washington's Oates, Bure was dealt near the March 2002 trading deadline as Florida sent him to the New York Rangers.

39. *NHL Image All.*

40. *Nice Shoes.*

41. *Ibid.*

42. The goaltender's philanthropic activities help to promote his masculinity of New Man. In addition to being the leader for the Capitals on their annual tour of Children's Hospital in Washington, DC, Kolzig has also established several programs that benefit local children. For one of these programs, Olie's All-Stars, Kolzig provides 10 seats for each home game at MCI Center in Washington, DC, for patients from Children's Hospital. These ailing children attend the games and sit in terrific seats in the lower level of the arena. One of the children rides the zamboni between two of the periods. Kolzig also created the Olie and Elliot's Great Saves Program along with Washington FM radio station 101.1 (DC 101) radio personality Elliot Segal. Kolzig and Segal pay into this fund for every save, win, and shutout Kolzig posts in a season. The team ownership then matched that amount, and donated the total — $25,000 for the 1999–2000 season — to Children's Hospital. Furthermore, along with Slapshot, the Capitals mascot, Kolzig "led the Capitals' Reading is Cool Program that brings reading to many school districts of the greater Washington/Baltimore area" (McGowan, 66). The Washington goaltender thus perpetuates his New Man mythology.

43. *NHL Image All.*

44. Whannel, 75.

45. The Penguins traded Jagr to the Washington Capitals following the 2000–2001 season. He has since moved on to another team.

46. *NHL Image All.*

47. Goffman, 45.

48. Tamar interview.

15

Social Class and Fishing: Fly Fishers vs. the Other

John F. Bratzel

I suppose that occasionally it happens, but I have never seen a newspaper sports section that has had a front-page headline reporting the catching of a fish. Indeed, fishing coverage, if there is any at all, is in the section right after bowling and before the used car ads. Even then, the articles that appear are usually purchased from some local freelance writer explaining the latest trends in a local lake. The only other reportage seems to be the annual drowning of an ice-fisherman. Serious discussion of the issues involved in fishing is effectively nonexistent.

Academia has not shown much interest either. There are a few books here and there on the phenomenon of hunting and fishing, but there are many more, I am sure, on baseball or, I suspect, even on NASCAR. The fact remains that hunting and fishing do not usually provide the basis for academic discussion.

This is unfortunate because a look at fishing, and specifically the presumed dichotomy between fly fishing and—for want of a better term— bass fishing or meat fishing, offers a chance for an examination of class in American society in an entirely different setting. Fly fishing clearly has an "elitist, selective,"[1] high-class appeal while bass fishing is considerably more common both in its frequency and in those who practice it. Fly fishing is deemed upper-class and sophisticated, environmentally sound, and technology-free or, to put it another way, natural. Bass fishing, on the other hand, is the fishing of the unwashed, lower-class masses; it rapes the environment and suffers from all the excesses of technological consumerism. Certainly there are elements of truth in this conception, but clearly the differences are not nearly as substantial as fly fishermen would have us believe.

The classic picture of fly fishing is a solitary individual standing in a beautiful, rock-strewn stream, dressed all in browns and greens, but absolutely no camouflage clothing, swinging a great arc of fishing line out behind him in anticipation of bringing it forward and delicately landing it — and the tiny fly that tied to the end of the line — gently on the water. The reason for the big loop is the essence of the difference between the two types of fishing. In bass fishing, the line is pulled out by the weight of the lure. In fly fishing, because the fly weighs so little that it could never pull the line from the reel, the fisherman is actually casting the line.

Both fly fishing and bass fishing have many variants. Both have hundreds of rod, reel, and line choices. Both also have seemingly unlimited bait choices. It is only a slight exaggeration to say that there are a million different kinds of artificial fly fishing flies. I suspect there are just about as many lures in bass fishing; moreover, in bass fishing, there is the addition of live bait.

The differences between the two types of fishing and who does each are where the controversy has its root. The problem is, however, that movies and literature have grafted onto fly fishing a quasi-religious, "green" quality. At the same time, these same sources posit bass fishing as crude and low class, environmentally destructive and high tech.

About a decade ago, the film *A River Runs through It*[2] was a big hit. It was based on a book by the same name written by Norman MacLean and published in 1976. It is not strange that the movie, more than the book, stimulated fly fishing all over the United States. The utterly glorious scenes of happy bonding and joy as father and sons fished in incredible natural beauty with the goal of besting rather than defeating their quarry could hardly fail to attract a following. Fishing was seen as a challenge in the picture, but it was really much more of an art. In fact, it was virtually a religion, a theme that often marks fly fishing literature. In *A River Runs through It*, to successfully catch a big trout was a sign that the fisherman was virtually predestined to heaven. Both sanctification and justification could be found in the quivering-cold body of a two-pound rainbow as it struggled in the net.

This film defined what fly fishing is, or at least is supposed to be, for many people. But if it glorified fly fishing, the movie could not possibly increase the already dominant self-congratulatory tones that already delineate fly fishing. In fact, even a cursory view of the literature reveals a combination of sanctimoniousness mixed with religious fervor.

The Orvis company is both the best known and most dominant name in fly fishing. The company markets very expensive rods and other equipment as well as a line of highly "preppy" clothes. In its basic book, *The Orvis Fly-Fishing Guide,*[3] the reader is offered a short homily that sounds like the dialog from a Horatio Alger novel on the difference between fly fishing and bass fishing.

> One early spring afternoon, I was walking the bank of my favorite river, searching for surface-feeding trout. A worm fisherman was carefully and methodically working one of the runs, and I envied his ability to place his worm right on the bottom.... [I am at a loss here to know whether this is sarcastic, but hitting the bottom with a weighted worm is not much of an accomplishment] I sat on the bank, keeping my eyes peeled for those characteristic rings on the surface of the water that indicate trout feeding on emerging insects.... Sure enough, about 1:45 I saw the sailboat wings of the mayflies glittering in the weak spring sunlight as they rode the currents, drying their wings.... It was the kind of opportunity that fly-fishermen often yearn for but seldom see.
>
> I waded out into the pool with a light gray dry fly, an imitation of the floating mayfly, tied to my leader. The normally elusive brown and brook trout of this river must have forgotten the lessons they learned last season. It seemed that every time I put my fly over a fish, it was taken. I was elated — so elated that I forgot about the worm fisherman sitting on the bank behind me until he started exclaiming: "Ooh! Oh my God! Oh!" Every time I hooked a fish, his awe became more apparent. Finally he gave in.
>
> "What kind of bait are you using?"
>
> "Dry flies," I said.
>
> "Live ones?"
>
> "No, artificials made out of fur and feathers."
>
> "I've been fishing worms all morning, couldn't even get a strike," he complained. "Usually worms work out pretty good."
>
> "Guess they just want flies today," I replied. "It isn't always this easy."
>
> He pelted me with more questions, while I played and released fish almost continuously. Finally the worm fisherman thanked me for my patience with his questions and began walking to his car, dejection showing in the slump of his shoulders. He turned to me once more.
>
> "Is it hard to learn?"

The only possible response that can be made to our bank sitter's questions is, "Hallelujah, a sinner has been saved; he has come to the arms of fly fishing and been delivered from the unspeakable damnation of 'worm fishing.'"

But if the Orvis Company, which, after all, wants to sell fishing rods, is willing to forgive and allow sinners to find salvation, others are considerably less kind, including Howell Raines, author of *Fly Fishing through the Midlife Crisis.*[4] Raines's book portrays fly fishing as a magical experience, an experience in which all aggression and anger are forgotten, where peo-

ple are at one with nature, and all is right with the world. Fly fishing is a
heady experience according to Raines, and the culminating act of catching
a fish in this manner represents perfect perfection, an organic communion
with his inner spirit. The quasi-religious nature of his ideas is even more
clearly revealed when he comments, "I begin to wonder if having fish shapes
around me is a way of staying in touch with the ideas of Jesus without having to go near the people who do business in his name."[5]

Ultimately, Raines is really offering a form of mystical escapism in
waders as the answer to baby-boomer, mid-life angst. But his zest for fly
fishing is that of a true convert, and like most converts, he not only evan-
gelizes, he castigates evil. For Raines, that evil is "fishing the 'Redneck way.'"
He describes it:

> The "redneck way" ... holds that the only good trip is one ending in many
> dead fish. These fish might then be eaten, frozen, given to neighbors or used
> for fertilizer. But fishing that failed to produce an abundance of corpses could
> no more be successful than a football season in which the University of
> Alabama failed to win a national championship. [6]

Bass fishing, according to Raines, is marked by competition, of trying to
catch the most and the biggest fish and has its roots in "lust and conquest."[7]

We have all heard about the "big one that got away," and I would be
willing to believe Raines if I had ever heard a fly fisherman brag about "the
little one that got away." To be fair, some fly fishers do talk about the total
experience as being as important as the actual catching of fish, but competitiveness and competition is not the goal of just bass fisherman. I remember one avid fly fisherman who crowed with absolute delight at landing a
big brown trout right in front of a number of other fly fishermen. And most
all fly fishing lodges have large paper charts that are updated daily during
the fishing season listing fisherman and their big-fish conquests. Some even
give out trophies. All have photos on the walls of particularly momentous
catches.

Obviously, many fly fisherman also fish for other species with their fly
rods, including bass and blue gills. Plenty of fishermen sit along the banks
and fish for trout with worms. Even though the fishing systems are not
exclusive, most serious fly fishermen associate themselves with trout fishing.
What makes this significant is that bass are plentiful and found in every
state, while good trout streams are rather rare. This rarity, with its concomi-
tant exclusivity, supports the higher-class status of fly fishing.

Along with the higher-class status comes a claim that fly fishing is more
environmentally friendly and technology-free. This contention is supported
by Richard Hummel in the book *Hunting and Fishing for Sport: Commerce,
Controversy, and Popular Culture.*[8] While it is true that bass fishermen tend

to embrace technology and regularly use sonar devices, temperature gauges and pH meters whenever they can, it is also true that these gadgets are almost impossible to use when trout fishing in a stream. That you cannot easily use technology, however, does not mean that it is not available; a little more digging reveals that seemingly every effort has been made to make as much technology as possible available to fly fishermen. For those times when it can be used, for example, a temperature gauge is available in "a flat black metal housing" from Orvis for $11.95 plus shipping and handling.[9] In fact, in some cases trout fishermen use float tubes with "Fishin' Buddy" depth, temperature, and fish finders attached to them. Add a motor, and you have a bass boat. In other words, the question is not so much how much technology is used, but whether new technologies are deliberately avoided by the purists.

The answer is "no," and a look at any Orvis catalog will reinforce that conclusion. For example, the newest must-have item this year is the new T3 Orvis fly rod. This rod, according to Orvis, "represents a breakthrough in Carbon Fiber Technology ... leveraging technology heretofore used only in the aerospace and defense industries."[10] It replaces the Trident fly rod, which used to be advertised for its titanium hardware and as being computer-engineered to dampen vibration in casting. Orvis bragged that it was called Trident because the engineers who designed it were the same people who built the (always environmentally friendly and technologically neutral) Trident nuclear submarines.[11]

In fact, fly fishing is replete with cutting-edge technology. Stores and catalogs offer Goretex waders, floating putty and malleable weights; there is even tippet made from fused spectra fibers that was originally invented to make bulletproof vests. A cursory look at fly fishing suggests that not only is technology very much a part of the sport, but much of it seems to have its roots in the military-industrial complex.

When it comes to being environmentally benign, one author says, "Within each fly fisherman is also the soul of a naturalist."[12] A nice idea, but the increasingly scarce redwoods and tropical woods that go into reel seats on rods seem to suggest an omission in environmental consciousness. The ultimate indignity in this regard, however, comes from an amazing description of the handle on a fly fishing reel. It is described as follows: "[The] impregnated rosewood handle is as durable as plastic with a classic look and feel."[13] In other words, their fine, rare woods are now apparently approaching the quality of plastic — a goal that very few people, for obvious reasons, would ever want to achieve.

One basis for the claim that fly fishing is somehow more natural and environmentally friendly seems based on the use of flies to catch fish. The idea is that your flies craftily mimic natural insects. All bass lures, on the other hand, do not. Spinners, in particular, look like nothing in nature. Fly fisherman scoff at such metal and rubber contraptions as being unnatural. On the other hand, the same lures that are scoffed at also catch trout quite well. Obviously, the true judge of what is natural is not the fisherman, but the actual fish, and they seem to make no distinction between the two types of lures.

"Flies only" areas and "catch and release" are common in fly fishing. Indeed, many fly fishermen by habit or by regulation use barbless hooks so fish will be less damaged. Many also quickly return the fish that they have caught back to the water. But just as fly fishermen do not necessarily want to end up with pile of dead trout, many bass fishermen do not want to end up with piles of dead bass either. The magazine *In Fisherman*, along with its associated television program and books, is an important opinion leader in fishing. It continually sings the praises of catch and release,[14] but in the big bass tournaments, the bass are always freed after they are weighed. In other words, catch and release is not solely a fly fishing attitude; it is increasingly marking fishing in general.

Finally, fly fishermen seem to revel in the idea that their sport is difficult and that it is based on skills won through hours of practice, careful crafting and choosing of baits, and years of study. Fly fishermen do have a point here. Learning to cast a fly is more difficult than tossing out a rubber worm, but it is not so hard that with a reasonable amount of effort it can't be mastered. Fly fishermen try to build an aura of great mystery around fly fishing. It just takes practice to learn. Moreover, the best bass fisherman also needs skill and perceptiveness to be successful.

In many respects, fly fishermen are trying desperately to distance themselves from bass fishermen. Theirs is not a blood sport. Theirs is a return to transcendental roots in which the fisherman finds him- or herself in the proper relationship with God and nature. Those who do not understand this are sinners— people to be disparaged and demeaned. At the root of some of this bias is a sense of class superiority fly fishermen feel over their bass fishing colleagues, but ultimately this type of thinking is quite destructive. Exclusionary sensibilities add little to a society that already suffers from other divisions. I hope in the future that fly fishers will lower their voices, if for no other reason than to stop scaring away the fish.

Notes

1. Richard Hummel, *Hunting and Fishing for Sport: Commerce, Controversy, and Popular Culture.* (Bowling Green, OH: Bowling Green State University Popular Press, 1994), 45.

2. Robert Redford, director, Richard Friedenberg, screenwriter: *A River Runs through It*, Columbia Pictures, 1992.

3. Tom Rosenbauer, *The Orvis Fly-Fishing Guide* (New York: Lyons & Burford, 1984), 7.

4. Howell Raines, *Fly Fishing through the Midlife Crisis*, (New York: William Morrow and Company, 1993).

5. *Ibid.*, 108.

6. *Ibid.*, 19.

7. *Ibid.*, 19.

8. Hummel.

9. http://www.orvis.com/store/product_directory_showcase. You will find this listed in the fly fishing section under accessories.

10. http://www.orvis.com/store/product_directory_chart_asp. The rod comes in a variety of sizes.

11. *Ibid.*

12. http://www.flyfishingforlife.net/philosophy.html. Fly fishing for life is an organization that takes businesspeople and others to exotic (and expensive) fly fishing destinations.

13. http://www.orvis.com/store/product_directory_showcase. This comment was made in the advertisement for Orvis's CFO reel.

14. See, for example, Al Linder, et al, *Largemouth Bass in the 1990s*, (Brainerd, MN: In Fisherman, 1990), 27–28.

16

Ali's Last Hurrah

Pete Williams

By 1978 Muhammad Ali had fought all of his greatest fights: the two with Liston, the three with Frazier, the two with Norton and, of course, the one with Foreman. He had been in barely perceptible but certain decline for at least five years, since the Bob Foster fight, when writers such as Jim Murray first noticed the speed and the reflexes were not quite what they had been. His most recent fight, the previous September against the hard-punching Earnie Shavers, had gone the full 15, and only a rally in that last round saved the victory and the title for Ali. He was 36, and he was ready for a fall.

It came in Las Vegas, on February 15, against a tough young ex-marine and recent Olympic champ, Leon Spinks. Although Ali was heavily favored, he had apparently not trained seriously, and he looked soft; Matchmaker Teddy Brenner said bluntly that he was too old to train effectively anyway, and that all he could do was lose weight. Angelo Dundee, Ali's trainer, was uncharacteristically irritable, and, even more unusually, Ali was not talking to the public, having taken, he said, a vow of silence. When he finally spoke again to reporters just before the fight, the copy he provided was less than sensational. "Many of the lines were reruns of better times," one writer said. "No surprise, really. His fights have told us how little he has left."[1] There was even an ominous publicity stunt, a computerized match between Ali (age 36) and Clay (age 24). Clay won it by KO in the eighth. None of these signs was good.

Leon Spinks was 10 years old when Ali won the title for the first time in 1963, which gave him the advantage of youth but also the disadvantage of inexperience. Ali, counting on the latter and aware that Spinks was not considered a particularly good fighter, had trouble taking him seriously. As a result, and for far too many early rounds, he clowned, danced, seemed too bored to throw punches, and leaned back against the ropes in a "rope-a-dope" effort to tire his man. By the end of round nine, Ali's cornermen were more than worried; they knew he was too far behind on points to win unless he knocked Spinks out, that even a last-minute rally a la the Shavers fight couldn't save him. Ali had a cumbersome number of advisors with him that night (someone counted as many as 18), and they all talked at once. Finally Dundee yelled, "Will you all shut the hell up!" and turned to Muhammad. "You got to go get him," he said. "You can't wait any longer. You've given him too many rounds. You've got to go get him now."[2]

In round 10, Ali tried. For the first time in the fight, Spinks started backing up. Ali hit him with several punches to the head but, although Spinks was hurt, he stayed on his feet; then, halfway through the round, Ali began to slow down, and Spinks came after him. Spinks was clearly the aggressor at the bell; a week before the fight Spinks had told a reporter, "My biggest credential is my birth certificate,"[3] and it was beginning to look like he was right. Although Ali never gave in after that, even winning two of the remaining five rounds, in effect, the fight was over. The last round was much like the 10th, the first half won by an aggressive Ali, the second half lost by an exhausted one. The fact that one of the three judges gave the match to Ali says much more about that judge's denial than about the fight, which Ali himself felt he had lost unambiguously.

If that judge was driven more by emotion than objectivity, his response was at least understandable, since the fight was incidental to what now truly did seem the end of Ali's career as both fighter and symbol. An old high school pal of boxing scholar Elliott Gorn phoned him as soon as the fight was over to ask, "Does this mean the sixties are over?" National magazines made it their cover story; the headline in one read, "The Greatest Is Gone." Ali himself was seen crying on his way back to his dressing room. Later, after the press conference, he had to walk through the lobby of the Hilton to get to his hotel room. A platoon of security guards linked arms around him, but it wasn't necessary. The people milling about moved aside quietly, respectfully, the way they would if someone asked them to make way for pallbearers with a casket. "You're still the champ," a few of them murmured. Ali tried not to listen.

From the hotel's discotheque, a singer cut through the smoky air with off-key bleats. From the hotel's casino, there were the 24-hour-a-day sounds of whirring roulette wheels and ice tinkling in empty glasses. Ali paid no attention to any of it.

He kept on walking, his head down so no one could get a good look at his battered, lumpy face. Sugar Ray Robinson offered his condolences. Ali said thank you with his eyes and moved on.

The elevator door was open when he got to it. He looked around at the security guards. "You guys don't have to protect me from nothing," he said. "Nobody want to touch me."[4]

Back in his room, Ali put on a striped robe and left the door to the corridor open. Anybody who wanted to come in to talk with him was welcomed. He only objected once, when one visitor too many called him "champ." He said that Spinks had beaten him in a fair fight, and that Spinks was the champ now. Pete Bonventre, who had spent several hours with Ali after he upset George Foreman in Kinshaha, said, "Ali knows how to lose more graciously than most sports heroes know how to win."[5] But then Ali said this: "I shall return. I'll let him hold the title for a few months and enjoy it. Then I shall return."[6]

The only question in anyone's mind was whether, in saying so, Ali himself was in denial. Was he looking at himself as a fighter, or as an icon — as a figure of history, or one of myth? Before going on, it wouldn't be a bad idea to briefly examine that distinction.

Any individual in the public eye, ergo every famous athlete, is assigned a mythical role by a public who will never know him or her, and the individual is regularly (probably inevitably) lost in the myth. Further, the myth often centers on a particular moment — an iconic performance — that becomes frozen in time. Very recently a man who had been born in Pennsylvania but who had spent most of his life in California died. He owned a restaurant in a small town on the West Coast. He was 81 and had lived a long and presumably varied life as an individual, somebody like you or me. He left his wife, two sons, two daughters, three brothers, a sister, thirteen grandchildren and seven great-grandchildren. His time on earth was ordinary, average, even pedestrian — nonetheless, he was given obituaries all over the country. The one in the *New York Times*, some 3,000 miles away from his suburban home, gave him three columns, two of which involved a photograph of the deceased catching a baseball next to the 415 foot sign in the outfield at Yankee Stadium a full 56 years ago. It's the only picture of him any of us has ever seen — he's crouched, trying not to bang into the fence, his left hand across his body and his gloved hand clearly holding the ball — and it's the only image of him that that ever was or will be printed. This was his iconic moment, the moment that, more than anything he ever did in his real world, defined his life; that picture is where he will live, timelessly, like Jack Nicholson's image on the wall at the end of the Kubrick movie.[7]

Now think of the heavyweights, of their mythical personae and the iconic moments that created them. The always-overrated Jack Dempsey, for example, has not just one, but at least three iconic fights, all of which convince us and flawed history that he was a man-killer: Jess Willard, Luis Angel Firpo and the second match with Gene Tunney. It doesn't seem to matter that, in the cold light of reality, Dempsey's gloves were loaded when he fought Willard, or that both Willard and Firpo were fourth-rate fighters, or that, after the overly publicized "long count," Tunney won going away. The image of Jack Johnson as someone who could utterly control a fight — Abe Attell once said "he could have called the round" on Marciano[8] — came primarily from two fights, Ketchel and Jeffries, in which he was in total mastery. Mike Tyson's image has been set, for bad and all, by one incident, and by one photograph from one particular fight. What sets Ali apart is not just that his persona is always so positive — it's that he has had such a great number of defining iconic moments.

As an individual athlete, of course, no one has ever suggested that Ali was anything less than one of the very best. As an icon, how many fights before that loss to Spinks might we claim for him as defining moments? It would be hard not to include the initial upset of Sonny Listen, the Big Bear, in Miami in 1964 and just as hard to ignore the rematch, if only for the famous photo, likely the most iconic shot of Ali ever taken, showing him standing and glowering over Liston. No one alive would omit the first Frazier fight, and although the second did not rise to the level of myth, the third, the "Thrilla in Manila," surely did. The first fight with Norton, in which Ali fought on gallantly despite a broken jaw, could be a judgment call, but I doubt if that little scrap that took place in the sub–Saharan jungle at about 4 AM Eastern Time fails to qualify. "That fight," said A. O. Scott in the *New York Times*, "may be the most mythologized sporting event of the last half-century." And it is certainly worth noting that Scott did not make that comment in the 70s, or 80s, or even in the 90s. He made it on April 11, 2003.[9]

> "I've lasted longer than the Beatles and the Supremes. Now it's just me and the Rolling Stones."
>
> — Muhammad Ali[10]

Ali arrived in New Orleans to sign for the September rematch with Spinks on April 10, and there were indications that he intended to take both his training and Spinks more seriously this time. When he got off the plane, he was low-key. "I'm not going to name him or call him nothing," he said, although he added that he did intend to prove himself, not just the greatest, but "the greatest of all time."[11] In training, Ali sparred 200 rounds. Reporters said this was at least four times as many as before the first fight, although Ali himself said he could only remember sparring not 50 rounds, but six. He clearly knew he had lost that first fight by discounting Spinks—

"I was fat, out of shape, tired," he said[12] — and this time he was, if anything, overcompensating. In his Pennsylvania camp, he was the first one up. Every morning at 5 am, it was Ali who rang the big bell that told everybody else to get moving. Then, while they dressed and got ready for the rigors of the day, he would go alone to a small white cabin he'd made into a mini-mosque for a half-hour of prayer and meditation. Sometime, every day, and as much as he had always hated this part of training, he would run, then force himself to run more. "I want to stop, but I can't," he said. "My chest burns, my throat is dry, I feel like I'm going to faint. My body begs me to stop. But I make myself run another mile, two more miles up those damn hills."[13]

In what Frank Sullivan's cliché expert would have called stark contrast, Spinks, who had taken the first fight seriously, was now coasting. Back in February, right after he won the title from Ali, Spinks had asked Butch Lewis, his manager, for "some money to party,"[14] and he began to fall in with a crowd that he considered glamorous, or at least cool (the entourage included the not-yet-famous Mr. T). While Spinks did train, he also embarked on what Jeffrey Sammons called "a widely publicized odyssey of arrests and lawsuits,"[15] including a number of drug charges. In early May, for example, the *New York Times* reported that Spinks had been arraigned on two charges of marijuana possession, adding that the date for his trial, August 10, would not conflict with his upcoming May 18 trial for possessing cocaine.[16] Spinks was complacent and cavalier even on fight night; Lewis had asked him to show up at the Super Bowl at 7, but Spinks didn't arrive until after 9 for a 10 PM fight.

Two days before the fight, final workouts for the two men were held at the Municipal Auditorium, and they were open to the public. Ali was scheduled first, around lunchtime, and he drew the larger crowd. After his workout, he promised (again) that he would win, no contest, and (again) that after he won he would most definitely and positively retire. Spinks arrived after Ali left, pulling up in a white Lincoln stretch, the disco inside turned up so high you could hear it through the closed windows. In the ring, after skipping to the same music for a while, Spinks tossed his rope away and began dancing in earnest, much to the delight of his fans. When he left he was taken not back to his room at the Hilton but to a mysterious house in the city, where he had chosen to spend the night away from the prying eyes of the press and, presumably, his trainers. Ali, on the other hand — well, the *New Orleans Times-Picayune* ran a story on the morning of the fight describing his visit to Felycyia Bradley, a lovely 11-year-old in the last stages of leukemia who had always been his fan. He seems to have cheered her up — she said he was "funny" throughout their talk — although just before he left, she admitted he had become serious. Arguably the world's most famous Muslim, Ali had told the little Christian girl to try not to worry, because Jesus was going to take care of her.[17]

Nonetheless, even if Spinks was running around town like a white-suited and drugged-up John Travolta while the teetotaling Ali was sowing the seeds of the Make-A-Wish Foundation, neither fact had much to do with a fight between a young man and one way past his prime. Jim Murray, who had been one of the first to realize that Ali was slipping as far back as 1972, wrote a story under the head, "Last Dance for Ali." The next day he looked at the aging fighter, naked in his dressing room and concluded that the icon had nothing on, that this old emperor was wearing no clothes. He said that if Ali couldn't score a knockout by round eight, he would likely lose. The day after that, in his last column before the fight, Murray could only be wistful about the ex-champ's chances. "There is a Santa Claus," he said. "Isn't there?"[18] Ali, meanwhile — was he speaking as individual or as icon? — was saying, "This will be my third coming. My first coming was in 1964 when I shocked the world by beating Sonny Liston. My second coming was when I upset George Foreman in Zaire in 1974. My third coming will be against Spinks tonight."[19]

And then, on the morning of September 16, 1978, Jim Murray was able to write, "Yes, Virginia, there is a Santa Claus"— which is not to imply that he thought the fight was close. Murray said he not only gave Spinks no rounds— the fight went the 15-round distance — but he gave him no minutes in any of the rounds. He said lynchings were less one-sided. He said Spinks was pitching a no-hitter, in that he never landed a punch; he said somebody should send him a picture of Ali, since he never got close enough to see what he looked like; he said, "Spinks spent the night throwing punches in places Ali had left several minutes before." When he later found out that two of the judges had each given Spinks four rounds, Murray said he'd be sure to turn down any invitations to go hunting with them. Ali, Murray said, would have had a tougher time with the heavy bag. If Spinks was representative of the talent in the heavyweight division, he said, Ali should be the first champ to retire wearing bifocals; he said Ali could beat Spinks again if he had to use a cane to climb into the ring. But, on the other hand, Murray said, if such a rubber match were arranged, it would be only fair to give the captain of the *Titanic* another shot at the iceberg.[20]

The crowd at the Super Dome (70,000, paying a then-record gate of $6 million) went equally over the top, rushing the ring after the final bell but before the decision and scaring Howard Cosell sufficiently that he was stripped of his polysyllabic sarcasm. Cosell announced that "this crowd pushing in on us" had made for "a bad situation." The police were trying to protect the people in the ring — even Ali was shoved — but Cosell said it was "almost impossible" for them to help. Although it might have been the hyperbole of a man accustomed to exaggeration, he did call the experience "the wildest scene I have ever witnessed." Cosell was not a New Orleanian, though, and he was probably too pious in his analysis of the highlight of the event, the sudden appearance in the ring of a young woman, in his phrase, "utterly disrobed." A repulsed Cosell, chalking this up to "bad fan behavior," seems to have ignored the possibility that male ringsiders had been tossing beads at their female counterparts.[21]

And the story should end right there, in perfect symmetry, with Ali adding a sixth and maybe even seventh iconic moment to the greatest mythical journey in boxing history, but we all know it doesn't. True, he had promised us during training that this hurrah would be his last. "I hurt all over," he had said. "I hate it but I'm taking it.... I know this is my last fight and it's the last time I'll ever have to do it. Just a few more weeks of pain and suffering to live good all the rest of my life, to always be champion."[22] Ali knew that if he beat Spinks, he would be going out on his own terms. He would be, as Murray put it, "not going gently into that good night," but raging "against the dying of the light. His light."[23] Had it happened that way, we could have kept the symmetry, not only in Ali's career, but also to an extent in the history of his sport in the city of New Orleans. Murray again:

> This is where it all began, this steambath of a city at the Mississippi's mouth. This is where "Gentleman" Jim Corbett de-mythologized the great John L. Sullivan, the burly immigrant's son who boasted he could lick any man in the house. This is where speed and footwork first dismantled brute strength in the first big fight where gloves were worn and the Marquis of Queensberry rules were enforced. This is where fighting became a speed sport and not a strength sport.[24]

So this city could have been, not only the place where modern boxing began — it was over in the Fauborg district, on Chartres, about a dozen blocks the other side of Esplanade — but also the place where the most important fighter of our time (and possibly, as he'd predicted, of "all time") made his triumphant exit. And if it couldn't happen exactly that way — if Ali should lose sight of the aging individual in his contemplation of the restored icon — we can still take some comfort in this final remarkable performance, and in the way he made us all feel when we finally went to bed, grinning at the ceiling, in the early hours of September 16, 1978.

Notes

1. Vic Ziegel, *New York Post*, February 15, 1978.
2. Pat Putnam, *Sports Illustrated*, February 27, 1978, 15.
3. Alan Goldstein, *Muhammad Ali* (London, Carlton Books, Ltd., 2000), 141.
4. John Schulian, *Writer's Fighters* (Kansas City, Andrews & McMeel, 1983), 15.
5. Pete Bonventre, *Newsweek*, February 27, 1978, 88.

6. *Sports Illustrated*, February 27, 1978, 19.

7. Al Gionfriddo, a very minor Brooklyn Dodger, made his famous catch of Joe DiMaggio's near home run in the sixth inning of Game Six of the 1947 World Series. He would never play another game in the major leagues. See the obituary in the *New York Times*, March 16, 2003. The movie to which I refer is, of course, *The Shining*.

8. Frank Graham, *New York Journal-American*, September 24, 1955.

9. In the *New York Times*.

10. Goldstein, 145.

11. *New York Times*, April 11, 1978.

12. Putnam, *Sports Illustrated*, September 11, 1978, 22.

13. Ibid.

14. Arlene Schulman, *The Prizefighters* (New York, Lyons & Burford, 1994), 132.

15. Jeffrey T. Sammons, *Beyond the Ring* (Urbana, University of Illinois Press, 1990), 228.

16. *New York Times*, May 5, 1978.

17. Molly Moore, *New Orleans Times-Picayune*, September 15, 1978.

18. Jim Murray, *Los Angeles Times*, September 13, 14 and 15, 1978.

19. Goldstein, 144.

20. Murray, *Los Angeles Times*, September 16, 1978.

21. Paul Atkinson, *New Orleans Times-Picayune*, September 16, 1978.

22. Putnam, *Sports Illustrated*, September 11, 1978, 22.

23. Murray, *Los Angeles Times*, September 13, 1978.

24. Murray, *Los Angeles Times*, September 13, 1978.

About the Contributors

Donna J. Barbie is a professor of humanities at Embry-Riddle University in Daytona Beach, Florida. Barbie completed a Ph.D. in American studies at Emory University, and published *The Making of Sacagawea: A Euro-American Legend* (1996). She was raised in North Dakota within a "golfing" family and began learning how to play about 2000. Marrying her sporting interest with her academic pursuits of American popular culture, she presented several sports papers at national and regional conferences, including the work on Tiger Woods, "Gender Wars in Golf," and "The Masters Tournament: Traditions and Conflicts."

John F. Bratzel is professor of writing, rhetoric and American culture at Michigan State University and graduate coordinator of the Latin American Studies Center. He has published widely in both popular culture and Latin American studies. Currently, he is the vice president and president-elect of the National Popular Culture Association, and is a member of the Executive Committee of the Consortium for Latin American Studies Programs. He heads the Latin American portion of the Less Commonly Taught Languages project that is organizing and coordinating the teaching of LCTL in the United States in the wake of events surrounding 9/11.

Tom Cook, Ph.D., has taught at Wayne State College in Nebraska for the past 15 years and earlier at several other colleges and universities in the South and Midwest. He also served as Wayne State's women's golf coach, concluding his coaching career in 1993 with three straight undefeated seasons. He has won his academic division's teaching award and has been nominated for a statewide teaching award. Fulfilling a longtime dream of teaching in China, Cook and his wife, Patricia, traveled to Hangzhou in 1998–99. They returned to teach in Changsha in 2001–02 and again for one semester in 2005.

Lane Demas is a history Ph.D. student at the University of California–Irvine. His research interests include 20th century popular culture, especially issues of race, ethnicity, and sport. In addition to his research on racial integration and segregation in collegiate football, he has also written on heavyweight boxer Joe Louis and Greek-American immigration.

Joseph Dorinson, professor of history at Long Island University's Brooklyn campus, where he has served as department chair from 1985 to 1997, has hosted several major conferences, resulting in his *Jackie Robinson: Race, Sports, and the American Dream* (M.E. Sharpe, 1998) and *Paul Robeson: Essays on His Life and Legacy* (McFarland, 2001). His most recent publications include essays on Frank Sinatra, Lenny Bruce, Milton Berle, Jerry Lewis, Jackie Robinson, and New York City on Film.

Barbara S. Hugenberg is an assistant professor and basic course director in the Department of Communication Studies at Kent State University in Kent, Ohio. Her research interest in American sports focuses on her observations of football and NASCAR fans. She is co-author of "If It Ain't Rubbin,' It Ain't Racin': NASCAR, American Values and Fandom," to be published in *The Journal of Popular Culture.* Her doctoral dissertation was an ethnographic study of Cleveland Browns fans upon the return of the team in 1999. She also co-authored "NASCAR's Bristol Motor Speedway: 'The Fastest Half Mile in the World,'" for *American Icons: People Places and Things That Have Shaped Our Culture* (Greenwood Press). Her research interests include organizational cultural studies, critical studies and popular culture.

Lawrence W. Hugenberg is professor of communication studies in the Department of Communication and Theater at Youngstown State University in Youngstown, Ohio. In addition to teaching communication skill courses, he also teaches courses in popular culture and cultural criticism. His research interests in American sports have included NASCAR, the Extreme Football League (XFL), and the World Wrestling Association. He is co-author of "If It Ain't Rubbin,' It Ain't Racin': NASCAR, American Values and Fandom," to be published in *The Journal of Popular Culture.* He also co-authored "NASCAR's Bristol Motor Speedway: 'The Fastest Half Mile in the World,'" for *American Icons: People, Places and Things that Have Shaped Our Culture* (Greenwood Press).

Brian Katen is an associate professor of landscape architecture at Virginia Tech. His work and research focuses on engaging the hidden layers of the everyday landscape. His research on vernacular gathering places in the Virginia landscape, including speedways, fairgrounds, mineral springs, and the state's African American landscapes, is revealing the everyday landscape of Virginia as an important, little-understood component of the larger historic Virginia and a significant resource for contemporary design.

Kimberly Tony Korol is a candidate for the interdisciplinary Ph.D. in theater and drama at Northwestern University and received her MA in theatre from the University of Maryland. Her research and teaching areas of specialty are Tudor theatre and performance and paratheatricals, including sports as theatrical event. She is currently completing her dissertation on the Maryland Renaissance Festival. Korol fervently hopes for the sakes of her son Walkir, who currently plays squirt hockey, that the NHL will come back stronger than ever after the lost 2004–2005 season.

Yasue Kuwahara, Ph.D., originally from Tokyo, moved to the United States upon graduation from Waseda University with a BA in English language and literature. She received an MA in American studies from California State University, Fullerton, and a Ph.D. in American Cultural Studies from Bowling Green State University. Kuwahara has taught courses on Japanese and American popular culture and the mass media at Northern Kentucky University since 1989. She also taught at

Xavier University of New Orleans. Kuwahara is the founder and director of the Popular Culture Studies Program at NKU. Her ongoing research focuses on U.S. influence on postwar Japan. She has authored book chapters and published articles in various journals, including *The Journal of Popular Culture*.

Michael S. Martin is assistant professor of history at the University of Louisiana–Lafayette. He received his Ph.D. in history from the University of Arkansas, and his BA and MA in history from the University of Southwestern Louisiana. He has published numerous articles on 20th century Louisiana history and the book *Chemical Engineering at the University of Arkansas: A Centennial History, 1902–2002,* and is currently revising his dissertation, "Senator Russell B. Long of Louisiana: A Political Biography," for publication. Martin lives with his wife, Amy, in Lafayette, Louisiana.

Kendra Myers is a summa cum laude graduate of Duke University with a BA in English and drama. After a career in the theatre in Atlanta, where she was named "Best Local Playwright," she received an honors fellowship to attend the University of Mississippi, where she earned her MA in Southern studies. Her thesis, "Drive: A Season in the Life of a Sprint Car Racer, or Confessions of a Dirty Girl," chronicles the experiences of a dirt-track racer in Memphis, Tennessee. Her articles and photographs on auto racing have appeared in *FlatOut* magazine, *The Southern Register,* and in the online journal SouthernSpaces.org, and she has delivered many papers and lectures on the subject. She continues to write, photograph, and get dirty in Oxford, Mississippi.

Arthur J. Remillard is a doctoral candidate in the Department of Religion at Florida State University. His dissertation examines the development of religious virtue in the American South from 1877 to 1920, and he is the managing editor of the *Journal of Southern Religion.* He has also cultivated an interest in religion and sport. In addition to the work represented in this volume, he has completed an ethnographic study on the religious experiences of competitive distance runners.

Bruce A. Rubenstein, professor of history and director of the Master of Liberal Studies in the American Culture Program at the University of Michigan–Flint, teaches courses in American history, including history of baseball and history of sport in the United States. He has authored numerous articles and co-authored three books with Dr. Lawrence E. Ziewacz of Michigan State University. His is currently completing two manuscripts dealing with the World Series.

Daniel Simone earned his BA in sociology at Rowan New Jersey College and his MA in history at North Dakota State University. Since 2001, he has presented numerous papers on auto racing, notably "Shifting, Swerving, and Turning: The Evolving Relationship between American Politics and Motorsports" and "NASCAR and New Jersey: The Morristown Races of 1951–1955." His article "Horsepower and Horse Tracks: The Fargo Auto Races of 1915" will appear in a forthcoming issue of *North Dakota History.* He is currently working on a Ph.D. in 20th century American history and environmental history at the University of Florida.

Joseph Stanton (Ph.D., New York University) teaches art history and American studies at the University of Hawaii at Manoa. His publication include the collections *Cardinal Points: Poems on St. Louis Cardinals Baseball* (McFarland, 2002) and *Imaginary Museum: Poems on Art* (Time Being Books, 1999); the anthologies *The Quietest Singing* (2000) and *A Hawaii Anthology* (1997); and poems and essays in such journals as *Poetry, Harvard Review, Aethlon, Elysian Fields Quarterly, Art Criticism, American Art,* and *Journal of American Culture.* He has published essays on Edward Hopper, Winslow Homer, Maurice Sendak, Chris Van Allsburg, John Berryman, and Donald Hall, and wrote *The Important Books: Children's Picture Books as Art and Literature* (Scarecrow, 2005). His works in progress include biographies of Stan Musial and Winslow Homer.

David R. Thompson, Ph.D., is an associate professor in the Division of Communication and Fine Arts at Loras College (Dubuque, Iowa). Thompson is coauthor of *Darlington International Raceway: 1950–1967,* featuring the photographs of Tom Kirkland, and wrote "Hot Wheels and High Heels: Gender Roles in Stock Car Racing," to appear in *Sexual Sports Rhetoric: Teaming Up Gender with the Language of Sport.* In Tianjin, China, he introduced American stock car racing to Asian scholars at "The United States and China into the 21st Century: A Symposium on History, Culture and International Relations." Known as "Turbo" to his students, he has raced stock cars in three states and taught courses on the history and culture of stock car racing. While in Texas, Thompson created a program to promote literacy at Longhorn Speedway in Austin. He has taught at Simpson College, the University of South Carolina, and Southwest Texas State university (now Texas State University).

James A. Vlasich is a professor of history at Southern Utah University in Cedar City, Utah, where he has taught for 24 years. He was named Professor of the Year (1986) and Distinguished Educator of the Year (1998). He has also served as Sports Area Chair for the Poplar Culture Association Conference since 1997 and appeared on a special edition of the NBC *Today* show for the 50th anniversary of the Baseball Hall of Fame (1989). He specializes in American Indian, sports, and American Southwest history. The author of *A Legend for the Legendary: The Origin of the Baseball Hall of Fame* (1990) and *Pueblo Indian Agriculture* (2005), he is a baseball fanatic, loyal Dodger follower and the father of two daughters who were former T-ball and softball champions.

Pete Williams received his doctorate from the University of Michigan and is professor of English at County College of Morris in Randolph, New Jersey. He is the son of golden-era sports columnist Joe Williams, whose articles he collected in *The Joe Williams Baseball Reader.* He also wrote two other books on sport, a biography of baseball's Bill Terry (*When the Giants Were Giants*) and a study of the psychology of myth-making (*The Sports Immortals*), as well as numerous sports-related articles and a few poems. He prays that the rumor that Steinbrenner will replace Torre with Valentine is untrue.

Index